ASPECTS OF BRITISH POLITICS 1904–1919

ASPECTS OF BRITISH POLITICS 1904–1919

DOREEN COLLINS

PERGAMON PRESS
OXFORD · LONDON · EDINBURGH · NEW YORK
PARIS · FRANKFURT

Pergamon Press Ltd., Headington Hill Hall, Oxford
4 & 5 Fitzroy Square, London W.1
Pergamon Press (Scotland) Ltd., 2 & 3 Teviot Place, Edinburgh 1
Pergamon Press Inc., 122 East 55th Street, New York 10022
Pergamon Press GmbH, Kaiserstrasse 75, Frankfurt-am-Main

First edition 1965
Library of Congress Catalog Card No. 65-21143

(2053/65)

CONTENTS

INTRODUCTION

I THINK a word of explanation about the purpose of this book is necessary since it is not intended to be primarily an attempt to write diplomatic history, nor yet a study of the First World War. What I have tried to do is to show the varied reactions to the changes in British foreign policy made necessary by her relative loss of power at the beginning of the twentieth century and the diminution of confidence in the handling of foreign affairs which was one of their results. Secondly, I have attempted to illustrate the effect of war both on the nature of foreign affairs and on the traditional machine for the execution of foreign policy which led in its turn to a sense of uncertainty and loss of morale within the Foreign Service. The ending of the war saw the desire both to extend true democratic checks over the foreign policy of the country and also to refurbish the Foreign Service that it might play an increasingly effective part in the modern world. It was a moment of hope when men desired to create a system in which there would be, not contradiction, but harmony between the needs of the people and the demands of government.

CHAPTER 1

INTERNATIONAL FRIENDSHIP

I

"The electorate is in fact the sovereign of England. The electors can in the long run always enforce their will." So wrote Dicey in 1885* in his analysis of how the constitution worked at the end of the nineteenth century. In seeming opposition to this, however, lay the undoubted fact that legal sovereignty in certain matters still remained part of the royal prerogative and thus within the discretion of the executive arm of the state. One of these matters was the conduct of foreign affairs. The Crown was acknowledged to be responsible for the making of war and the declaration of peace, and the signature of a treaty did not depend upon the sanction of Parliament "even the conduct of negotiations with foreign powers are exempt from the direct control or supervision of Parliament". In consequence the Cabinet retained supremacy in the field of all foreign affairs: "it is not Parliament, but the Ministry, who direct the diplomacy of the nation, and virtually decide all questions of peace or war".†

The reconciliation of these two seemingly opposed conditions he found, not in law, but in constitutional conventions which had as their ultimate object "to secure that Parliament, or the Cabinet which is indirectly appointed by Parliament, shall in the long run

---

* Dicey, *The Law of the Constitution,* 5th edn., pp. 359 and 70.
† Dicey, *op. cit.,* p. 393.

give effect to the will of that power which in modern England is the true political sovereign of the state".* As examples of such constitutional maxims he quotes with approval "Treaties can be made without the necessity for any Act of Parliament; but the Crown, or in reality the Ministry representing the Crown, ought not to make any treaty which will not command the approbation of Parliament."† "The action of any Ministry would be highly unconstitutional if it should involve the proclamation of war, of the making of peace, in defiance of the wishes of the House."°

If Dicey can fairly be taken as representative of thoughtful opinion concerning the control and conduct of foreign affairs in the latter part of the Queen's reign, then it can be seen that a matter of critical importance is the question of fair play. If the working of the system depends upon the executive acting in accordance with constitutional morality, of equal importance is the assurance, in all circles outside the executive, that anything else would be unthinkable. In this way, a delicate balance may be obtained between the necessities of democracy and freedom of negotiation. If confidence is once shattered by the belief that the rules go unheeded, then the swing of the pendulum is likely to be excessively violent for the executive has not been misguided concerning a matter of policy but morally contemptible. A further point can be found in Dicey which can help to account for the quality of reaction should such unfortunate circumstances occur. Far from viewing the powers of the Cabinet resulting from the survival of the prerogative as a potential threat to the sovereignty of Parliament, his verdict was precisely the opposite. It resulted in an increase in the authority of the House of Commons for the "Ministry in all matters of discretion carry out, or tend to carry out, the will of the House".+ "If government by Parliament is ever transformed into government by the House of Commons,

* Dicey, *op. cit.*, p. 358.
† Dicey, *op. cit.*, p. 351.
° Dicey, *op. cit.*, p. 351.
+ Dicey, *op. cit.*, p. 394–5.

the transformation will, it may be conjectured, be effected by use of the prerogatives of the Crown."*

Secure, therefore, in the belief that the Cabinet was the protector and safeguard of the people, the conduct of foreign affairs caused no fundamental disquiet. Isolated attempts were made from time to time to bring matters up to date. Thus in 1886, it was moved in the Commons that "it is not just or expedient to embark in war, contract engagements involving grave responsibilities for the Nation, and add territories to the Empire without the knowledge and consent of Parliament" but the loss of the motion by four votes led to no further action at the time.† It is also true that the Radical tradition had always thundered against the accustomed methods of handling foreign affairs, finding in this field a splendid opportunity to display nineteenth century oratory. "When you come to our foreign policy, you are no longer Englishmen, you are no longer free, you are recommended not to inquire. If you do, you are told you cannot understand it; you are snubbed, you are hustled aside. We are told that the matter is too deep for common understandings like ours – that there is a great mystery about it."° The system, however, was strong enough to withstand both the rolling rhetoric of this form of criticism and its associate of the attack upon the Diplomatic Service (see p. 57 *ff)* for both were contained within the security of constitutional propriety. By 1914, the confidence which this engendered had been shattered and in consequence the objects and conduct of foreign policy, the politicians and civil servants who attempted to make and execute it were torn viciously apart until the failure of communication between accuser and accused was almost complete. This sorry degeneration is a many-sided story but it is easier to see today that under all the faults of omission and commission of statesmen and the beliefs, interpretations and exaggerations of their detractors lay the fundamental fact of the relative decline

* Dicey, *op. cit.*, p. 397.
† *Hansard,* 3rd Series, Vol. 33, Col. 1386.
° John Bright at Glasgow in Dec. 1858.

in British power. It was this that created the real dilemma for a democratic foreign policy, for the security of the nation now necessitated actions which yet further limited her freedom of manoeuvre and which in consequence made a mockery of ultimate Parliamentary control.

Certain conclusions, which together formed the tradition of foreign policy, follow fairly obviously from Dicey's remarks. If the elector were ultimately king, then no form of secret agreement between Britain and a foreign power and no action which would prejudice the ultimate responsibility of the Commons fell within the rules. In return the executive might fairly be allowed a degree of latitude in its overseas dealing not accorded to it in domestic matters. The tradition of continuity in foreign policy, intended to express the needs of the country rather than a narrow party interest, obviated further drawbacks of political democracy. It will readily be appreciated that the smooth working of such principles is much enhanced if at home the political ethic which divides parties is not so very different and if abroad Great Britain is not under pressure. The luxury of developing the theory that all foreign policy is a bad foreign policy; the conception of Britain as the arbiter of Europe keeping the peace because no other state could ever be sure what she might do; the glory of splendid isolation itself were but the privileges of power. A country which is above the battle, which feels itself strong and secure and which has confidence in its own capacity for self-help has no need of much in the way of agreements and, equally, is spared the necessity to formulate its foreign policy objects very clearly. "Peace and trade" is good enough.* Within such a framework suspicion of the executive was largely dormant for no action that it took was likely to cause serious harm; whilst at the same time the executive had little temptation to indulge in subrosa practices which were of first class national importance.

Changing world circumstances destroyed British freedom of

* And such conditions make internal political agreement on the objects of foreign policy so much easier.

action and thus the essential premise upon which a theory of democratic foreign policy had been erected. The need to enter the hurly-burly of international politics necessitated a reconsideration of the national interest and in particular faced Great Britain with the concrete problem of the nature, significance and implications of international friendship. The world was growing smaller and events everywhere were likely to affect the European situation. "Peace was changing from a broad assumption to a narrow margin"* but too often this hard fact went unrecognised. These altered circumstances are clearly illustrated by the story of the Anglo–French entente. Signed originally as a settlement of certain limited colonial differences, within two years it had faced Great Britain with the possibility of her participation in a war in Europe. Could there be clearer evidence of the extent to which the world had contracted and simultaneously grown less secure for her? Under such circumstances the classical theory of foreign policy control required re-thinking. The conception of the country's freedom of action safeguarded by the ability of the House of Commons to take ultimate decisions on peace and war could have no meaning in a world in which security might be shattered overnight by events on the Franco–German frontier. If this had become the British frontier too, then her elementary duty was to consider how she was to protect it if the need arose. This had perforce to involve her in a relationship with France which was indeed an "entangling alliance" and whose details it would have been impolitic in the national interest to disclose. The conditional clause, however, is an important one. Not everybody accepted the validity of the analysis upon which it depended. The way was thus opened for searching scrutiny of the objects and conduct of British foreign policy. As international tension increased, the argument steadily became more acrimonious for during the few years remaining before 1914, observers of foreign affairs saw only too clearly the increasing possibility of war. Whilst the debate exposed the extent to which the assumptions about the handling

* R. Vansittart, *The Mist Procession,* p. 57.

of foreign affairs were false, it also laid bare the unrealistic nature of much of the criticism of that handling in so far as it was based on a non-recognition of the connection between traditional principle and a particular set of circumstances which had vanished, never to return. Isolationism was no longer a viable policy but the isolationist attitude of mind, a hang-over from days when freedom of manoeuvre still existed, was present in the country and clearly and strongly expressed.

Nevertheless, with whatever degree of awareness of the larger issue, from the turn of the nineteenth century Great Britain officially abandoned isolationism in favour of international friendship. By that date, it was clear that her basic interest was in peace, for her days of expansion were over and she was now concerned both to maintain and consolidate her position and to ensure a peaceful environment in which her trading interests might flourish. Whilst there was no disagreement on such broad policy objectives, considerable differences of opinion arose as to the method of fulfilment. It is a familiar point that during these years, Great Britain was not only isolated and unpopular but uncomfortable because of it and that these circumstances compelled the British government to take certain positive steps to improve the country's international standing. The cloud of general unease which lay over her foreign relations did not prove easy to dispel. It led her first of all to look for a friend in Germany but when this approach failed her attention turned to France where the desire for a friend coalesced with a more specific line of policy, namely the need to liquidate particular disagreements through which war, or acute tensions, might come.

The signature of the entente in 1904 was welcomed by all sections of opinion in the country. Whilst it was actually signed by the Conservatives, it appealed also to liberal and to trading interests as a mature act of policy which would ease certain frictions surrounding British trade, and which two democratic countries should not tolerate between them. It was later, and particularly from the Agadir crisis onwards, that it became, in their eyes, a "foreign entanglement" and in itself a cause of

international difficulty. Specifically, it was welcomed by Grey* whose memories of tensions with France whilst he was a junior minister were sufficiently strong for him thoroughly to approve the policy. At this early stage, there was no recognition that a severe and unexpected price might be demanded or that it would be for the Liberals to determine whether this price was to be paid. Indeed, it was not long before Grey, when back in office, carried this general policy one step further. The other major source of tension was to be found in Anglo–Russian relations and in 1907 Grey completed an entente similar to that which his predecessor had signed with France. The Anglo–Russian entente, however, was always a more controversial piece of work at home on the grounds that better relations had been obtained at the expense of the Persians and a shot in the arm for Russian tyranny. The completion of the triangle through a comparable Anglo–German entente proved beyond the British government. In essence this was because there were but few outstanding issues between them which were susceptible to negotiation and a solution of those that were had in fact been found by 1914. There were two real issues between the two countries and the British government found neither negotiable. The first was the navy. "What really determines the Foreign Policy of this country is the question of sea power. It is the Naval question which underlies the whole of our European Foreign policy."† Thus said Grey and it was not a matter upon which anyone disagreed with him. Even those who most disliked his policy had no doubt that the supremacy of the navy must be maintained. The *Economist*, not a particular supporter, agreed that the British fleet must be clearly and indubitably stronger than that of any other power° as did the Radical members of the Cabinet. "It was of course impossible

* To become Foreign Minister in the new Liberal government in December 1905.

† Grey to Imperial Defence Conference, May 26th 1911. *British Documents on the origins of the War,* Vol. VI, Appendix V. Hereafter referred to as B.D.

° 13th July, 1912.

not to have an uneasy feeling that the German battle fleet was built with the design of challenging British naval supremacy."* "The Radical section of the Cabinet were just as much alive as their Imperialist colleagues to the menace which rival warship programmes involved to the good relations they were anxious to maintain with Germany as well as with all other nations."† The second was the bid for German hegemony in Europe. Thus the German offer to cease the naval competition in return for British neutrality in a European war was also considered too high a price to pay. "We discussed the result of the visit in the Cabinet on Haldane's return, but we had to realise that political formulae are not safe."° Here opinion in the country was less united, both on the reality of the German threat and on the extent to which it might fairly be discovered in the successive crises which shook Europe before the war.

If the first broad strand in British policy was to eliminate disagreements betwen herself and the major European states, the second was to assist in the maintenance of relationships between the European powers themselves. War between any of them could only damage British trading interests, was unlikely to be isolated and would face Great Britain in an acute form with her perennial problem of preventing any one power becoming supreme in Europe. As the crises on the Continent became more frequent, so the danger for Great Britain became more acute. In general terms, Grey's policy was directed towards obtaining a solution on the assumption that each nation's interest in peace overcame its interest in obtaining a temporary victory. Since the ramifications of each event were wide and liable to touch each European power, Grey in the main favoured the conference as a diplomatic method. When his assumption was correct the method worked, when it was false, the technique was barren. In retrospect he wrote "The only sound basis for such an agreement [i.e.

---

* Lloyd George, *War Memoirs,* Vol. I, p. 10.

† George, *op. cit.,* p. 7.

° Grey, *Twenty-five Years,* Vol. I, p. 253.

between the Triple Alliance and the Entente] would have been a sense in the Great Powers that the common interest of all of them in peace was so great as to transcend the special interests of each, and a belief on the part of each that the other Powers felt this and could be trusted. Militarism did not believe this. It held the contrary view – that the opposing interests of nations are the dominant factors, and that their tendency to attack each other can only be kept in bounds by armaments; that peace can be secured not by justice, not by desire for it, not by agreements, but only by armed force."*

Once outstanding issues with France and Russia had been settled the danger of war for Britain came in two ways. The direct threat of the German navy where all agreed that British supremacy must be maintained, and the indirect threat, infinitely more subtle in the manner of its fulfilment, of a Germany victory over France and Russia, whether by war or diplomacy, by provocation or direct aggression. It was here that the decisive cleavage of opinion arose between the government and the radical elements in British society. All were agreed on the basic need of the country in a peaceful world and the development of British trade. All were agreed that her safety, her trade and her whole international position depended directly on the navy. All were agreed that the general line of policy contained in the liquidation of irritating disagreements was sound. Where opinion disagreed was on the analysis of German behaviour and in consequence on the tactics to be pursued as particular problems arose. These differences crystallised over the question of the importance of France to Britain and here one can distinguish three broad groupings of belief. The first was that of the Foreign Office which had no doubt that Germany constituted a real threat to the independence of Great Britain, albeit at one remove and that the most effective way to restrain her from executing that threat would be to convert the ententes into direct alliances. From the official side, two themes stand out with stark clarity. The first is the growth of

* Grey, *op. cit.,* Vol. II, p. 51.

suspicion of Germany and her motives and the second the development of the view that the independence of France must be considered a vital national interest and therefore treated as if it were the independence and security of Great Britain. At the other extreme was the radical viewpoint that Germany was no menace and that the support which Great Britain tended to give her entente partners was provocative and carried the danger of creating the threat she feared. Thus the further away one moves from the hub of the wheel the less the acceptance of the reality of the German threat, the greater the readiness to put the best rather than the worst construction on her actions, the less the recognition of the importance of France. It is not to be expected that everyone will think alike and it might fairly be argued that a function of free discussion is to allow the expression, not only of diversity of judgement, but of differing moral standards upon which those judgements are based. On this occasion, those who were immediately responsible for British action thought primarily of the national interest in the practical sense of the security of the country, whilst those with no direct involvement thought mainly in terms of the obvious interest of all men in peace. Ultimately, these were arguments which derived from two different views of the nature of the international world and between them it was difficult to obtain a satisfactory point of contact. One consequent disadvantage was the conflict of opinion, the hesitations and doubts when the possibility of action arose.

Finally, in the middle, with all the disadvantages thus entailed, stood Grey. His view of German policy was not so clear cut as either of the extremists. He wanted to do nothing to offend Germany or to make it more difficult for her pacific elements to prevail; in particular, he had no wish to give either France or Russia the carte blanche which an outright alliance would entail. On the other hand, he could not afford to let the German position in Europe grow steadily more powerful so that ultimately Great Britain might have to face a stronger enemy. In consequence, he found it necessary to support both France and Russia against Germany, in order, at one remove, to retain the independence

of Great Britain. There could therefore be no doubt in his mind that if war should actually come it was in the British interest to fight for France. "My own opinion" wrote Grey on the early 1906 crisis "was, that if Germany forced war on France in order to destroy the Anglo–French Agreement, we ought to go to the help of France."* These three broad ideas can be seen in action through a survey of Anglo–French relations from the signing of the entente to the outbreak of war. Unfortunately, the circumstances of 1914 obscured the problem and with the return of peace British policy was once again hampered by the lack of clarity apparent in the country on the degree of importance to be attached to the independence of France.

II

On 8th April 1904, the series of agreements known as the Anglo–French Entente were signed in which, *inter alia,* the recognition of British predominance in Egypt was matched by acceptance of the French position in Morocco.† Under the latter agreement Great Britain recognised

> ... that it appertains to France ... to preserve order and to provide assistance for the purpose of all administrative, economic, financial and military reforms which it may require ...

and agreed

> ... not to obstruct France in any action she might take for such a purpose providing that such action does not interfere with British trading rights.

Article 9 stated that the two governments would "afford to one

* Grey, *op. cit.,* Vol. I, p. 77.
† The Egyptian side of the bargain is largely ignored in what follows.

another their diplomatic support in order to obtain the execution of the clauses of the present Declaration".

A secret annexe provided that in the event of either government finding themselves "constrained by the force of circumstances to modify their policy" in respect of Egypt or Morocco then the principles of commercial liberty, free passage at Suez and the non-fortification of the Gibraltar coast were to be respected. Furthermore, accepting that there was no immediate intention to change the capitulations or judicial system, Great Britain agreed to consider French suggestions for such reforms in Morocco if and when they were made. Finally it was agreed that certain areas of Morocco should fall to Spain if the Sultan should cease to exercise control.

It was not the content but the signature of the secret articles that was significant. In fact the annexe only took the published agreement one stage further and the latter itself foreshadowed the predominance of France in the not unlikely situation of Morocco breaking up. Nevertheless, it did commit an ostensibly democratic country to an obligation of which it knew nothing and on these grounds must be condemned. Its most important diplomatic ill-effect was to contribute its quota to the growth of international suspicion. This was because the knowledge of a secret agreement soon leaked out in diplomatic circles and Germany for one was afraid that there was more in it than was actually the case. Bülow feared that it contained clauses concerning the Rhine frontier* and it obviously lent colour to the rumours in Germany in 1905 of an Anglo–French alliance. The clauses were finally alluded to in the Temps of November 11th, 1911; officially published by Great Britain and presented to the Commons on November 24th and acknowledged by Grey in debate on November 27th "We have laid before the House the secret Articles of the Agreement with France of 1904. There are no other secret engagements. The late Government made that Agreement in 1904.

* See Bülow to Metternich, June 4th, 1904, quoted H.G. Nicolson, *Sir Arthur Nicolson, bart., First Lord Carnock,* p.149. Hereafter Carnock.

They kept those Articles secret, and I think to everybody the reason will be obvious why they did so. It would have been invidious to make those Articles public. In my opinion they were entirely justified in keeping those Articles secret, because they were not Articles which commit this House to serious obligations . . . For ourselves we have not made a single secret article of any kind since we came into office."*

The secret annexe did harm at home as well as abroad. The suspicion and its later confirmation that all had not been told destroyed some degree of domestic confidence in the capacity of governments to act responsibly. Had it been published in 1904, it is unlikely that any but a very small minority would have rushed to the championship of the Moors as against the predatory Europeans on the lines of the reaction to the Hoare–Laval pact not so many years later. The age of self-determination had not yet arrived and it is noticeable that the book most critical of British policy in Morocco, namely E. D. Morel's "Morocco in Diplomacy"† was a great deal more concerned with the fact that Germany had not had her cut, than with the fact that the Moors should be left unmolested.

As it was, Great Britain was committed to diplomatic support for France in an area where trouble was likely and which could not be isolated from the main currents of international affairs. Thus to view the problem for her as one of providing diplomatic support for France without it appearing to be anti-German in character and as one which would not have wider implications than had been intended in a settlement of differences was in itself too simple. It took time, however, for this to be realised and the pace of recognition was not the same for everybody. Indeed, some people never learnt this lesson. Circumstances made it impossible to treat the entente as an isolated incident and since Morocco was in fact an international problem, it was not

* *Parliamentary Debates,* 5th series, House of Commons, Vol.32, Cols.57–8. Hereafter this series is simply *Hansard.*

† Published 1912. It was later reprinted as *Ten Years of Secret Diplomacy.* References to the latter are to the 6th edn. of 1920.

possible for Great Britain to prevent others interpreting her actions in terms of their significance for international groupings. Thus in turn Britain was faced with a further problem. Having signed the entente it was now necessary to maintain it in the face of action by a third party. Specifically this meant the need to decide whether German policy in Morocco was concerned with her commercial interests therein or with the desire to expose the weakness of the Anglo–French relationship. If her true object were to break up the entente then, once Great Britain had recognised her own need of support, it is difficult to see that she had any effective alternative policy but to attempt to prevent Germany succeeding in this aim. The newness of the Anglo–French relationship must also be remembered since this increased the sensitivity of France to any appearance of backsliding. It was necessary for those actually handling day to day affairs to take great pains to prevent such suspicions.* The obverse of such an attitude to France was the need to present an impassive face of rectitude to Germany that British conduct might arouse no fears. We cannot know whether a more sympathetic attitude to Germany would have altered events in any way, but coldness does not normally win confidence or quieten distrust. If the latter is unfounded, special attention is often necessary to remove it. This Great Britain did not provide. A recurring example of this is the question of the press. On more than one occasion the German Ambassador considered he had reason to complain of the hostility of the British press but neither Lansdowne nor Grey would ever say more than that the British government had no control over the newspapers.† Again, during the Moroccan crisis of 1905–6, the British line of diplomatic support for France was clearly understood by all, including Germany, from the start. This led the British delegate at Algeciras to refuse to act upon the German suggestion that he should urge a compromise on France. The only reply he felt himself able to give was that it

* See e.g. Grey, *op. cit.,* Vol.I, pp.104–110.
† See e.g. B.D., Vol.III, Nos.99, 229.

was not for Great Britain to determine the terms that France should accept but to support her in what she herself had determined.*

The official expectation was not that Germany would draw the conclusion that Great Britain was hostile but that she would cease to trouble once she had realised she could not break the Franco–British link, but whilst policy-makers placed the relationship with France as the foremost of their worries, internal critics saw only the face that British policy turned to Germany and deduced from it that Britain was anti-German. They thus neglected to consider the implications of international friendship and the fact that this is not likely to be rated very highly if it does not mean support in a crisis. The Radical argument before the war was often that the country should be an ally of none and a friend to all and in consequence the issue of practical help to a friend was not publicly canvassed. Many people still wanted the independence of action of isolation, long after isolation had gone.

The reception of the Agreements by France was generally welcoming but the German reaction was more dubious. On the Continent their implications in terms of European politics were perhaps more clearly seen than in England. A *Times* despatch from Paris on the signing of the entente was significantly headed "The Isolation of Germany" and already in April the French Ambassador had raised with Lansdowne the question of the possibility of a British rapprochement with Russia. Both Bülow and Holstein held the view by late 1904 that Great Britain was definitely unfriendly towards Germany and might possibly attack her. Whilst the initial German reception of the entente might be described as reserved but not unfriendly she began to feel more uneasy as the summer went by. A sign of the developing German attitude was reported by Nicolson "In the autumn of 1904, . . . I received one morning a visit from . . . Herr von Kühlmann, who mentioned to me in the course of conversation that his Government did not consider that the Anglo–French Agreement had any official

* B.D. Vol.III, Nos.265, 362.

existence: it had not been officially communicated to the German Government, and had not consequently been officially accepted by them. France and Great Britain were of course at liberty to settle their differences, but these were matters between those two countries alone, and in no wise affected the rights and interests of third parties".*

It is now time to turn to Morocco itself. By the end of the nineteenth century Morocco was entering the international arena. The European powers had genuine commercial interests there whilst the state of the country was such that neither life nor property, whether foreign or native, was adequately protected. Other interests, however, were super-imposed upon material ones. Great Britain desired to protect the Straits of Gibraltar by preventing the fortification of that part of the African coast; France saw in Morocco the consolidation of her North African empire of Tunis and Algeria; Germany, the late comer in colonial expansion, saw possibilities here too, whilst Spain, who possessed certain rights in Morocco, wished to hang on to a last remnant of her greatness overseas. Inevitably the situation in Morocco would have to develop because of its unstable nature; equally inevitably the European powers could not divorce their interests in the Moroccan question from their foreign policy as a whole. The tensions and suspicions between them were bound to be reflected in their Moroccan policies to some degree; in the event these pressures were to prove the more important in determining the outcome for Morocco.

Given the opening up of the country by outside interests, the possibilities of internal reform and the attainment of reasonable stability were but two; an agreed international solution which would be presented jointly to the Sultan and supervised on behalf of the international community and one which was based on an individual national interest. By the entente agreements France had obtained recognition from Great Britain and Spain of her prerogative but German acceptance had been bought neither by

* Carnock, p.159.

consultation nor by compensation and it was in accordance with current standards of State behaviour that she should feel both humiliated and hurt. Against a background of increasing internal chaos and public recognition of the need for reforms to establish a stable and peaceful Morocco, France proceeded to consolidate the position diplomacy had afforded her, Germany to initiate clumsy manoeuvres of somewhat doubtful purpose and the Sultan of Morocco to exploit the increasingly obvious dissensions between the European powers. A deteriorating situation increased suspicions on all sides and especially after the Kaiser's visit to Tangier in March 1905. In short, France saw Germany waving the big stick and attacking her position in Morocco; Great Britain saw a move out of all proportion to German professed interests which were commercial and which could be safeguarded by negotiation if France accepted equality of trading and industrial rights. If Germany had a further interest, this could only be the desire to obtain a Moroccan port or to break up the entente, or both. Neither of these was Great Britain prepared to consider and her attitude began to harden.

In April 1905 Germany began to sound the powers concerning a conference on Morocco and thus the possibility of internationalising the question. France was opposed to this and Great Britain supported her. That month Lansdowne, via Bertie, expressed to France his opposition to Germany obtaining a port in Morocco. "You are authorised to inform Minister for Foreign Affairs that we should be prepared to join French government in offering strong opposition to such proposal and to beg that if question is raised French government will afford us a full opportunity of conferring with them as to steps which might be taken in order to meet it."*

This suggestion was seized on with eagerness by the French and followed up by Cambon in London on 17th May, 1905. Lansdowne was still anxious that Franco-British policy should be concerted.

* B.D., Vol.III, No.90.

"I observed" wrote Landsdowne of this conversation "that the moral of all these incidents [not only those in Morocco] seemed to me to be that our two Governments should continue to treat one another with the most absolute confidence, should keep one another fully informed of everything which came to their knowledge, and should, so far as possible, discuss in advance any contingencies by which they might in the course of events find themselves confronted."*

Cambon and Delcassé seem to have genuinely believed that Lansdowne was offering France an alliance and, in view of this encouraging support, Delcassé was in favour of standing out as the German attitude to France became more threatening. At a French Cabinet meeting on 6th June, he therefore took the view that Germany was bluffing and that France could afford to withstand her. The majority view, however, was against him and for the first time the critical question was raised that, even were she willing, Great Britain was in no position to give effective support to France. If Germany attacked, she could not in fact prevent France from being over-run. Here, then, was indeed a turning point for it was to fill the empty gap that the military conversations were soon to be proposed.

This episode, leading as it did to Delcassé's resignation, increased mutual suspicions between Great Britain and Germany. Great Britain saw that Germany had bullied France out of all proportion to her interests in Morocco. Germany, crediting the rumours of an offer of an offensive/defensive alliance and noting the hostility of the British press, inclined to the view that Great Britain was her real enemy. German fears were thus increased and she was ever more determined to detach France from friendship with Great Britain whilst she in turn was increasingly resolved to maintain the Gallic bond.

On 7th June Germany accepted the Sultan's invitation to a conference. On 8th June the British Cabinet discussed Morocco, decided to reserve its position on this proposal and to exchange

* B.D., Vol.III, No.94.

ideas with France. When France agreed to the arrangement, Great Britain fell into line. By the September, Franco–German agreement on the agenda had been reached and the conference finally opened in the New Year. This long period of delay saw further German actions which both deepened British suspicions and strengthened French opinion of the need to stick fast to the entente. Their effect, therefore, was further to solidify the alignment and not to weaken it.

Before the conference actually opened, important political changes had taken place in Great Britain. On 5th December, 1905 the Liberals came to power under the Premiership of Campbell-Bannerman. Asquith went to the Exchequer, Grey to the Foreign Office and Haldane became Secretary of State for War. Parliament was dissolved and the government scattered until the results of the general election of 12th January 1906 at which a Liberal majority was returned. It was during this interregnum when Grey was at the Foreign Office for three days a week only and when no Cabinet was meeting that certain important events occured.

This Liberal government represented two schools of thought roughly identifiable with the pro- and anti-Boer groups of the South African war. In broad terms the pro-Boer party (Campbell-Bannerman, Morley, Lloyd George) were against a forward policy in external relations and opposed to British support of any power if this might draw her into European tensions. The anti-Boer party (Asquith, Grey, Haldane) although they had not at this stage considered the possible implications of the friendship with France yet possessed greater familiarity with a more hard-headed conception of what might constitute the national interest. In an assessment of Grey's foreign policy it is important to remember that he had always to consider the domestic situation and the need not to offend the Radical section of his party.

Considerable uncertainty existed outside the new government over its likely attitude to foreign affairs and the extent to which its predecessor's positive policy towards France would be continued. Although Campbell-Bannerman was known as a francophil many thought his government would soon lapse once again into isolation. France, in particular, was alarmed and concerned lest the Lansdowne attitude of prior consultation should die. Thus on 10th January 1906, Cambon called on Grey to inquire how far diplomatic support at Algeciras would go and whether, if Germany attacked France, British military assistance would be given. Grey replied that he was unable to promise anything regarding armed support, that he was not in a position to consult his colleagues and that until the poll had been held the verdict of the country on Liberal policy would not be known. Lord Loreburn* claims that the Cabinet could in fact have been called together perfectly easily; even so the further point that the government had not as yet been confirmed in office still holds. Cambon was asked to repeat the question after the elections, which he did. Meanwhile, on 10th January, Grey gave it as his personal opinion that although the circumstances of the case would affect the British attitude, if there were direct German agression on France on a matter arising out of the entente, public opinion would be strongly moved in her favour. Finally, Cambon asked for unofficial naval and military conversations in case the necessity of support arose. Grey agreed.†

Grey found it necessary, too, to clarify to the German Ambassador the view point of the new government. He warned Count Metternich on 3rd January° that if trouble arose between Germany and France over Morocco he, Grey, thought British public opinion would be strongly pro-French.

As is well known, the Cambon conversation was never repeated to the full Cabinet. It went to the Prime Minister and to Lord Ripon, the leader of the House of Lords, to Bertie the Ambassador in Paris and to Asquith. Grey also spoke to Haldane in order to put the military conversations in train. On 21st January, Campbell-Bannerman wrote to Grey "When would you like to have a Cabinet? ... Would you like the answer to the French to be

* *How the War Came,* p.80.
† B.D., Vol.III, No.210.
° B.D., Vol.III, No.229.

confirmed by a Cabinet before it is given?"* Nothing was decided within the next ten days and on the 1st February Grey was called from London because of an accident to his wife which proved to be fatal. With the passing of the acute diplomatic crisis the matter, presumably, faded from mind. The military talks which were set in train in 1906 were not disclosed to the Cabinet till 1912.

On 31st January a second interview with Cambon was held at which the Frenchman came for his answer. Grey refused to be drawn into a definite commitment. He pointed out that a proper defensive alliance could not be kept secret but must go to Parliament for agreement; it would imply prior consultation by France on her Moroccan policy so that, if need be, we would "be free to press upon the French Government concessions or alterations of their policy which might seem to us desirable to avoid a war". He repeated his personal opinion that if Germany attacked France, Britain could not remain neutral and he told Cambon that he had so informed Metternich.†

It is, of course, true that in these conversations Grey promised nothing more than diplomatic support; this was contained in the original entente agreement as was public knowledge. Nevertheless, the open discussion of the possibility of war did point to the existence of a developing situation which it would have been wise to disclose.

At this time too, an important change took place in the Foreign Office. Sanderson retired and was replaced as Permanent Under-Secretary by Charles Hardinge on 2nd February. Hardinge held a more dynamic view of his office than his predecessor and he was known to hold the belief that German policy was generally aggressive and that he was opposed to it.°

On 16th January the Algeciras conference opened. Great Britain was represented by Arthur Nicolson, the Ambassador at Madrid, who had previously spent a period in Morocco. His instructions

* Grey, *op. cit.*, Vol.I, p.86.
† B.D., Vol.III, No.219.
° Lord Hardinge, *Old Diplomacy*, p.122.

were to "cordially support the proposals which your French colleague may bring forward with a view to the improvement of the existing state of affairs, and you should encourage your Spanish colleague to adopt a similar attitude. You should at the same time take care that no measure of arrangement is sanctioned which might impair the rights and privileges secured to Great Britain in that Declaration".* This policy had previously been agreed with the Prime Minister. A private letter had also gone from Grey to Nicolson to the effect that the writer believed Germany intended to refuse France her special position in Morocco for which the entente had promised British support. Thus if Germany succeeded in preventing France obtaining what she wanted it would be a great blow at the entente; if France, with British help, were to obtain her object then the prestige of the entente would be enhanced. "Our main object therefore must be to help France to carry her point at the Conference."†

Within the context of this broad instruction, Nicolson was left very much on his own as to how he was to conduct himself at the conference but it implied a steady support to be given by him to the French delegates, even sometimes against his better judgement as to the concessions that France might well make. Behind the scenes Nicolson did a great deal to persuade the French to come to an amicable compromise but at the conference table he was always prepared to support their view. Neither was he prepared to urge the French delegate to a solution which was unacceptable under the implied threat of a British weakening of support. This was the testing time for the entente and Britain was dealing with a sensitive partner; one who, moreover, was being threatened with war by a stronger neighbour. She was only too ready to see in any British moderation proof that the entente meant nothing. Nicolson was, therefore, in a delicate position for Great Britain did not wish the conference to end in failure, especially one that could be laid at the doors of France. He had

---

* B.D., Vol.III, No.193.
† B.D., Vol.III, No.200.

thus to try to persuade France to be reasonable but not to carry persuasion so far that she felt let down or that Germany could claim a diplomatic victory. His actions, which he certainly had to determine for himself as the situation developed, were always based upon the instructions he had received.

The proceedings of the conference at first dragged seriously. They were as difficult and awkward as the prior posturings of the participants would lead one to expect and although an agreement was reached by April, it is clear that the effects of the conference were bad. The episode constituted an important step away from fluidity in international groupings. Germany had found that Austria–Hungary was her only true friend; Great Britain was more firmly attached to France and at the conference Russia and Italy had generally supported her also. Nicolson was left with strong suspicions of German motives and with an acute dislike of her bullying methods. Although the seeds of this attitude had been sown earlier, 1906 was the turning point for him; after this he became steadily more conscious of a German menace. Eyre Crowe, in the Foreign Office, reviewed the situation and the implications of Algeciras for Franco–British and Anglo-German relations in a document drawing attention to the growing seriousness of the situation.*

III

In view of the threatening attitude which Germany adopted after the signing of the entente, French governments had to consider the possibility of war. They were therefore concerned to translate the principle of support into the terms of practical assistance from Great Britain. In particular, it was necessary to have prepared plans which could be put into action immediately on the outbreak of war because of the anticipated speed of the German attack. It must be remembered that all countries considered that a

* B.D., Vol. III, Appendix A. See p.86 below.

European war would be short and characterised by swiftly moving armies; for the French, therefore, the important factor was the amount of land assistance which could be provided within a few days. Only plans which had been laid beforehand could hope to be effective and an approach was thus made by France to arrange for this prior planning.

Whilst military preparations to fight on the Continent were a novel proposition for Great Britain, it is possible to detect signs of a growing readiness to contemplate changes in the traditional methods of defence which implied the belief that she could no longer fully rely for the protection of the Empire upon her naval weapon but that she would additionally require an army prepared for large-scale fighting on land. One of the most important members of this school of thought was Col. Repington who, in January 1905, became Military Correspondent of *The Times* and who conceived it to be his duty to create a climate of opinion favourable towards increased military strength. It was to him that the questions of British military assistance to France and the British action should Belgium be invaded were raised at the turn of the year. From Repington the matter passed both to political and Service circles. The practical issue had thus, at last, been placed squarely before the British.

On 10th January, as previously explained, Cambon took the matter up with Grey and asked for unofficial communications between the Admiralty, War Office and the French attachés on what action might be taken if the two countries were allied in war; it being recognised that such talks would commit neither government. "I did not dissent from this view" wrote Grey. This request was reinforced by a despatch from Bertie received on 18th January 1906 to the effect that, whilst there was no desire in France for war and therefore very little chance she would invade Morocco relying on British support, there was great mistrust of Germany. In the French view, the German danger would be counteracted if Germany knew that in the last resort Great Britain would stand by France. Without such an assurance there was danger of a revulsion of French feeling against Great

Britain. This despatch was not circulated at that time to the Cabinet but to Ripon and Campbell-Bannerman only.* Grey wrote to the War Office on 15th January expressing his official agreement that the talks should start, which they did.

Campbell-Bannerman agreed to the talks reluctantly. His view was more down to earth than Grey's for he saw that discussions might in effect commit Great Britain. "But I do not like the stress laid upon joint preparations. It comes very close to an honourable undertaking: and it will be known on both sides of the Rhine."† Grey on the other hand always held that these discussions were important on a tecnical level only and in no way prejudiced the principle of whether assistance ought, in certain circumstances, to be given or not. True to his conception, Grey showed no interest in the talks, "What they settled I never knew".°

Asquith, when Prime Minister, was informed of the conversations by Grey in a letter of 16th April 1911, and Asquith's opinion at that time seems to have been similar to Cambell-Bannerman's He wrote to Grey on 5th September 1911, "Conversations such as that between Gen. Joffre and Col. Fairholme seem to me rather dangerous; especially the part which refers to possible British assistance. The French ought not to be encouraged, in present circumstances, to make their plans on any assumptions of this kind".+

The conversations continued. Lloyd George was informed of them in 1911 but the rest of the Cabinet not till the following year when he claims that the majority were "aghast".+ Presumably Grey's view of Olympian detachment did not appeal to them. This deception made the Radical section of the Cabinet more suspicious of Grey and played its part in making his job of obtaining unanimity in 1914 more difficult.

A side-light on the British view was expressed to Cambon by

* B.D., Vol.III, No.213. See also J. A. Spender, *Life of Campbell-Bannerman,* Vol.2. p.256.

† Spender, *op. cit.,* Vol.2, p.257. To Ripon, Feb. 2nd.

° Grey, *op. cit.,* Vol.I, p.94.

\+ These letters are quoted in Grey, *op. cit.,* Vol.I, pp.94–5.

× George. *op. cit.,* Vol.I, p.50.

Sanderson shortly after the latter's resignation. His view was that the conversations could imply no more than that the governments should consult together, this being the limit to which the British government could properly bind itself without "in some way making Parliament aware of the obligations that it was incurring" and no government, in his experience, had gone beyond that. The Cabinet, he said, could give no pledge which would be morally binding on the country to go to war in some circumstances without telling Parliament. He added an interesting practical point to the effect that statesmen were agreed that it was unwise to bring hypothetical cases and desired action in them before the Cabinet for discussion was then on the level of principles and opinions inevitably differed, whilst in a concrete case unanimity was very much more likely to be obtained.*

IV

The Agadir crisis of 1911 continued the story of Morocco as a factor in the events leading up to the war and is a decisive landmark in Anglo–German relations since the general public in both countries was for the first time brought face to face with the imminent possibility of war between them. For the five years separating these two Moroccan crises had seen events which had increased the divisions between Germany and Great Britain and which were further evidence of the increasing decay of the international order.

There are three matters which appear as of outstanding importance in these intervening years. The first was the signing of the Anglo–Russian entente which committed Great Britain more closely to the side of the Dual Alliance. Once again, the entente was a removal of difficulties in certain limited areas rather than a sign that Britain would henceforth be in accord with Russia over international problems. Nevertheless, from the British point

* B.D., Vol.III, No.220(b)

of view, the advantage was not purely imperial for the known weakness of Russia presented the constant danger that she would be drawn into a German alliance. If this in turn were followed by French absorption into a European bloc then the isolation of Great Britain would be complete. To secure Russia to the entente side, however, could only be done indirectly, not only because of public opinion at home, but also because Russia would not have agreed to any documents which could have been construed as anti-German as indeed the Convention was not.

Relations with Russia on matters arising out of the Convention continued from time to time to cause distrust but its importance as a factor in the European balance of power was established when, on October 6th, 1908, Austria–Hungary announced the annexation of Bosnia–Herzegovina. Grey was afraid that if he did not support Russia, Isvolsky would be forced to resign and his place taken by someone unfavourable to the Anglo–Russian entente. He thus supported the Russian demand for an international conference but he refused to reply to a Russian enquiry as to what Great Britain would do if "a crisis arose in the Balkans and Germany took the part of her ally". The only certain help upon which Russia could call was from her ally France whose attention at that moment was fully engaged over an incident in Morocco which once more was poisoning her relations with Germany. Russia, therefore, had no alternative but to accept the Austrian action in the Balkans under the threat of a German diplomatic ultimatum and the matter was settled by March 1909.

Although the central powers had won a diplomatic victory the price they paid was high. Russia had been made to feel an inadequate protector of the South Slavs and was less likely to be willing to be humiliated in the future. She had been made aware, too, that the German link was a weak one and that her better course would be to build up her relations with the entente powers. At the same time Austria–Hungary had discovered she was able to take her own decisions in the Balkans and that in the last resort Germany would have no other course than to support her. In the Balkans therefore Grey's policy was directed in the following years towards keeping the peace so that Austria and Russia would not find themselves in the position of supporting opposing factions and unable for prestige reasons to withdraw from exposed positions. When war in the Balkans did come, he concentrated on a settlement which would satisfy both parties. Nicolson was left more than ever convinced of the reality of the German threat to dominate Europe, fearful lest the Anglo–Russian entente would wither and that Russia would soon be expected to make further concessions in the Balkans, demands she would not be able to resist alone. Hardinge's view was very similar. Both men appreciated the weakness of Russia and the danger that, without support, she might be sucked into the orbit of the central powers and thus both were anxious to see the ententes become alliances.*

During this crisis in European affairs, the British public and Parliament became very alarmed about the German navy.

The first German naval law was introduced in 1897, and the following year the Kaiser declared that Germany's future lay upon the water. Although at first this caused Great Britain little or no anxiety it was an issue which always contained the seeds of danger for it was one on which Great Britain in the last resort would not compromise. It was an article of faith that the maintenance of the British position depended upon the maintenance of her sea power. The size of the necessary British building, however, was a matter of acute domestic controversy with the Radicals constantly attempting to cut down the naval estimates, whilst at the same time accepting the principle of British supremacy at sea. In 1904 Sir John Fisher became First Sea Lord and together with Earl Cawdor, his political chief as from the following year, put through two important changes. The first in time was the redistribution of the fleet so that it was concentrated nearer home and potentially able to protect Great Britain against a German navy in the North Sea. From then on the fleet was divided into three. The Mediterranean Command based on Malta, the Atlantic

* Carnock, p.308. Also Hardinge, Memorandum, April (?) 1909, B.D., Vol.V, Appendix III.

based on Gibraltar and the Channel Command based on the home ports. This was a weakening of strength in the Mediterranean and was a policy approved by the Committee of Imperial Defence. The entente with France from then on had a strategic as well as a diplomatic justification for the French fleet based on Toulon would compensate for the loss of British strength. It also meant that the Admiralty kept a close watch on German Moroccan policy to ensure that she did not obtain a potential base in this area.

The second half of the Fisher–Cawdor policy was the Dreadnought programme. The first of these new ships was launched in 1906 under conditions of great secrecy but the original project, designed to place Great Britain in a position of incontestable superiority, was soon abandoned for a more modest policy. By 1909, the Admiralty was in acute state of anxiety lest the country, for a few months of 1912, be actually inferior in Dreadnoughts, though not, of course, in other naval vessels. When realised by the public this possibility caused much alarm. An increased programme was agreed to under the pressure of a thoroughgoing naval scare whose critical phases ran concurrently with the crisis in the Balkans.

Fleet building continued on both sides and all efforts to do a deal to stop it failed. From July 1910 to May 1911 Anglo–German negotiations on fleet limitation were tried but no bargain could be struck. The German quid pro quo was a guarantee of British neutrality in a European war and this Great Britain was not prepared to give.

In addition to these troubles, Morocco had continued to be internally unstable and an international bone of contention despite the Act of Algeciras. French forward action to deal with disturbances continued to be looked on askance by Germany. Tension between France and Germany in 1907 over the bombardment of Casablanca and later the recognition of the Pretender to the Moroccan throne was followed by the more serious episode of the Casablanca deserters befriended by the German Consul in September 1908. A period of acute ill-will followed which was again smoothed over and in December of that year Franco–German negotiations on their Moroccan interests were opened. These led to an agreement of 1909 whereby German trading interests and the predominance of French political ones were recognised. Although welcoming the détente, Grey was not entirely happy for fear the agreement meant that German commercial interests were to obtain an unfair share to the detriment of others. Grey had no intention of allowing the British interests in Morocco to be ignored, thus foreshadowing his attitude in the 1911 crisis.

In December 1910 a French ship was sent to the closed port of Agadir in Southern Morocco thus causing a fluttering of the diplomatic dovecotes as to what the move presaged. In Germany the Pan-Germans were outraged at what seemed to them to be yet another threat to their country's legitimate interests but the German government at first tried to soothe them down. The internal situation in Morocco at that time and in the ensuing months was very unstable and the French reacted by sending troops to the country with the objects of restoring order and protecting the Europeans. In March 1911 troops entered Casablanca and Rabat and in April a French column was sent into the interior, towards Fez. This last action was too much for Germany. On 1st July, the Panther arrived and anchored off Agadir. The crisis was on.

The British interest in Morocco in 1911 lay at two levels. On the one hand were her commercial interests in the country itself, on the other Morocco as a factor in international affairs. In this latter context her interest again needs to be divided into two. The first was the need to prevent Germany obtaining a port or at the least to obtain satisfactory conditions should she do so, and the second was the need to support the ententes. By 1911 the international situation for Great Britain had worsened. The naval rivalry with Germany meant that for her own sake she could not afford to see the ententes weakened and there was danger of this. The occupation of Bosnia–Herzegovina pointed to the fact that war might come through an Austro–Russian clash in the Balkans rather than through a direct Franco–German conflict. The maintenance of peace was more difficult, albeit as necessary to the over-riding British interest, than a few years earlier but the makers of British policy were more alive than previously to the danger of obtaining it at the expense of weakening her friends. In Morocco, although Grey had welcomed the signs of Franco–German rapprochment in 1909 he was aware of the possibility of this taking place at British expense both in respect of her commerce, and as a symptom of international isolation. He did not want peace at the price of France veering to the German orbit. In 1911, this dual attitude is clearly to be seen.

Grey's reaction, therefore, to the news of the despatch of the Panther, a reaction which was supported by his officials, was that Great Britain must have a say in any new arrangement in Morocco. He, therefore, informed the German Ambassador that he and the Prime Minister considered the situation so important that it would have to be discussed by the Cabinet before they could express an opinion on the British reaction.*

The Cabinet was summoned for 4th July. Despite the differences of opinion in the Cabinet on foreign affairs it did not speak with a dual voice. It agreed that, whilst for Great Britain to send a ship would be taking too violent a step, a firm stand should be taken towards both France and Germany. France should be told that Great Britain would fulfil her treaty obligations in any diplomatic discussions with Germany and in which she would expect to play a part, whilst Germany should be told that Great Britain could not be disinterested in what was happening in Morocco. Grey thus reported to Metternich that Great Britain must be concerned in a Moroccan settlement both because of her own interests there and because of her treaty obligations to France. She would recognise no agreement come to without her.† Arthur Nicolson wanted a stronger line than this as is disclosed in his letter to Hardinge of 5th July 1911. Believing this was the latest

* B.D., Vol.VII, No.347.
† B.D., Vol.VII, No.356.

move in a carefully thought out plan, he wanted a ship sent out at once to Agadir. He expressed himself as not sorry for the episode on the grounds that it would serve as an eye-opener as to the true nature of the German intentions.*

Meanwhile Franco–German negotiations on a settlement, which had begun earlier, were continuing. The German demands at first were very high for compensation elsewhere in Africa. On 18th July a report of them was received in the Foreign Office. Crowe minuted "This is a trial of strength . . . Concession means not loss of interests or loss of prestige. It means defeat. . . . The defeat of France is a matter vital to this country. Therefore it will be of little use for H.M.G. to consider in detail the particular conditions which might or might not be put up with, before deciding the larger and dominant question whether England is prepared to fight by the side of France if necessary."† This too was Nicolson's view though there was no doubt in his mind that Great Britain must support France at this crisis.

A fortnight went by and no reply came from Germany to Grey's remarks of 4th July. The Foreign Secretary grew anxious lest Germany failed to recognise the legitimate British interest in the matter and afraid lest the British "long ignorance and silence combined must lead the Germans to imagine that we don't very much care . . . I think therefore it is essential that I should on Friday be authorised to make some communication to Germany . . . that . . . we must become a party to a discussion of the situation".°

On Friday, 21st July, Lloyd George, as Chancellor of the Exchequer, was due to make a speech at the Mansion House and it was in this public statement that the seriousness of the British interest was reasserted. As a leading member of the Radical section of the government, his firmness was obviously of high significance in displaying its unity. What is of equal importance is that he determined his attitude for himself. His consultation

* B.D., Vol.VII, No.359.
† B.D., Vol.VII, No.392 attached minute.
° Grey to Asquith, B.D., Vol.VII, No.399.

of Grey and Asquith merely gave him their approval* and there was no general consultation of the Cabinet. The speech was followed by an explanation from the German Ambassador as to the reasons for the German action. Negotiations between France and Germany continued but for some months the danger of war remained and as a result the British war preparations became more efficient, notably as a result of the meeting of the Committee of Imperial Defence on 23rd August. The negotiations finally reached a satisfactory conclusion. The German acceptance of the French political influence in Morocco was bought for an area of French West Africa and by the conventions of 3rd November, 1911 Morocco ceased to be a factor in European affairs.

On 27th November an important debate on foreign affairs was held. Not only was there serious concern over the recent crisis but the secret clauses of the Anglo–French entente had been revealed. It thus seemed that the whole conception of Parliamentary responsibility had been thrown overboard and inevitably raised the suspicion that there were other secret agreements of which the country knew nothing. Asquith reassured the Commons "the world is now in possession of the whole of our Treaty obligations on this subject. There is no secret arrangement of any sort or kind which has not been disclosed to the public".

With Europe tottering from crisis to crisis and with German naval building getting ever more alarming, the Cabinet welcomed the knowledge that the Kaiser would be glad to see an important British Minister in Berlin with whom matters of difficulty might be discussed. In February 1912 Haldane visited Germany but found it impossible to arrive at any satisfactory agreement. He did not, however, return home quite empty-handed for he bore the draft of the new German naval law which, in default of any political agreement, came into being on 14th June 1912.

The Haldane mission alarmed the French and the draft law the Admiralty. France could hardly afford to see Great Britain

* Grey, *op. cit.*, Vol.I, pp.224–5. George, *op. cit.*, Vol.I, pp.43–4.

neutralised in the event of a European conflict and on 15th April 1912, Cambon called at the Foreign Office to ask for a definition of the British position "when the moment arrived". This Nicolson could not give.* He pointed out that the government would require to preserve its complete liberty of action for the future. Furthermore, there was in Great Britain at the time a widespread desire for an understanding with Germany. Although this feeling was a vague one any "proposals so to reshape our understanding as to give it more or less the character of an alliance" would be construed as anti-German. Grey and Asquith approved his words.†

Meanwhile the Admiralty had posed the question of the proper British reaction to the draft navy law. With an increase in the German navy a greater concentration of the British fleet in home waters would become necessary in order to protect the country but this would obviously denude British strength elsewhere. Arthur Nicolson gave his views on 6th May 1912 concerning the political aspects of the Admiralty problem. He concluded that there were only three possibilities open to Great Britain and of these only one was practical. She could increase her navy in order to guard both home waters and the Mediterranen, a solution which he dismissed as being far too costly. Secondly, she could ally with Germany to prevent the necessity of concentrating in the North Sea. This he rejected for three reasons. Germany would be the senior partner and British safety would depend upon German goodwill; secondly Scandinavia, Holland and Belgium would be drawn into the German orbit and thirdly it would antagonise France and Russia and thus the British position in the Middle East and in India would be imperilled. Finally she could come to a naval understanding with France "the cheapest, simplest and safest solution".° This document was discussed by the Cabinet and it was decided to adopt this third solution which, indeed,

* He had succeeded Hardinge as Permanent Under-Secretary on 23rd November 1910.

† B.D., Vol.VI, No.576.

° B.D., Vol.X, Part 2, No.385.

was only an extension of the Cawdor–Fisher policy of 1905 which had already given a strategic justification for the entente. In September, the French government announced its intention of concentrating its fleet in the Mediterranean and this fact encouraged rumours that the entente was likely to be made a formal alliance. Although this was not so, certain members of the British government were not blind to the possible binding effect of the naval arrangements on future British policy. Thus Winston Churchill wrote to the Prime Minister "The point I am anxious to safeguard is our freedom of choice if the occasion arises, and consequent power to influence French policy beforehand". This would undoubtedly be impaired if France could say that they had concentrated in the Mediterranean because of naval arrangements made with Great Britain. This, in his view, was not true for the dispositions of the French fleet were the best that could be made for them. Neither was Great Britain relying on France to maintain her position in the Mediterranean. Consider "how tremendous would be the weapon which France would posses to compel our intervention, if she could say, 'On the advice of and by arrangement with your naval authorities we have left our Northern coasts defenceless. We cannot possibly come back in time' ".*

In October that year, the military conversations with France and Belgium were revealed to the Cabinet. Under the pressure of this alarming disclosure and the danger of a *de facto* commitment because of the naval rearrangements, the Cabinet thought it proper that the nature of the relationship with France be put in writing. This was done through an exchange of letters between Grey and Cambon an 22–23rd November 1912.† These letters agreed that military and naval conversations had been carried on "It has always been understood that such consultation does not restrict the freedom of either Government to decide at any future time whether or not to assist the other by armed force. We have

---

* *The World Crisis,* Vol.I, pp.112–13.
† B.D., Vol.X, Part 2, No.416.

agreed that consultation between experts is not, and ought not to be regarded as an engagement that commits either Government to action in a contigency that has not arisen and may never arise. The disposition, for instance, of the French and British fleets respectively at the present moment is not based upon an engagement to co-operate in war.

"You have, however, pointed out that, if either Government had grave reason to expect an unprovoked attack by a third Power, it might become essential to know whether it could in that event depend upon the assistance of the other.

"I agree that, if either Government had grave reason to expect an unprovoked attack by a third Power, or something that threatened the general peace, it should immediately discuss with the other, whether both Governments should act together to prevent aggression and to preserve peace, and if so what measures they would be prepared to take in common. If these measures involved action, the plans of the General Staffs would at once be taken into consideration, and the Governments would then decide what effect should be given to them."

This formula pleased both sides. The British conscience was quietened into the belief that there was no obligation to France. France, reading the obligation to consult, felt Great Britain had gone to the utmost except for a formal alliance in providing an offer of help. So misleading can a mutually agreeable form of words be.

V

The early summer of 1914 was a peaceful time for Europe. The main causes of tension were minor ones arising from the aftermath of the Balkan wars and there was no reason to suppose that any problem in this area would prove more intractable to patch up than in the past. Anglo–German relations were reasonably good and indeed certain specific issues between the two countries seemed to have been settled. Agreement over the Berlin–Baghdad Railway was awaiting signature in July 1914 and long negotiations over commercial interests in Africa appeared to be yielding results and were continued until war was imminent; furthermore these matters had been discussed amicably and rationally.

The murder of the Archduke on 28th June came, therefore, for Great Britain and for Europe out of a comparatively clear blue sky. The immediate reaction, although one of shock and realisation of the situation's gravity, did not include a belief that this was something special in the way of Balkan crises. For nearly a month no openly significant move was taken for Europe was waiting upon the official Austro–Hungarian reaction as expressed in the compensation which she would ask for from Serbia and which she was recognized as being entitled to require. Gradually, during this waiting period, the belief gained ground that Austria–Hungary was preparing an ominous document which would have repercussions throughout Europe.

On 23rd July the Austro–Hungarian ultimatum to Serbia was sent. Its terms were recognised as being in themselves a provocation. Grey wrote that it "seemed to me the most formidable document I had ever seen addressed by one State to another that was independent".* Nevertheless the Serbian reply of 27th July accepted practically the whole of it and expressed willingness that the Hague Tribunal should pronounce upon the remainder. This reply was rejected by Austria–Hungary who declared war on Serbia on the 28th. The following day Russia announced partial mobilisation and general mobilisation on 30th July.

Public opinion in Great Britain during the crisis was not bellicose. The majority were expecting a way of keeping the peace to be found and, if it were not, wanted Great Britain to be kept out of the war. "Overall, public opinion, and most of its leaders, were instinctively opposed to military intervention on behalf of European countries."† It was only gradually that thought became crystallised around certain central themes, namely the problem

*B.D., Vol.XI, No.91.

† *The History of The Times*, 1912–48, Part I, 1912–20, p.205, hereafter *The Times History*.

of whether there existed an aggressive German desire to dominate the continent; the extent to which it was a British interest to maintain France and the meaning of the obligation to Belgium. On these issues all shades of opinion were expressed. At one extreme lay those who believed with *The Times* that the country's obligation was to come out strongly in favour of the ententes and at the other those who wanted her to keep out of the war whatever happened. With such a range of opinion, the government was forced to act warily for fear of splitting the country on the most basic issue possible but in any case the Cabinet was not in a position to take a firm line for the divisions of opinion in the country were reflected therein. As the Cabinet was the prisoner of the country, so Grey was held by the Cabinet. The Foreign Secretary's views were more clear cut than those of most of his colleagues amongst whom a strong pacifist element existed; thus far from Grey bullying the Cabinet into following his lead precisely the opposite was true. He had to conform to their opinions and match his pace according to their doubts and hesitations lest the Cabinet should break up and Great Britain be left with no decisive voice at a vitally critical stage. Cabinet discussion only gradually moved from the possible ways of preventing war altogether, at which stage the attitude Great Britain should take if war were to come was ignored, through the realisation that war was probable and concern with the nature of the British interest in it, to the final stage when the invasion of Belgium settled the matter for practically all in favour of intervention.

Grey's policy was first of all to preserve the peace but if this proved impossible then he believed both honour and interest demanded that Great Britain should support France.* Once the first aim proved impossible his efforts were directed towards getting this point of view accepted by his colleagues and at such a time and in such a way that the country was united that the help be effective.

The views of the Foreign Office underwent a change as the

* Grey, *op. cit.*, Vol.I, p.312.

crisis continued. Originally Nicolson had thought of the matter as an issue between Austria and Serbia and expected the storm to blow over,* but with the terms of the Austrian ultimatum it became obvious to him that it was a quarrel which could no longer be isolated. Russia could not ignore events and allow Austria to progress further in the Balkans. Thus indirectly Great Britain was involved through the damage to the entente which might result if Russia was defeated with or without a war. On 24th July,† Eyre Crowe expressed this viewpoint clearly and carried it through to its conclusion. The real danger was that the crisis was in fact the German bid for hegemony in Europe. Since France and Russia were evidently disposed to accept the challenge, the only hope of peace would be through deterring Germany from her attempt. He suggested that the only possible method open to Britain to achieve this would be to mobilise the fleet if either Austria–Hungary or Russia mobilised so that Germany would understand Britain intended to support her friends. He was quite clear that, if war came, Great Britain must not stand aside for she could not afford either to allow Germany to win or France and Russia to achieve victory without her. Grey, however, took the view that this analysis was somewhat premature and he was not yet able, of course, to announce that Great Britain would take such action because of his political difficulties.

By the time that France began to press for a clarification of the British position, Nicolson saw quite clearly that is was Britain's duty to intervene. Furthermore, he believed it her interest and the longer it was left the harder the task that would face her. On 31st July, therefore he urged on Grey the need for mobilisation,° and on the following day he acted as the mouthpiece of France to Grey on the subject of her perilous naval position.+ By August 2nd, with reports that Germany had invaded France

* B.D., Vol.XI, No.40 (minute).

† B.D., Vol.XI, No.101 (minute).

° B.D., Vol.XI, No.368. The precautionary period of the Committee of Imperial Defence was already in operation.

\+ B.D., Vol.XI, No.424.

Nicolson was quite clear that Britain must support her. Grey, however, was still depended upon Cabinet opinion. "At such a time, and on such an issue, he who spoke must not go one inch beyond what the Cabinet had authorised".* Churchill states† that there was complete agreement in the Cabinet upon every telegram Grey sent and upon every step which he took. At the first stage of the crisis the Cabinet had refused to look the implications of possible British intervention squarely in the face and it was not until 3rd August that it could speak with a clear voice.°

As soon as it appeared that the crisis was a European one, Grey attempted to obtain agreement on some form of mediation, such as a conference or a joint démarche at Vienna. It would be tedious to recount the details of his suggestions since they came to nothing but it would certainly be unfair to suppose either that Grey, the puppet of his permanent officials, accepted the idea of war without a struggle because the Foreign Office was determined on a show-down with Germany or that he weakly considered war inevitable and therefore did nothing to stop it. To characterise his conference proposal as "a timid and half-hearted approach, and at the first difficulty it encountered it was abandoned by its distracted author"+ is to neglect the pressure towards peace exerted by Grey in the ensuing days.

On 24th July, Grey spoke to Lichnowsky suggesting that Germany, Italy, France and Great Britain should offer mediation between Austria–Hungary and Russia. This was done upon his own, not Cabinet, responsibility. He did not tell Lichnowsky whether, if war came, Great Britain would participate "and I

---

* Grey, *op. cit.*, Vol.I, p.339.

† *The World Crisis*, Vol.I, p.214.

° An indication of the greater community of view between the Conservatives and some Liberals than the Liberals as a whole is given by the action of the Tory leaders on 2nd August, that is before the invasion of Belgium. The Opposition had approved the pre-war entente policy and had normally supported Grey's actions. Now, a letter was despatched to the Prime Minister to express the view that France and Russia should be supported and pledging Opposition support for such policy. The Cabinet, to whom this document was submitted, was not yet ready for decisive action so that it is impossible to claim any practical, as opposed to theoretical, significance for the letter.

\+ George, *op. cit.*, Vol.I, p.60.

could not say so".* This was followed by Nicolson's suggestion of 26th July that it was time to propose a conference of disinterested ambassadors in London† and to ask for a suspension of military operations by Austria–Hungary, Serbia and Russia. This invitation was despatched that day but rejected by Germany on the 27th July. This refusal to take any seriously active step to restrain Austria awoke grave suspicions of the real German intentions in Nicolson.° Although the following two days saw German attempts to exert a restraining influence on her partner, it was now too late for them to have any effect. Grey, however, continued to hope that war might yet be averted and made further proposals for mediation on 30th and 31st July and the 1st August, but his efforts for peace can really be said to have failed with the rejection of his proposals for a conference. From then on, war appeared increasingly probable and his growing concern was to see that Great Britain came to the support of France.

He was not yet in the position of being able to give Cambon the assurance that she would. Those who complained at the time, and afterwards, that Grey ought firmly to have told Germany that Britain would enter the war to save France, thus preventing its occurence,+ forgot that the Cabinet did not take this view. They ignored too, another problem which faced Grey; namely the danger of allowing France and Russia to precipitate war. This was a fear shared by the Foreign Office as is shown by Eyre Crowe's minute of 30th July. If Great Britain were to take such a step the government might "*induce* and *determine* these two Powers to choose the path of war".× Whilst, therefore, Grey was anxious to prevent Great Britain being used in this capacity, if France and Russia took the decision to go to war themselves, then the Foreign Office believed it would be to both duty and interest to fight with them. "The whole policy of the *Entente*

* B.D., Vol.XI, No.132.

† Thus repeating the successful method of the Balkan wars.

° B.D., Vol.XI, No.174 (minute). No.239.

\+ Since German military plans discounted British efforts, the argument is doubtful.

× B.D., Vol.XI, No.318 (minute).

can have no meaning if it does not signify that in a just quarrel England would stand by her friends."*

Meanwhile, on 25th July, Churchill had visited Grey to enquire if the international situation was bad enough to keep the fleet in being rather than to disperse it after its summer manoeuvres. As a result the fleet was maintained in a state of readiness in the hope that this would show to the world that Great Britain would not in all circumstances remain neutral. From 27th July onwards the Cabinet met constantly to discuss the situation as events gathered speed but the majority, at this stage, were still opposed to British entry into war. Against this background Grey spoke to Lichnowsky on 29th July. He warned the German Ambassador against being misled by the friendly tone of Anglo–German conversations into a false sense of security, and that he must not count on Great Britain standing aside. Grey also spoke to Cambon warning him that Great Britain would not necessarily feel obliged to enter a war. He pointed out that whereas British public opinion had felt a moral obligation to support France over Morocco, this was an Austro–Serbian quarrel in which no such obligation arose. Even if it became an Austro–Russian one, Great Britain would not feel necessarily bound to take a hand. If Germany and France also became involved, then Great Britain had not yet made up her mind what she intended to do.

On the same day the German Chancellor made an offer to Great Britain. In return for British neutrality then "in the event of a victorious war, Germany aimed at no territorial acquisitions at the expense of France".† But Germany was not prepared to give such an assurance concerning the French colonies and she could not say what would be necessary towards Belgium but "provided that Belgium did not take sides against Germany her integrity would be respected after the conclusion of the war".

Eyre Crowe minuted that it was clear that Germany was practic-

* B.D., Vol.XI, No.369. Memorandum by Eyre Crowe, 31st July 1914.
† B.D., Vol.XI, No.293.

ally decided on war and that she was likely to violate Belgian neutrality.

Grey refused this offer on two grounds. Firstly the terms implied that France would lose her position as a great power and this would be contrary to the British interest and secondly such a bargain would be an irrevocable disgrace.

On 30th July Cambon called on Grey to recall the Grey–Cambon letters with their agreement to consult if the peace of Europe were threatened. He asked what Great Britain would do in the case of German aggression against France. After a Cabinet meeting at which the question of Belgium was discussed for the first time, Grey replied to him the following day. Great Britain was not at this stage prepared to give a pledge concerning her actions if war should come. In any case it would be for Parliament to decide what she should do and at that time neither Parliament nor public opinion felt that any treaties or obligations were involved although, of course, future developments might well alter this view. He quoted the neutrality of Belgium as an example of the developments he had in mind. Great Britain could therefore make no promise to help France but she was sending an official enquiry to Berlin and Paris asking for an undertaking that Belgian neutrality would not be violated.* That day Nicolson urged on Grey the importance of mobilising the army so that, if Great Britain were drawn into war, she would be prepared for immediate action. Grey agreed that the Cabinet should consider this "early tomorrow".

On 1st August, Germany declared war on Russia, France began to mobilise and Belgium announced she would defend herself if attacked. The British Cabinet could shirk no longer the problem of what it was prepared to do in support of France, and it is from that day that a shift in view within the Cabinet may be detected. An indecisive Cabinet was held in the morning after which Grey interviewed Cambon. Grey pointed out that France was entering the war by virtue of the Franco–Russian alliance

* France acceded to this request; Germany did not reply.

by which Great Britain was not bound and whose terms were not known to her. The Cabinet was not yet prepared to propose to Parliament that the British Expeditionary Force be sent to the Continent. France, therefore, must come to her own decisions as to her next actions.

Cambon refused to transmit this reply to his government. Agreeing that there was no formal obligation on Great Britain yet Cambon held that it was an overwhelming British interest and duty to support France. That afternoon, through Arthur Nicolson, Cambon reminded Grey of the dispositions of the French and British fleets. Since 1912, as a result of the growing intimacy of the entente, the French fleet had concentrated in the Mediterranean and had left the defence of her northern coasts and the Channel to Great Britain. There was now nothing but the British fleet to prevent the Germany navy sailing down the Channel and bombarding France.

Grey accepted that this issue was a matter which required urgent decision and at the evening Cabinet he proposed that Germany be told that Great Britain could not allow this to happen and by the following morning the Cabinet had agreed that this should be done. Such a decision was surely a decisive step for it brought Great Britain at least halfway towards the battle arena. The Cabinet had been faced with the problem of moral obligation to France and had perforce to determine the action such obligation demanded. It had concluded that this action should be positive.

Meanwhile, Churchill had been told by Grey after the Cabinet that he had verbally informed Cambon of the intended British warning. Churchill, therefore, on his own initiative but with the knowledge of Asquith, Grey, Haldane and Crewe, ordered full fleet mobilisation that night.

The Cabinet was still divided on Sunday morning with the possibility of majority resignation in protest against a decision to enter the war on the side of France. No clear decision was taken on what to do if Belgium was invaded although it was now known that Luxemburg had already been entered by the German army thus seriously decreasing the likelihood that Belgium would escape unscathed. That afternoon the British refusal to allow the passage of German ships through the Channel or the North Sea in order to attack the shipping or the coasts of France was sent to both Germany and France. German acceptance of this note in return for British neutrality was received on the following day. This was, in fact, the only direct commitment to France on Britain's part when Grey spoke to the House of Commons on Monday afternoon when the guarantee was made public. This decision to give a certain degree of support to France was nevertheless too much for certain members of the Cabinet who resigned from the Government in consequence, although only two found it necessary to persist after the invasion of Belgium.

On Sunday evening the German ultimatum was received by Belgium. It stated that if Belgium was prepared to adopt an attitude of benevolent neutrality in war towards Germany, she in turn would guarantee Belgium and the Belgian possessions for the peace and would evacuate Belgian territory, and indemnify her, after the war. If Belgium refused this, she would be treated as an enemy country.

Belgium decided to withstand attack and that night the German declaration of war on France was despatched.

This situation together with an appeal for diplomatic intervention from the King of the Belgians to King George V, faced the British Cabinet on Monday morning. All its members, save Burns and Morley, agreed that the Belgian efforts must be supported if Germany would not be restrained and this decision was to be supported in the country by all but a very few. This Cabinet also formally sanctioned the mobilisation of the fleet and agreed to the main lines of the speech which Grey was to deliver to Parliament in the afternoon.

The immediate matter of substance between Germany and Great Britain had thus become the independence of Belgium and upon this interest and debate now largely crystallised to the detriment of discussion upon surrounding and deeper issues which the one clear-cut problem had absorbed. Belgian neutrality had been effected by two treaties of 1839, the first between. Great

Britain, Austria, France, Prussia, Russia and Belgium and the second between the five great powers and the Netherlands. They were identical in terms. By these treaties, Belgium had accepted the obligation to observe neutrality at all times and towards all states whilst the five great powers guaranteed the fulfilment of this pledge.

There had been discussion in England from time to time as to whether this pledge was individually binding on each guarantor irrespective of the action of the others and on each occasion it had been decided that it was.* Thus in 1908 Grey asked the Foreign Office for its opinion as to whether the guarantee would hold if Belgium acquiesced in her own subjection. Crowe believed that it must since the guarantee ultimately arose from the fact that it was an interest of the guarantors to preserve Belgian neutrality. Hardinge hastened to add a rider to this inflexibility: "The liability undoubtedly exists as stated above, but whether we could be called upon to carry out our obligation and to vindicate the neutrality of Belgium in opposing its violation must necessarily depend upon our policy at the time and the circumstances of the moment."†

When Grey faced Parliament on Monday afternoon he therefore took the line that it was free to make its own decision as to British action. In the event his speech was well received and his policy endorsed by the vast majority. Grey therefore went straight ahead. An ultimatum was despatched to Germany on 4th August demanding a reply to previous British requests to respect Belgian neutrality and expiring at 11 p.m. G.M.T. It was not thought necessary to summon the Cabinet to consider the formal terms of the ultimatum or to declare war on Germany.

Superficially, therefore, Parliament had asserted its supremacy, but whether the conception of freedom of decision upon such grave issues under conditions of great urgency and mounting excitement could be considered as anything but derisory is, of

* Since it was only a guarantor who was in practice likely to violate Belgian neutrality, no other interpretation was really possible.

† B.D., Vol.VIII, No.311.

course, another question. And this in turn raises a further problem, for if it was in fact an illusion then it is necessary to shed some light on the problem of whether this was the responsibility of government or of circumstances over which no one in the country could exercise any effective control. But before deciding this question it is necessary to look rather more closely at the actual handling of government business in the field of foreign affairs.

CHAPTER 2

DEVELOPMENTS IN WHITEHALL

I

The period of tenure of the Foreign Secretaryship by Sir Edward Grey was of great importance to the Foreign Office and its status in the machinery of government. It was an era which saw both the crystallisation of its responsibilities and the emergence of powerful forces which were to lead to its partial supersession. Although it rallied from the depths to which it had fallen at the close of the first world war, the Foreign Office could never hope to acheive again that high and solitary eminence in the responsibility for foreign affairs that had once been accorded it. This was largely because of the growth of a different environment to which the machinery of government had perforce to be adapted and which compelled a greater diffusion of interest in Whitehall than had been necessary hitherto. Whilst the war was the biggest single cause of this development, signs of the change were already apparent in earlier years and to such external pressures must be added a loss of confidence in the ability of the department to pursue the country's objectives in a proper manner. Although it is no longer feasible for the Foreign Service* to claim that it alone possesses the capacity to advise upon, or to execute, policy

* The Foreign Office and the Diplomatic Service at this time were technically distinct and a "Foreign Service" as such did not exist. I have, however, used the term to cover them both when the occasion demands to avoid cumbersomeness of expression.

in the field of foreign affairs, to arrive at the position in which an ex-Permanent Under-Secretary can write "I can recall no major issue on which my advice was taken"* reduces a Department of State to a position of triviality from which neither community nor officials can benefit. It may be that the events here chronicled were in part responsible for this situation.

The abandonment of *laissez-faire* in favour of deliberate governmental control in the nineteenth century necessitated the development of a Civil Service competent to serve the needs of the community as a whole and manifestly open to recruitment on the basis of talent rather than of birth. Although this process was reflected in developments in the Foreign Office and Diplomatic Service, they were much slower to respond to the changing nature of society than the home departments. That this was so was due to two main reasons. Firstly reformers were concerned far more with domestic matters than with foreign affairs as the arena within which the battle for a democratic society should be fought. Certainly isolated international issues were of great importance in which both government policy and execution were criticised, especially when this appeared to be based on forward action and an over-indulgence in limited wars. But the second half of the 19th century did not face Great Britain with any issue which appeared to threaten the very existence and security of the state and there was thus no need to think out very clearly the nature of the national interest. In so far as the Foreign Office and the Diplomatic Service became subject for debate the matter was thus seen in terms of the attack on privilege rather than the proper objects of foreign policy. At this time, criticism revolved round the Diplomatic Service rather than the Foreign Office since the whole structure of the former, despite limited reforms, remained one necessitating an independent income.† As late as 1914 the MacDonnell Commission could sum up the position thus: "the Diplomatic Service is effectually closed to all His

* R. Vansittart, *The Mist Procession,* p.550.

† But also because the Foreign Office had much less authority than later.

Majesty's subjects, be they never so well qualified for it, who are not possessed of private means".*

The second reason for delay was the strength of the belief in diplomacy as necessarily the preserve of an aristocratic milieu which alone could produce the qualities needed by the diplomat. Bagehot's view† that "There is one kind of business in which our aristocracy have still, and are likely to retain long, a certain advantage. This is the business of diplomacy... The old-world diplomacy of Europe was largely carried on in drawing-rooms, and, to a great extent of necessity still is so" was still adhered to in one form or another by the dissenting members of the MacDonnell Commission: "It therefore seems to us a mistake to suppose that, in recruiting for the Diplomatic Corps, it will be possible altogether to ignore social position and the possession of some private means as elements of consideration".° "The primary qualification for the Diplomatic Service is a capacity to deal on terms of equality with considerable persons and their words and works. ... Ordinarily, however, this capacity is a result of nurture in an atmosphere of independence. ... the present constitution of society provides this atmosphere of independence only where there is financial independence."+ Nevertheless during the nineteenth century the Diplomatic Service, albeit somewhat ponderously, began to show signs of adaptation to meet the twin criticisms of overprivilege accompanied by inefficiency.×

The number of ambassadors and heads of missions paid and appointed by the state was very small in the first half of the nineteenth century and it was still standard practice for them to take into their houses young men who wished to spend a few months abroad, possibly with a view to entering the Diplomatic Service themselves but this was not a necessary precondition.

---

* Royal Commission ot the Civil Service. 5th Report of the Commissioners, Cd.7748, p.15.

† *The English Constitution.* 1872 ed. The House of Lords, pp.119–20.

° Sir H. W. Primrose and Mr A. A. Booth.

\+ Mr A. Boutwood.

× See p. 75 onwards for the connection between this charge and trading problems.

Whilst these young men were looked upon as part of the ambassador's family rather than as his subordinate staff, it came to be generally recognised that an ambassador would normally have such assistance which was of benefit to all parties including the state. It was, however, essentially an informal system in which personal factors were of first importance; thus the ambassador's recommendation was essential in determining whether a young man should be sent out to him or not. It was not until the 1830's that these arrangements received some official recognition with the provision of payment for these assistants after a long, unpaid probationary period, but the method of appointing them still remained the same. Here, in these early arrangements, can be distinguished two ideas which were to dog the service for many years and which, in their original form, outlived the period of their usefulness. Firstly the lack of any salary in the early years and secondly the idea of a personal connection either in the service itself or related circles in order to get in at all.

In the middle years of the century a number of changes were made in this system to try to bring it more into line with modern ideas. None of these were very drastic or added up to a thorough going spring cleaning of the service which, for the period under review, it never had. In 1855, Palmerston agreed to the introduction of more formal methods of recruitment which resulted in the introduction of a qualifying test in French and handwriting. Neither this test, nor the corresponding examination for the Foreign Office "was of a character calculated materially to raise the efficiency of the service or to widen the area from which candidates were drawn".* The report of a Select Committee of 1861 led to regulations which established the need for a tighter qualifiyng test and laid down that after four probationary years (unpaid) as an attaché a satisfactory candidate should receive a post as Third Secretary at £150 p.a. and from that date his position should be pensionable. In order to be so appointed he had to speak good French and understand it and one other

* Cd.7748, p.3.

language. It was decided that before going abroad at all a short period would be spent in the Foreign Office and in the later stages of a man's career voluntary exchanges between the service and the Foreign Office were to be permitted subject to the consent of the Foreign Secretary who was also allowed to order a temporary exchange of duties.

It is these changes that really mark the establishment of diplomacy as a recognised profession by creating for the first time a proper ladder of promotion up which young entrants could expect to mount as time went by. Public criticism, however, had not been stilled, indeed if anything it became more pointed since diplomacy, by virtue of these changes, had become considerably more expensive to the public purse. It was, of course, a period when the whole problem of the Civil Service was a public issue and dissatisfaction with the Diplomatic Service was cogently expressed in the House of Commons on the grounds that it was a closed body, recruiting on favouritism from a privileged class and that it was often inefficient since promotion by seniority alone did not give adequate scope to ability. Once again a Select Committee was requested to investigate. Despite the fact that in 1870 open competition had been established for the larger part of the Civil Service, the Committee approved the existing arrangement of nomination followed by a qualifying test for the Diplomatic Service. It looked forward, however, to greater freedom of exchange with the Foreign Office, hoped that promotion to more important posts would go to ability rather than seniority and considered matters of pay. The regulations of 1872 which followed this report accepted the need for an examination but laid down that a United Kingdom university degree would exempt a candidate except for précis writing, handwriting and French. Third secretaries passing an examination in public law were to receive an extra £100 p.a. as were those whom their Heads of Mission certified as having a competent knowledge of Russian or certain other non-European languages where such were the vernacular. The salaries of second secretaries were put on a definite scale and a minimum salary of £500 p.a. was laid down for secretaries of

Legations. Annual reports from Heads of Missions on second and third secretaries and on attachés were to be considered before promotion or increase of pay was granted. The probationary period for an attaché was reduced to two years.* In 1880 limited competition amongst nominated candidates was introduced but it was still not the same competition as used for the Foreign Office which by now was recognised as having the stiffer examination. This had not always been the case.

Although the following years saw a process whereby the Diplomatic Service and the Foreign Office moved more closely together, association rather than amalgamation was all that was acheived.

The Ridley Commission on the Civil Service (1886–90) was the first official body to propose unification, a recommendation which was to be repeated by the MacDonnell Commission (1914) and finally achieved in 1919. Furthermore, the Ridley Commission condemned the unpaid probationary period and the general inadequacy of salaries which together operated as a property qualification but of its recommendations the only one adopted for the Diplomatic Service was the assimilation of its examination with that of the Foreign Office in 1892.

It is reasonable that it should have been found difficult to assimilate the Diplomatic Service to the normal pattern of the Civil Service and that modernisation should have taken longer if only because its members were scattered over the globe and had to be acceptable abroad. It was nevertheless unfortunate. In the early years of the twentieth century the Foreign Office overhauled itself and became a streamlined organisation fitted to live in the modern world but nothing equivalent happened to the Diplomatic Service which remained one in which promotion was uncertain and slow and where the young entrant had little opportunity to show his abilities. Coupled with the property qualifi-

* Nevertheless, climbing up the ladder remained appallingly slow. Thus C. Hardinge entered the Diplomatic Service in 1880 and took 15 years to reach the salary of £400 p.a.

cation this meant that, especially after 1906, the Foreign Office was more attractive to new recruits and competition to get in was more acute.*

II

Until 1857 the Foreign Office was staffed by political patronage but from then on a system of limited competition was introduced on subjects suggested by the Foreign Office and approved by the Civil Service Commission. This arrangement was to last, in some form, until 1919. A basic preliminary to entry to the examination was approval as a suitable person by the Secretary of State with the intent to ensure that each employee should be a "fit and proper person to be entrusted with the affairs, often delicate and confidential, of the British Foreign Office".† This fear of leakages did much to delay the delegation of routine matters, such as copying of documents, to the subordinate staff.

The examination originally developed independently of that for the Home Civil Service but initially was of a very low standard consisting of orthography, précis writing, French translation and handwriting of which the last was the most important. The standard was lower than that for the Diplomatic Service, did no more than keep out the obviously incompetent and made very little change in the nature of Foreign Office recruitment. It was not until 1871 that the test became a reality and for the next twenty years it was far harder to get into the Foreign Office than the Diplomatic Service as far as the examination was concerned; in consequence, the home department considered itself the superior. It will be recalled that in 1892 the examinations were fused and at the same time changes were made in the syllabus which resulted in a heavy emphasis upon a knowledge of modern languages. In

* D. Cooper, *Old Men Forget,* states that at this period there were usually about twenty candidates for the Foreign Office. In 1911, when he sat for the first time, there was only one vacancy. In 1913 there were four.

† Ridley Commission, 1886–90.

consequence, a tendency developed for intending candidates to omit a university career in order to live abroad to acquire the necessary fluency. Thus the service laid itself open to attack on the grounds of a narrow education, a lack of knowledge of the institutions of this country and the closing of opportunity to young men who could not afford to live abroad and study.

In 1905, under Lansdowne, the examinations were partially assimilated with that for Class 1 appointments in the Home Civil Service, the main remaining difference being now the need to obtain extra high qualifications in French and German. This assimilation did not mean, however, the interchangeability of aspirants. The candidate still opted for the Home Service or one of the foreign departments and indeed the language qualification successfully ruled out the person who had not made special preparation for it. In consequence, the failed foreign service candidate could not be considered for the Home Civil Service. Furthermore, although candidates for the overseas branches now took the same examination, they still entered either for the Diplomatic Service or the Foreign Office and did not compete against each other. Nevertheless, the change in the examination meant that candidates were well advised to pursue a more normal education through the universities and reflected opinion that this broad, general education was the best training for the Civil Service generally. Thus from 1906 onwards the normal pattern was for a young entrant for either service to go to a university and then spend one or two years abroad. The great merit of the Foreign Office over the Diplomatic Service, however, was that, once in, one was paid. Competition therefore was very acute and it was not to be expected that the ability to be found there would be content for ever with an exclusive pre-occupation with routine matters, and the turn of the century saw the growth of strong, internal pressures for the use of the Foreign Office as a more significant participator in policy making.

The necessity for prior nomination always caused great difficulty because, whatever its validity, it was a system which lent itself to the suspicion that selection was wielded as a weapon to maintain the Foreign Office as an exclusive social preserve. Although nomination had been token of the hands of the Minister by the creation of a Selection Board in 1907 the belief remained widespread. Thus the *Economist* complained* that patronage was still rife and that Grey had made no attempt to make a career in the Foreign Office "open to the talents" or to introduce a system of selection on merit. The MacDonell Commission too reported that it was the weight carried by parents and sponsors which counted rather than the qualites of the candidates themselves. Certainly the arrangements, which were complicated, were open to abuse either by the Minister or the service since no rules were laid down by a third party to guide them or any form of outside check imposed. It does not follow that the position was exploited. From 1907 onwards an intending candidate had first to obtain nomination by the Secretary of State. This depended upon his being recommended by persons known to the Minister or by persons of standing who knew the candidate personally, but the Board then became responsible for interviewing and selecting the applicants who appeared most suitable. Its recommendations then went to the Secretary of State who normally accepted its decisions. The candidate was then free to sit the examination.

The Board consisted of the Permanent Under Secretary, as Chairman, and the Principal Private Secretary to the Secretary of State. These were the permanent members and they were assisted by one or more members of the Diplomatic Service and the head of one of the political departments of the Foreign Office. The Assistant Private Secretary was secretary to the Board.

Through this system the more obvious forms of political or personal pressure on the Foreign Minister were prevented but it still allowed the possibility or, perhaps more importantly, the appearance of patronage. The Foreign Office officials,† by the vehemence of their protestations to the MacDonnell Commission, appear to have been very sensitive to the charge that the Board

* 12th October 1912.

† Minutes of Evidence submitted to the MacDonnell Commission, Cd.7749; see e.g. Evidence of Tyrell and Nicolson.

was influenced in its choice of recruits by matters of social standing and pointed out that the Board deliberately refrained from enquiring at interview about a man's parents for this very reason.* Real power obviously still remained with the service through the composition of the Board and it appears to have been generally accepted that the word of the private secretary was of great importance.† The situation seems to have been that only persons from a very small social class of the community ever troubled to apply so it is a little difficult to know if the Board was really unbiased or not. Thus the MacDonnell Commission reported that, in the years between 1908 and 1913 (i.e. since the introduction of the Board of Selection) 25 out of 37 (67%) of the applications for attachéships were from Eton and all but a very few of the rest had been to expensive public schools. Only in one case was a university other than Oxford or Cambridge represented. It also reproduces (Appendix LXXX) a combined table of competitors for clerkships and attachéships during the same years. Of 86 applicants 50 were from Oxford, 24 from Cambridge, 11 were from no university and 1 had been to Edinburgh for three months. (In a few instances, individuals from the first two universities had also studied at London or foreign establishments for short periods.)

Transfer between the Diplomatic Service and the Foreign Office was now taking place to a greater extent although it was inevitable it should be voluntary in nature as long as the young diplomat had little or no pay. Nevertheless, of the seven senior clerks in the Foreign Office in 1914, 6 had seen service abroad and even Tyrell, the private secretary, had spent 6 months at the Rome Embassy. Hardinge, who became Permanent Under-Secretary in 1906 had had a previous diplomatic career as had his successor, Arthur Nicolson. Lord Bertie was sent to the Paris Embassy in 1903 from an Assistant Under-Secretaryship and Spring Rice,

* Except in so far as was necessary in order to determine his nationality, e.g. if candidate had an obviously foreign name. See Crowe's evidence, particularly Qs 37118 – 37148.

† See, for example, Q 39,455.

Ambassador at Washington until 1917, found useful employment in the Foreign Office at the outbreak of war whilst awaiting transport back to his post. Eustace Percy who entered the Diplomatic Service in 1910, returned to the Foreign Office in 1914. There was thus, despite the obstacles, considerable coming and going and plenty of experience in the Foreign Office of the needs and scope of the diplomatists and of knowledge at first hand of foreign states, their governments and attitudes.*

Until 1906 the Foreign Office was essentially a subordinate adjunct of the Secretary of State and in organisation changed little from its first formal constitution in 1782 until the first world war. The growth in international business and contacts in the nineteenth century had little effect upon it except in numbers, reflecting both the limited conception of the proper field of governmental control and the dominating personalities of the Secretaries of State. The Diplomatic Establishment in 1796 was 15, increasing to 46 in 1861 and to 52 by 1914.† The personnel were allocated to different departments which were created according to the needs of the time and modified as necessary. Thus by the 1880's there were eight departments, Eastern Europe (held to be the most important in the nineteenth century and covering Russia, Turkey, the Balkans, Persia and Egypt); Western

* In view of the claims of writers about the lack, or the frequency, of transfers, the following figures may be of interest that the reader may judge for himself. A perusal of the Foreign Office list for the years before the war gives the following information:

Year	Transfers abroad from Foreign Office (mainly to Diplomatic but occasionally to Consular Services).	Transfers from abroad to Foreign Office (mainly from Diplomatic Service but occasionally from Consular Services).
1906	6	2
1907	2	1
1908	7	3
1909	7	3
1910	3	2
1911	3	3
1912	6	2
1913	3	2
1914	3	5

† See note, page 67.

Europe; America and the Far East (or China Department); the Slave Trade; the Commercial; the Consular; the Treaty and the Chief Clerk's. Each Department was presided over by a Senior Clerk; the Parliamentary Under-Secretary of State supervised the work of the Commercial Department whilst the Permanent Under-Secretary and the Assistant Under-Secretary divided the rest between them. In 1876 a Legal Assistant Secretary had been added as a direct result of the increasing use of arbitration as a method of settling international disputes and the increase of international trade which brought British subjects more into contact with foreign governments and could often involve the British government.

All the work of the political departments was done by the Diplomatic Establishment. Lower Division clerks and later supplementary clerks found their way into the domestic departments but their entry on the political side came very slowly. Even as late as 1890 fears were expressed that if such subordinate clerks saw confidential papers, foreign governments would soon begin to infiltrate their agents.* The Foreign Office, greatly daring, began

† These figures are broken down as follows:

1796	1861	1914
1 Secretary of State	1 Secretary of State	1 Secretary of State (1 Parliamentary Under Secretary)
2 Under Secretaries	1 Under Secretary of State	1 Permanent Under Secretary
1 Chief Clerk	1 Parliamentary Under Secretary	3 Assistant Under Secretaries (4th added during year)
1 Senior Clerk	1 Assistant Under Secretary	
1 Senior Clerk (paid less than the first)	1 Chief Clerk	1 Controller of Commercial (Consular) affairs
9 Junior Clerks	8 Senior Clerks	7 Senior Clerks
	8 Assistant Clerks	10 Assistant Clerks
	25 Junior Clerks	28 Junior Clerks
15	46	52

Source: Cd. 7748, page 8.

* Sir Philip Currie (P.U.S until 1893) thought this might happen if open competition were introduced for the diplomatic establishment, which conjures up a most interesting picture of spies swotting up their Greek.

to use lady typists in the 1890's for copying work; at first they were restricted to non-confidential material but later became more widely used.* However, there was nothing strange in the junior clerks of the Diplomatic Establishment doing the typing when it was thought necessary. This reluctance to use less qualified persons for routine work led ultimately to an absurd situation in which the Foreign Office took a significant share of the country's most educated young men in order to employ them on tasks well below their capacities. Such an arrangement could not last.

By 1914, there were seven main departments in the Foreign Office: the Eastern European, the Western European, the Far Eastern, the American, the Consular, the Commercial and the Treaty. These were still staffed by the Diplomatic Establishment although a few second division clerks were to be found in the Treaty Department. In addition the office contained the internal departments: the Chief Clerk's, the Librarian's, the Registry and Parliamentary. The Legal Adviser still had no legal department. Since 1906 a certain amount of routine work had been removed from the political departments to the Librarian's and the Registry where it was dealt with by second division clerks.

Although in form the Foreign Office remained relatively unaltered, the use that was made of it underwent fundamental change. This was the result of several factors. During the second half of the nineteenth century, suggestions were heard concerning the need for wider recruitment and greater responsibility for the Foreign Office† as part of the movement for an expanded and efficient civil service; this combined with growing internal dissatisfaction and with an enormous increase in the volume of international business which had to mean a greater spread of work and the percolation of responsibility downwards simply in order to keep on top of the job. This increase in the volume of work

* However, Lockhart tells us that "In 1911, there were still elderly gentlemen who wrote fastidiously with quill-pens". *Memoirs of a British Agent,* p. 45.

† See, for example, some of the opinions of the Select Committee of 1870 suggesting that clerks should comment on despatches.

is commented on by all authorities and was continuous throughout the century. Thus Mr Baillie Cochrane in the House of Commons on 4th July 1862 stated that the number of despatches had grown from 10,000 in 1830 to 75,000. Writing of 1880, Charles Hardinge says "The Foreign Office was a very different place from what it is now. The work was infinitesimal by comparison".* Despatches numbered73,819 in 1890 and 108,904 in 1902; an increase of nearly 35%.

To leave the matter there, however, is to take but a narrow view. The real justification for the changing role of the Foreign Office lies in the changing world in which it had to live. The importance of the home-based department both absolutely and relatively to the scattered Diplomatic Service was much increased by the speed up of communications which inevitably curtailed the freedom of manoeuvre of the man on the spot in favour of more detailed instructions from home. "Diplomatists have, I know, little power nowadays" wrote the young Nicolson as long ago as 1878† already conscious of the changing context within which his profession had to operate.° This development increased pressure on the central process of decision making at a time when international developments were necessitating a greater involve-

* Hardinge, *op. cit.*, p. 11.

† Carnock, p.18.

° This is not in fact quite the same as saying that the diplomat was becoming redundant for his essential functions are personal negotiation and the supply of accurate information to his home government. These still remained. The increased speed of communication really did two things. Firstly it enabled him to be bypassed if this were demanded by other pressures. Secondly it removed his isolation from home. This latter is only to be considered a drawback if it is thought tha basic policy decisions are rightly the function of the man on the spot. His remoteness certainly gave him a greater latitude if he wished to use it; on the other hand it left him with inadequate direction if he did not. During the years 1810–12 the Foreign Minister and his under-secretary "honoured His Majesty's minister plenipotentiary at Constantinople with sixteen despatches, and not one of these valuable documents had any bearing upon the intricate and momentous negotiations which Canning was then conducting at the Porte". (S. Lane-Poole, *Life of the Riht Honourable Stratford Canning*, Vol.I, p.128). His closer contact with home should surely make him more not less effective. Nevertheless the opinion has always been widespread that since the nineteenth century the diplomat has been reduced to the level of a post office.

ment for Great Britain in international affairs. The spaciousness within which splendid isolation could be adopted as a policy was giving way to a world in which problems could not only arise in any part of the globe but could have repercussions upon, or be affected by, what was still the central core of world politics, namely the European balance of power. The field of interest of foreign affairs was thus enlarging and at the same time becoming more complex as the inter-relationships between events became more intricate.

The government of the day must act. However complex a problem with which it is faced and however uncertain the information at its disposal a decision must be taken even if it is to do nothing at all. In order that a body of men can take a decision on a matter about which their knowledge is recognisably limited it must be reduced to a simple and easily digested form. There is no time for a subtle discussion of infinite shades of meaning and nuance. "A man who makes a five minute speech in a Cabinet is voted a bore straight away."* Obviously the more vital the decision the greater the length of time devoted to it but there is often not time for general debate on the larger, fundamental issues which underlie a limited and particular problem. Those who are immersed in day to day affairs and who are under pressure to take a decision have little time or inclination to determine their actions by reference to first principles. The belief in such reference, and indeed awareness of basic principles, was the driving force behind Crowe's desire to turn the Foreign Office into a thinking machine. Even with such assistance at hand, the Foreign Minister may have neither time nor inclination to draw upon it at such a fundamental level. "A Minister beset with the administrative work of a great Office must often be astounded to read of the carefully laid plans, the deep, unrevealed motives that critics or admirers attribute to him. . . . If all secrets were known it would probably be found that British Foreign Ministers

* Lloyd George. H. C. Paper 161 of 1931, Q. 1010. See also Lloyd George, *The Truth about the Peace Treaties,* Vol.I, p.113. "Cabinet speeches are traditionally brief. The usual contribution lasts a maximum of five minutes".

have been guided by what seemed to them to be the immediate interest of this country without making elaborate calculations for the future."* The function of being the thinking machine for the Cabinet and of producing advice and guidance for it on any subject at a moment's notice and of acting on Cabinet decision must become more important as the pressure of Government business grows. This took place for British foreign policy at a time when the compression of international society made decisions increasingly more critical.

These threads mingled with the demand from within the Foreign Office that talent should be more profitably used. In the nineteenth century, clerks were employed on routine matters such as the copying of despatches,† cyphering, sending reports to diplomats abroad and seeing that incoming ones reached the Foreign Minister. There was not so much change by 1914 for the juniors.° As long as Salisbury remained effectively responsible for foreign policy there was no possibility of change for he ran the affairs of the country as an extension of those of the Hatfield estate and used the Foreign Office as little more than a postal convenience. The work of his staff seems to have revolved round the problem of getting despatches and messages on the Hatfield train or even further afield when Lord Salisbury was holidaying on the continent. Not unnaturally, records of what he did are often lacking.+ Very little of importance in these days went below the Permanent Under-Secretary and Salisbury expected very little in the way of advice from him. What suggestions he did get related to routine rather than policy matters. Lansdowne, too, was temperamentally disinclined to share responsibility. He was notoriously secretive in behaviour, a habit of mind which extended

* Grey, *op. cit.*, Vol.I, p.6.

† Writing the Queen's copy by hand because she disliked typewriting; drying it in front of the fire because she liked the ink to be dark.

° See Duff Cooper, *op. cit.*, p.45. The young Foreign Office clerk "expecting to be initiated into the mysteries of diplomacy" in fact spent his time (de)cyphering and typing. He entered the Foreign Office in 1913. See also R. Vansittart, *op. cit.*, p.43.

+ See Cecil, *Life of Salisbury*, Vol.IV, p.21.

to his colleagues as well as to his civil servants; thus Hardinge described him as "not an easy Chief to serve owing to his very reserved nature".* This attitude of mind accorded well with that of Sanderson who held the Permanent Under-Secretaryship from 1894–1906, "a well-stored official of noted and unoriginal ability".† He did not consider that giving advice to the Foreign Secretary was the proper function of the Foreign Office official and Grey describes him as being "not prompt to initiate policy, but he was wise in counsel and in advice, and indefatigable in carrying it out, an admirable draftsman of an important despatch".° The Foreign Office was also by-passed by the system of private letters whereby the Foreign Minister was in direct and personal correspondence with ambassadors and heads of missions and which the Foreign Office itself often never saw. The same practice was carried out by the Permanent Under-Secretary. Thus Nicolson, appointed in 1910, had a voluminous correspondence not revealed to his subordinates.+

This system had been under attack for many years and possibilities of change were canvassed within the Foreign Office itself. The arguments of the reformers were that it was necessary to satisfy the just claims for greater responsibility emanating from the younger members. With the high standards of intellect and education now being demanded for entry, it was illogical not to provide work which would give both stimulus and responsibility and the opportunity to prove intellectual capacity. It also meant the Foreign Office ran the danger of losing (or presumably never getting) its better members especially since other departments, the Treasury and the Colonial Office being cases in point, did provide such opportunities for their new entrants. Promotion was also very slow. The average length of service before a man became an assistant undersecretary was 15½ years and again, in comparable departments such as the Colonial or Indian Offices, it was very

* Hardinge, *op. cit.*, p.122.
† Vansittart, *op. cit.*, p.45.
° Grey, *op. cit.*, Vol.I, p.88.
\+ R. Vansittart, *op. cit.*, p.99.

much less. At the same time, it was claimed, devolution of responsibility would give relief to the under-secretaries and above, and would lead to a quicker despatch of business. Efficiency would be improved, particularly if the junior members were given definite areas of responsibility so that the department could produce relevant material and advice very much more quickly for there would already be in existence a body of expert opinion on particular problems. Thereby the department would meet the complaint that it was often slow to produce necessary information and was less efficient than other Foreign Offices, notably the German.*

Sanderson was not happy about these proposals. He believed that far greater oversight by the higher officials was necessary than in most government departments because of the serious consequences of a mistake. He was against the freeing of the Diplomatic Establishment from all routine work on the grounds that this would mean second division clerks would be in a position to see all papers if they were concentrated in a general registry removed from higher control. The main responsibility of the department, he thought, was to see that the work was properly done, not that young men were given intellectual satisfaction. Lansdowne, however, in 1903, expressed himself in favour of reform and of the devolution of responsibilities at all levels. In consequence, an internal committee was appointed to look at the despatch of business in other public departments to see if it would be possible to delegate routine matters to second division clerks and to use the Diplomatic Establishment more fruitfully. The committee reported in favour of the system used in the Colonial Office of minuting on despatches as they were received. In 1905, a memorandum on reform† was sent to the Treasury and formed the basis for the introduction of more systematic and business-like methods in the following years, particularly whilst Hardinge, an energetic administrator, was Permanent Under-Secretary. The aim

* Which was much larger.

† Eyre Crowe played a prominent part in this.

was now to find a method of work which would ensure that, on any subject, past knowledge and developments would be easily accessible and that a clear picture of relations with all other countries and between them would be constantly up to date. On the framework of this clearly set out picture, the Foreign Office would add its own view as to action in the particular circumstances as they arose.

The three elements contained in this view of the role of the Foreign Office were put into effect. Firstly, internal reorganisation created a general registry manned by subordinate staff which made the back history of a question more readily accessible. In theory little of routine work, beyond cyphering, was left to the Diplomatic Establishment. Secondly, Heads of Missions were required to submit an annual report on the affairs of the country in which they were residing. This report included an assessment of the country's relations with foreign powers. Thirdly, it led to the practice of having "experts" in particular subjects in the various departments and gave an opportunity, previously lacking, for the younger members to express opinions.

This memorandum was of enormous importance. As its suggestions were acted upon a profound change took place in the Foreign Office and in its significance. It changed from "a stuffy family business into an efficient Department of State".* The power of decision, at any rate on important matters, still remained at the highest level of the Permanent Under-Secretary and the Foreign Minister but matters requiring action were now accompanied by comment and advice expressing the opinions of persons who had often spent years studying the particular subject. It was now possible for there to be a Foreign Office opinion as distinct from that of the Foreign Minister.

Grey thus became the first Foreign Secretary for whom recognised and established Civil Service advice was available. In part this situation had arisen because it had become increasingly

---

* Carnock, p.325. But lost something of family intimacy in the process. See Vansittart, *op. cit.*, p.153.

difficult for one man to be knowledgeable about the whole span of foreign relations and for him to have to rely upon his specialist advisers for guidance so that he in turn might guide his colleagues. For a few years before the first world war the Foreign Office was recognised as being the pre-eminent source of this advice. It was a responsibility which was soon to be shared by both unofficial advisers and other government departments. The rise of the Foreign Office was new and provided a fresh element for the attack on the conduct of foreign affairs; namely that a Civil Service Department was usurping the true function of government. There is no clear dividing line between tendering advice for the decision of another and over-persuasion to take a preferred course and it was the belief of the radical opposition that the Foreign Office had overstepped the permitted limits and that Grey was but the mouth-piece of those whom he should have controlled.

III

Before leaving the question of departmental structure and the extent to which it adapted itself to the changing needs of society; it will be convenient to deal with the problem of trade since here again administrative arrangements remained archaic long after the need for modification had been recognised. Once more, criticism of an old fashioned structure sprang from a far deeper question, namely the relative loss of British industrial power and consequent discussion as to the proper degree of interest to be shown in trade by the British government. For those who felt it should be more direct and positive, the lackadaisical arrangements of the diplomatic machine provided yet one more cause of dissatisfaction with the country's administrative arrangements for handling overseas matters. It is an important question too, because trade was both one aspect of foreign affairs and one which could be claimed by another department of state as more properly its concern. The rivalry between Board of Trade and Foreign Service over the control of trading matters was thus an early challenge to the latter's claim to be the department in control of the country's external relations; a challenge which was bound to become more serious with the outbreak of war and the growth of active governmental participation in the economy both then and later. In the years before the war, however, trade formed an uneasy no man's land between them where the problem of demarcation was never really solved. The association between the Board of Trade and industry naturally inclined that department to the view that it was a suitable and more appropriate instrument for the support of trading interests abroad; but this was a dagger pointed at the heart of the older department, part of whose *raison d'être* had always been to serve as both the symbol and reality of the willingness of the government to protect its citizens overseas. There was in any case the further complication of the existence of the Consular Service which pursued an uneasy life as a poor, and not very respectable, dependant of the Foreign Office which yet was not prepared to give it up. From about the middle of the nineteenth century, one can find the recurrence of a number of fairly concrete issues revolving round the problem of the role of the government in the British pursuit of trade and the appropriate machinery to pursue this role; the relations between the Board of Trade and the Foreign Office; the relation between the Consular Service and the two home departments; the relation between political diplomacy and trade and thus between a diplomat and the consul abroad.

As the nineteenth century drew to a close, Great Britain found herself increasingly aware of the growth of other nations to industrial maturity and the great importance of trade to the maintenance of the British political position. In order that her trading interests should be both maintained and strengthened, the argument was heard that the governmental machine should take a greater and more positive interest in matters of commerce than heretofore. Hence came the charge that traditional organisation, in addition to its other failings, was also inefficient. An indication of the way the wind was blowing was a motion introduced into the House of Commons on 18th February 1870 which proposed that the Consular Service should be removed from the Foreign Office to the Board of Trade. "It should be remembered" said Mr Holmes "that this country was not now in the same relative position to other countries that it was 20 or 30 years ago. Formerly we were far ahead in respect of trade and commerce but now other nations were nearly ahead of us." An aristocratic Diplomatic Service would inevitably despise the merchant and trader and remain unaware of their significance. Arthur Nicolson, who could write "I like our upper mercantile men. There is so much energy and sense about them. I think they are the very marrow of England".* was recognised by his biographer to be the exception to the rule. Some concession to this change in need was made by the creation in 1864 of the Commercial Department to form a loose link between the consuls and the Board of Trade and to symbolise the awareness of the Foreign Office concerning commercial matters.† Further liaison with the Board of Trade was attempted through the practice of attaching young entrants to the Consular Service to the Board for a short period before sending them abroad and it was also recognised that the Board was responsible for guiding the Foreign Office on commercial conditions in, and policy towards, other countries.° No formal method of co-operation existed between them until 1917 when the Department of Overseas Trade, jointly responsible to both, was created.

In the field, the Diplomatic Service made some attempt to move with the times by the appointment of commercial attachés as from 1880 but on such a limited and superficial basis as to be almost laughable. Thus by 1906 such attachés were to be found at Paris, Berlin, Vienna, Madrid and Constantinople; between them they were supposed to cover the whole of the European continent and to be responsible for the acquisition of knowledge of trading conditions in their allotted area which could be passed home and ultimately to British trade. When it is realised that the

---

* Carnock, p.54.

† It ensured too that commercial negotiation would be executed by the Foreign Office, not the Board of Trade.

° The Board had its own representatives in the Dominions.

MacDonnell Commission found one man trying to cover Germany, Holland, Denmark, Sweden and Norway and that there was no commercial attaché anywhere in the American continent, it will be appreciated that this process had not gone very far. Furthermore, the position of these men in the service was unsatisfactory. They were not part of the regular Diplomatic Service but appendages to particular missions, often recruited from the Consular Service. In consequence they had no regular career or promotion prospects. Additionally they had an impossible job. To cover such extensive areas adequately would have meant perpetual travel, considerable proficiency in a number of different languages and a significant amount of time spent at home in order to keep in touch with British industrial development. In practice, the missions all too often piled the routine commercial work upon them thus making it impossible for them to leave the capitals at all.

In 1906 a new system was tried. The European attachés were based on London* and now divided their time between special investigations abroad and contacts with British manufacturers. The old system inevitably remained for the more distant posts but an attempt was made to relieve the attachés of routine work. This did not altogether meet the case either and the complaint was now heard that they did not spend enough time abroad. The MacDonnell Commission thus recommended that they should once more be part of a mission but that their capacity to travel freely should not be impeded and that they should spend at least three months a year at home.

The Consular Service was in reality the overseas machine for the assistance and support of British trade. Prior to 1914 it was divided into three services: the Far Eastern, the Levant and the General. Each was recruited and organised separately and linked with home through the Consular Department of the Foreign Office. From 1872 the Far East and Levant services were recruited by open competition but this was changed to limited com-

* Except for Paris and Constantinople.

petition following the recommendations of the Ridley Commission.* These services recruited young men between the ages of 18 and 24 who went to distant and obscure parts of the globe as members of an organisation which was sufficiently large and well run to offer them definite prospects of promotion and the possibility of satisfying their abilities and ambitions. It was these services which contained, and perhaps helped to produce, the great personalities one associates with the name of the British Consular Service of the past. The General Service was a different kettle of fish, less satisfactory for the people who worked in it or for the purposes it was meant to pursue. In consisted of two branches: the salaried career service recruited at home and the unsalaried, often referred to as the trading branch, consisting of local persons, not always of British nationality, who were willing to take on the position for prestige reasons in areas where there was not enough work to justify a salaried appointment. It was this last which was peculiarly vulnerable to criticism, more especially through its heavy reliance upon unpaid volunteers, many of them foreign, who could hardly be expected to have the interests of British trade very much at heart.†

The difficulty of organising a career service had always been held to lie in the need to recruit persons with previous commercial experience, often of a highly specialised nature and of a particular area, and therefore recruitment by an examination in early manhood was an unsuitable instrument of selection. Appointments were by nomination. The Ridley Commission had seen no real way out of this dilemma but wanted to see recruitment by examination as far as this was practicable and a reorganisation of grading within the service to give better promotion prospects. However, by the turn of the century, entry was still being made by nomination to men between the ages of 25 and 50. The Commission also suggested that recruits to the service should spend a period

* The MacDonnell Commission wanted to change it back again.

† e.g. before the war, out of 653 unsalaired representatives no less than 45 per cent were of foreign nationality. See Mr Pennefather, 9–3–16, *Hansard*, Vol 80, Col. 1804.

in the Commercial Department of the Foreign Office or in the Board of Trade before going abroad. The next attempt to devise a better system came from the Walrond Committee of 1903 which, through a selection device of nomination (after public notice), examination and interview, aimed to catch two groups of men in early manhood, the university product and the young man who had spent four or five years in business. The age limits for entry were therefore fixed at 22–27. After recruitment, the Committee recommended that a period be spent in the Commercial Intelligence Branch of the Board of Trade before the new entrant went abroad. After a year he should be required to take an examination in the language of the country where he was working.

Whilst a number of internal reforms were carried out in the ensuing years, the General Service remained one causing considerable disquiet both to members of it and outside persons who, for whatever reason, were interested in its performance at a time when British overseas trade was increasing and the duties of consuls becoming more onerous. The problem came under scrutiny yet again by the MacDonnell Commission. This body decided that the aim of recruiting persons with previous business experience had not been fulfilled and thought that the best policy would be one of early recruitment followed by a fairly lengthy study at home of British trade and business. It therefore recommended open competition at senior clerical level, to include two modern languages, to be taken at 18 or 19. This would be followed by 2 years study of industry and commerce and an extended period in the Foreign Office and Board of Trade. At about 21 years old, the recruit would go abroad as an assistant at one of the larger consulates before getting more independence. Arrangements would need to be made for him to keep in touch with British industry throughout his career. Unsalaried appointments would perforce have to continue for areas where British interests were small and a whole-time salaried officer would obviously be uneconomic; but it hoped that, where this was necessary, every effort would be made to find a British subject. It also recommended that the inspectorate should be strengthened and normally filled by promotion from the Consular Service. It did not recommend amalgamation with the Diplomatic Service but thought that interchange could become more frequent.

Unfortunately, there appears to be substance in the common view that the Diplomatic Service at this time was contemptuous of trade and thus of those who were concerned in it. In part this attitude was given negative encouragement by the fact that recruits to the service were not examined in economic matters and therefore had no incentive to understand them,* but this is not a full explanation for it. It probably resulted from an amalgam of many reasons, partly class, partly selection necessities, partly tradition, and a general laissez-faire approach, not confined to the Diplomatic Service, which saw no necessary connection between business and state activity. Whatever its cause it existed. "With the Embassy in St Petersburg we had practically no contact. . . . But between the two British Services there was an impassable gulf. . . . In the archives of the Moscow consulate there is – or was – a letter from a certain British Ambassador, . . . Dear Mr ---, Please remember that I am not here to be bothered with questions about trade."† It was feared that the knowledge and experience of the consuls were often ignored by the Diplomatic Service. It was well known, claimed the *Economist,*° that the consular officers in the Near East and elsewhere were a great deal better informed than the Diplomatic Service and no effort had been made to increase the business and commercial acumen of the Foreign Office and Diplomatic Service. This superior attitude of the diplomat to trade seems to have taken a long time to die. "As for Mr Adams, he flourished too early, for in those days commercial attachés were decidedly looked down upon by the regular diplomats. He was a man of great ability and trenchant speech, who found it hard to conceal his impatience with what he considered the super-

* Political economy makes its first appearance as a possible examination subject in 1908.

† B. Lockhart, *Memoirs of a British Agent,* p.78. He became British Vice-Consul in Moscow in January 1912.

° 12th October 1912.

ficiality of the Chancery. . . . The Commercial Attaché was not asked to dinner at the Embassy."*

Underlying these changes, investigations and criticisms of the official machinery for handling trading matters was, of course, a deeper problem. They reflected both the growing importance of British overseas trade and the slowly developing view that if, in addition to the benefit to private individuals, it was a national asset contributing to the country's greatness and the 'stability of the empire', then the state could no longer remain as disinterested as had once been assumed. It was a period, too, of growing uneasiness in the face of increasing competition and such factors focussed on the specific problem of whether British officials should do more to discover and encourage openings for British traders and, if so, how far such positive help should go. Opinions ranged from the older view, held in general by the services concerned, that assistance to, and not promotion of, trade was their proper function to those at the other extreme who wanted officials to adopt an active sales technique to dispose of British goods as, so they claimed, continental officials, and especially German, were increasingly doing. Majority opinion, however, was not ready to accept the equation consul equals commercial traveller, and the MacDonnell Commission believed that there was no real evidence that British officials were less active than others in furthering commercial interests; indeed on the contrary, the Foreign Office, Diplomatic and Consular Services shewed "a real and increasing sense of the importance of the services which consuls can and do render to the British commercial community". In addition to the assistance of British trading communities, the glimmerings of official recognition that the political arm of the State should properly provide backing for sound British investment overseas can be detected. "I regard it as our duty, wherever bona fide British capital is forthcoming in any part of the world, and is applying for concessions to which there are no valid political objections, that we should give it the utmost support we can,

* L. E. Jones, *Georgian Afternoon,* p.109. He is writing about 1923.

and endeavour to convince the foreign government concerned that it is to its interests as well as to our own to give the concessions for railways and so forth to British firms who carry them out at reasonable prices and in the best possible way."*

IV

The smooth working of government business is obviously much eased if good relations exist between the political head of a department and its permanent members and thus, by implication, between the government of the day and the civil service. It is here that great differences existed for the Foreign Office before and after the war. Before 1914, the men in the Foreign Office were self-confident and assured, by the end of the war they often felt ignored and correspondingly resentful. Such ease of contact was greatly helped by the fact that both politicians and civil servants came from similar social backgrounds; moved in very similar circles and seemed to find no difficulty in filling either political appointments or top civil service jobs as occasion demanded. The outstanding example of this is Charles Hardinge, a friend of the King's but also a career diplomat, who passed not only from the Permanent Under-Secretaryship of the Foreign Office to become Viceroy of India but also back again. The major drawback is the unfortunate appearance that may be given to those outside the magic circle and it well becomes those on the inside to take infinite trouble to prevent any suspicions arising concerning their activities or to deal with them as soon as possible should they be expressed.

Between Grey and his staff existed a close harmony of relationship. The members of the Foreign Office respected him as a man principle and high moral code, neither was he the sort of person whose control would at any time be harshly felt.† But this under-

* Grey, 10–7–14, *Hansard,* Vol. 64, Col. 1446.

† See e.g. Hardinge *op. cit.,* p.122. Vansittart, *op. cit.,* pp.109–110.

standing did not prevent the development of differences of emphasis over policy between the Foreign Minister and his staff, which became more marked as the war drew nearer. On the major issue of the need to maintain peace all were at one and the differences on tactics could not disguise the large element of common ground which existed between the Foreign Minister and his chief advisers which was of infinitely more significance. To both Grey and Nicolson the outbreak of war in 1914 was a major tragedy which they had spent years trying to avoid, albeit by methods discounted by their critics.* They both considered the outbreak of war a catastrophe of the greatest magnitude for a civilised world; both held a view of international relations based upon mutual respect, the limitation of interference in other states' affairs and the use of international courtesies and diplomacy as symbols of international politics in which all could play their allotted part and war was not total.

In the years before 1914, the Foreign Office contained some decisive men whose backgrounds often entitled them to friendships at the highest levels and who had very definite views on the right course for British foreign policy. Charles Hardinge became P.U.S. in 1906 at the time of the Algeciras conference. He was a firm and recognised supporter of the entente policy whose appointment immediately aroused the suspicions of the German Ambassador,† and whilst at the Foreign Office was wholeheartedly in favour of Grey's Russian rapprochment. If Morocco had shewn to Grey and the Foreign Office the need to support France against German pressure, the Bosnian crisis of 1909 displayed the weakness of Russia. A memorandum from Hardinge on this matter put the Foreign Office point of view. Although he personally toyed with the idea of an alliance "Were England the ally of either France or Russia the political equilibrium and peace of the

* Grey to Page: "Thus the efforts of a lifetime go for nothing. I feel like a man who has wasted his life". B. J. Hendrick, *Life and Letters of Walter Page,* Part 1, p.315.

† Hardinge, *op. cit.,* p.122, "He suspected me, and rightly so, of opposition to Germany's aggressive policy".

Continent would probably be maintained", he recognised that public opinion was not prepared for this for it "does not yet sufficiently grasp the danger of Germany's ambitious designs".*

Hardinge was succeeded by Arthur Nicolson in October 1910. By that time, he too had come to see foreign affairs in terms of the central problem of a German menace to international society which he believed could be best dealt with by the conversion of the ententes into alliances as a public deterrent to Germany.† His appointment, also, was unwelcome to the central powers.° Lichnowsky reported that he "was no friend to Germany, but his attitude towards me was scrupulously correct and courteous. . . . He too did not want war, but as soon as we advanced against France, he no doubt worked in the direction of an immediate intervention".+

In his viewpoint Nicolson was supported by Eyre Crowe who, from being the head of the Western Department, had in addition become an Assistant Under-Secretary in 1912. Here was a man whose powers of analysis and incisive thought were developed far and away above those of most of his colleagues. The 1907 memorandum stands out in the British documents as a masterpiece of logical and long-term thinking, the perfect justification for his 1905 arguments for reform. It is not to be wondered at that it created a stir in a newly emancipated department in a country where decisions are normally taken on an empirical basis. Crowe inevitably developed a clear cut view of foreign affairs and, once having prepared his analysis, the proper course of action thereby followed. There is, however, no glimpse in Crowe's work of the old saying that politics is the art of the possible or of the fact that Grey was not his own master. Crowe, writes Nicolson,+ "had an unfortunate habit of indicating to the Foreign Secretary,

* B.D., Vol.V, Appendix III.

† Carnock, p. 305 (refering to Nicolson's attidute in 1909); p. 351 (to 1911); p.402 (to 1913). B.D., Vol.V, No. 764.

° Hardinge, *op. cit.,* p.190.
Vansittart, *op. cit.,* p.93.

+ Lichnowsky, *Heading for the Abyss,* p.69.

× Carnock, p.327–8.

and his colleagues in the Cabinet, that they were not only ill-informed but also weak and silly". It is not surprising that outside critics, seeing a man in a position of responsibility who combined contempt for the amateur with superior intellectual ability came to distrust the influence he wielded. "The warning only got Crowe tarred as a fireband",* and did his personal position no good. A perusal of Crowe's famous document, however, makes any suggestion that it can be used as evidence for the view that the Foreign Office was aggressively inclined in general, or irresponsibly anti-German, untenable. To Crowe, the British interest was in peace "the general tendency of British governments to take advantage of every opportunity to approach more closely to the ideal condition of living in honourable peace with all other states. . . . the national policy . . . is so directed as to harmonize with the general desires and ideals common to all mankind".† It behoved Great Britain, nevertheless, to be aware of the possibility that German might be aiming at hegemony in Europe for she could not afford to run the risk of this and wake up to the fact when it was too late. Great Britain must therefore prevent any extension in German power. At the same time, any legitimate interests of Germany regarding trade or shipping should be met in order not to provoke her. Experience, he wrote, has shown that one-sided concessions are no good for they only whet the appetite for more. This had been particularly important in the case of Germany. He closed with the hope that Anglo–German relations might improve now that it was clear that Great Britain was serious about her friendship with France and that Germany could not exploit any differences between them.

It would therefore be fair to say that for about eight years before 1914 there had been a consistent Hardinge–Nicolson–Crowe policy which saw Germany as the threat to the maintenance of that peace which all at home desired and which believed that a clarification of the British position, which would leave no doubt

* Vansittart, *op. cit.*, p.64, who points to the significant fact that the memorandum was ignored as the basis for policy.

† B.D., Vol.III, Appendix A.

in German minds that Great Britain would resist any aggressive move, was the best step Britain could take to ensure it.

Grey, on the other hand, was not prepared to go so far. Although not blind to the German danger, yet he was not prepared to assume that Germany was deliberately bent on making war and had therefore not given up hope that each international problem, as it arose, would be susceptible to a peaceful solution. Another problem worried him. He saw two European camps and the necessity for Britain to retain her freedom of action for as long as possible in order to be sure that she in fact came down on the right side, if the time came. Although he became increasingly aware that it was the Franco–Russian side that would need support, he could never banish from his mind the fear that, with Great Britain's allegiance secure, the entente powers would themselves initiate aggressive action and bring on the war he wished to avert. His remarks to Parliament in 1911 make this position quite clear: "our friendship with France and Russia is in itself a guarantee that neither of them will pursue a provocative or aggressive policy towards Germany . . . Any support we would give France and Russia in times of trouble would depend entirely on the feeling of Parliament and public feeling here when the trouble came, and both France and Russia know perfectly well that British public opinion would not give support to provocative or aggressive action against Germany."* Grey also believed in the Concert of Europe and that united action between the great powers was the way to prevent a general war. Time and again, therefore, he advocated the conference as a method of settling a dispute, in 1906, in 1911, in 1912 and in 1914. Such an attitude makes one disinclined to join an alliance which must inevitably be directed against a particular enemy. He even deprecated the use of the term "Tripe Entente" for fear that this would help to crystallise the basically unnatural division of Europe.†

Grey had his lieutenant in the Foreign Office in his private

* 27–11–11, *Hansard,* Vol.32, col.59.
† Carnock, p.308.

secretary, William Tyrell, who found himself in perfect agreement with Grey on the need to maintain the maximum of fluidity in international relationships for as long as possible and hence to retain the possibility of influencing them.

It was thus true that there was a 'Foreign Office policy' which differed from that of the political heads of the government. It is worth noting however Lichnowsky's opinion that, of all the Foreign Office officials, it was Tyrell who counted for most with Grey and far more than Nicolson* and it was Tyrell who was noted for his efforts to achieve an understanding with Germany. "He became an convinced advocate of an understanding. He influenced Sir Edward Grey, with whom he was very intimate, in this direction."† The fact is, too, that it was Grey and not Nicolson who saw his policy followed. The ententes were not turned into alliances and uncertainty remained as to Britain's position up to the very last moment before the war began. The Foreign Office view did not prevail over that of the elected representatives of the country and could not have done with a Cabinet which contained such varying views on the nature of foreign affairs.° The system had been established that the Foreign Office should express its view, as indeed the progressives had earlier demanded and it was illogical now to criticise it for so doing. It always remained up to the government to accept or reject that advice.

Superficial appearances supported the view that the Foreign Office ran Grey rather than the other way about. Grey by nature was a modest man to whom public life was a necessary obligation because of his favoured birth rather than the mainspring of his actions. "Indeed, partly owing to his dislike for urban life and his consequent perpetual wish to get out of office, he was politically completely disinterested. For all the years in which he was connected with the Foreign Office, I don't think there was a single day in which he would not have welcomed resignation.

* Lichnowsky, *Heading for the Abyss*, pp.69–70.
† *op. cit.*
° See pages 125–6.

He held office because he thought it his duty to do so, and for no other reason."* Without any suggestion that he neglected the proper business of his office, which he did not, such detachment enabled him to spend considerable time away from London, even at critical periods. Thus the weekend of 26th July 1914 found him in Hampshire and it was actually Nicolson who suggested the time to propose a conference to save the peace had come. Here was no departmental chief who could not tear himself away from the office. As his health grew worse, his absences grew more frequent thus encouraging the appearance of having abdicated responsibility to his permanent officials but it is as well to bear in mind his own statement that "I did not, however, regard anything expect my own letters and official papers as deciding policy".†

Similarly he had a very high sense of the essential responsibility of his office as the main source of inspiration in foreign affairs vis-a-vis the Cabinet. He considered the Foreign Secretary as the most important person shaping foreign policy;° even the Prime Minister was no more than an equal.+ This belief alone could well have discouraged him from explaining his views, much less dealing with the differences between them and those of his colleagues and this aloofness was accentuated by his overall political detachment through which he remained apart from day to day party skirmishes and played very little part in Cabinet discussion on other issues. Indeed, he found this a suitable opportunity for drafting his despatches.

This had the disadvantage that he remained an enigma to the radical wing of his party; open to the appearance of weakmindedness and the charge of indifference. He never really overcame its underlying suspicion and distrust of him as the agent of undesirable policies and, indeed, made no effort to do so. There

* Lord Robert Cecil, quoted G. M. Trevelyan, *Grey of Fallodon,* p.309.
† B.D., Vol.VI, p.ix.
° Grey, *Journal of the Royal Institute of International Affairs,* July 16th, 1930.
+ Grey, *op. cit.,* Vol.I, p.119.

was thus a certain lack of confidence in him which was enhanced by his desire to keep Great Britain's international agreements loose and undefined, for the inability to find a focus for coherent criticism is extremely exasperating when one wishes to complain. It was Grey's misfortune, as a proponent of the middle way, to lend himself to attack both from those who thought he went too far and from those who felt he did not go far enough.

The essential subordination of the Foreign Office to the Cabinet is in fact clearly demonstrated by the Agadir crisis and by the events of 1914. Both these occasions faced the country with the prospect of war with Germany and in consequence evoked a virulent attack upon the men handling the conduct of foreign affairs. The 1911 crisis brought out well the differing strands of thought in the country on international affairs. To the Radicals it was a typical example of the fire-eating Foreign Office egging on the forward party in France and consequently running the risk of war when British interests were not involved, whereas to Nicolson and Crowe it was a clear cut issue of a German bid for supremacy in Europe. In fact it was the Cabinet, meeting three days after the Panther arrived, which decided upon a definite line of action to be followed towards both France and Germany, which was neither that of Nicolson, (or expressed in terms of Crowe) nor that of the outside pundits. The Lloyd George speech, which is normally taken as the critical statement of British policy was not influenced by the Foreign Office and although it is usually read as implying a tough line with Germany,* it could equally well be read as a warning to France. Again in 1914, British policy wavered until the Cabinet had made up its mind and, in any case, the material obligation if there were one, arose out of the military and naval obligations for which the Foreign Minister and the Committee of Imperial Defence must at the least share the responsibility with the Foreign Office.

* And thus Morel, of course, believed he was the mouthpiece of the Foreign Office. *Ten Years of Secret Diplomacy,* p.146.

V

A further consequence of British loss of power was the need for her to bring her defence thinking up to date. This generalised need began a process whereby, as defence plans were crystallised, British freedom of political decision was further curtailed. It thus precipitated another dilemma for the control of foreign policy in a democracy since defence planning is inevitably secret. In consequence, it encourages the undesirable aura of mystery which surrounds foreign policy whilst the amount of influence exerted by the military arm of the state is difficult for the outsider to assess. He is likely to assume the worst.

At the close of the nineteenth century, attention had begun to turn to problems of the defence of the colonies and of the United Kingdom, but the conception of rational defence planning was an unfamiliar one which many found distasteful and what headway the reformers made was in consequence slow. Nevertheless, as Great Britain's international unpopularity became self-evident, the climate of opinion became sufficiently favourable for the movement to progress from the creation of small, uninfluential committees, grudgingly set up to discuss specific situations, to the appreciation of the need for some machinery which could consider the defence of the empire, including the mother-country, as a whole and which could engage in long-term, continuous study. Whilst today, this idea appears but an elementary and precautionary conclusion, the reaction of the time indicates very clearly the extent to which people's minds were soaked in peace and their unwillingness to face the very difficult problem of the compatability of democracy with efficient defence preparations. Defence thinking in peace time must inevitably have a momentum of its own, even if it is limited to articulating possibilities that have not previously been brought out into the open forum of discussion. It was this sort of danger that critics had in mind when they opposed the movement for reform in the Service Departments for fear that it would unleash an uncontrollable militaristic monster. The attitude of Campbell-Bannerman is particularly interesting since he was gradually led to accept not only this but also the need for some overall defence machine and, when Prime Minister, played his part in the development of the planning machinery. Back in 1890 however he had reacted very strongly against the proposal that there should be a Chief of Staff in the War Office responsible for preparing plans for military operations which to him was little different from openly planning an aggressive war. There is "no room for 'general military policy' in this larger and more ambitious sense of the phrase".* This was a line of thinking which continued well into the twentieth century. Whilst the active war-mindedness of British generals was probably an exaggerated fear, it would seem inescapable that increased rigidity in foreign policy flows from defence planning since in practice it is impossible to make plans for the use of military and naval forces or for the mobilisation of the civil economy without some pre-conceived idea of the type of war that is going to be fought, who it is going to be fought against, and who is going to be an ally. Unfortunately, the problem is not solved by the refusal to consider its necessity.

The dividing line between discussion of defence in general and of defence problems in a particular situation is obviously a very fine one and once splendid isolation had given way to the entente with France the framework within which defence was to be organised was changed. The new direction of British foreign policy gave an impetus to defence thinking along certain lines and as this in turn progressed even further so it became more difficult to consider any *volte-face* in foreign policy. Thus the naval reorganisation begun by Fisher in 1904 and continued through the years till 1910 was, we are told, "necessitated by the reorientation of our foreign policy resulting from the Entente with France and Russia and the rise of the German menace".† It was followed by the further naval planning of 1912° and thus resulted in the problem of the protection of the French northern

---

* J. Spender, *op. cit.,* Vol.1, p.118.

† Hankey, *The Supreme Command,* Vol.I, p.21.

° See Chapter 1, p. 42 *et seq.*

coasts in 1914, when Cambon could claim that it was at British request that France had moved her fleet to the Mediterranean on the understanding that Britain would undertake the protection of the Northern and Western coasts. In consequence the Cabinet had perforce to give France a guarantee of naval protection if Germany did so attack her.* In fact, the further defence plans between countries are co-ordinated the greater must be the similarities in foreign policy. The two factors work upon each other and in the pre- 1914 period this meant Great Britain being increasingly closely committed to one side of the Continental alliance system. Attempts at easing Anglo-German relations, which were tried, were never taken so far as to be at the expense of France. The original decision was a political one but, in view of the international circumstances in which that decision operated, it led inevitably to closer technical co-operation and this in turn crystallised and made more definite the direction of British foreign policy.

Thus from a general survey of the defence of the empire, the Committee of Imperial Defence was led to the development of specific plans for the mobilisation of strength should Great Britain be concerned in a European war and on the assumption that she would be allied with France. This line of thinking had for some years been common ground at least for the heads of the Foreign Office, Admiralty and War Office, their political chiefs and the Prime Minister as regular participants in governmental policy.† Lord Hankey's description° of the successive stages of development of the Committee bears out the conception of planning as containing an inner momentum as it passed from the stage of creating itself and formulating the fundamental principles of defence to that of specific plans and the perfection of detail. It is

---

* B.D., Nos. 424 and 487.

† Hankey, *op. cit.*, Vol.I, p.59 contains a comprehensive list of the names that spring most readily to his mind. He states Lloyd George was rather detached from the detailed war preparations and his attendance was apparently rather sporadic.

° Hankey, *op. cit.*, esp. Chapters V, VI, VII.

apparent* that by 1908 considerable service planning for the contingency of a German war had been undertaken and from then on the problem for the Committee was to try to obtain some overall co-ordination of what were still relatively isolated parts. By the following year, the major lines of a master plan had been laid, and the ensuing years were preoccupied with polishing the components.

There was thus an element of truth in Morel's charge that a climate of "war mindedness" had been created by development of military plans in that only one war was seriously envisaged: "from January, 1906, onwards, our secret military and naval commitments to France were the spinal column of our foreign policy."† Those who were concerned were under increasing pressure to think of foreign affairs along certain given lines but one must be careful not to read too much into this and the use of an emotionally charged word is unfortunate. "Warmindedness" does not have to mean a belief in the inevitablity of war,° much less the desirability of a preventive or aggressive war, but it is clear that the concept of war with Germany had become a daily and familiar companion in official circles for many years before 1914. This whole process was probably helped by the fact that, since foreign affairs did not normally occupy the centre of the stage in Cabinet discussions, it was natural that the Committee itself, concerned as it was with military and naval preparations, should come to occupy an important position. Within its structure, the influence of the Service Departments was very great and as the Committee obtained its own Secretariat, these posts were filled by service officers. It was from this source that the impetus towards planning came in the early years.+ Consider, too, Henry

* Hankey, *op. cit.*, p.64.

† E.D. Morel. *The Secret History of a Great Betrayal*, p.16.

° Though see p.108 for N. Angell's view.

\+ e.g. see Hankey, *op. cit.*, p.65 which displays very clearly the Service itch to get on with the job. The impression left by Lord Hankey is that, at an early date, the conception of a war with Germany had become a working basis for policy in Service circles, becoming increasingly accepted with the passage of years. See e.g. p.21, p.64, p.77.

Wilson at the War Office who combined close links with many politicians and strong, personal pro-French predelictions. His relations with the French General Staff became increasingly close and much of his own time was spent in France and Belgium getting to know the ground over which the British Expeditionary Force might be asked to fight. Certainly in one sense this activity was commendable but it contributed its share to the widening gap in both thinking and feeling, between official circles on the one hand and the general public and the radical thinkers on the other whose preoccupation was with the arts of peace.

The immediate origin of the Committee of Imperial Defence was the setting up by Salisbury in 1895 of a Defence Committee as a Cabinet Committee to examine defence problems generally but the inadequacies of the British military machine exposed by the Boer War led to the demand for a more formidable organisation and the old Defence Committee under Balfour's premiership was reconstituted in 1903 and took as its title the Committee of Imperial Defence. In a speech in the Commons in March 1903 the Prime Minister described its function. It was to be responsible for surveying the military needs of the whole empire and to submit them to continual review so that the necessary strategic decisions would constantly be kept up to date. Secondly it was to be different in organisation from the old Defence Committee for it was to keep detailed records of its decisions and the reasons therefor, for the information of the Cabinet, the administration and for the successors of both. Thus for the first time a coherent body of knowledge, constantly being supplemented, was established and a pattern of working and organisation flowed from this original concept of its scope.

Originally it had a permanent nucleus of the Prime Minister, the Lord President, the Secretary of State for War and First Lord of the Admiralty, the first Sea Lord, the Commander-in-Chief, the Heads of Naval and Military Intelligence. It was recognised that the Foreign Secretary, the Colonial Secretary and the Chancellor of the Exchequer would need to keep in frequent touch and that other Cabinet Ministers would be invited as the needs of the moment dictated. Balfour changed this in 1903 to a system whereby the Prime Minister was the only regular member, entitled to call upon any other person to attend the meetings as he thought necessary. Thus no vested interest concerning the right to attend or to exclude others was allowed to grow and the utmost flexibility of membership, necessary as the scope of discussion grew ever wider, was established from the start.*

At first secretarial services were provided by the Foreign Office where the meetings were held. As the work got into its stride, however, it was appreciated that a permanent staff was required to provide the necessary continuity of knowledge in view of the ever changing membership and the natural change of governments and individual political and staff appointments. Thus Treasury minutes of May and July 1904 made a permanent staff of one secretary and two assistants possible for the first time. Sir George Clarke, later Lord Sydenham, became the first secretary, to be succeeded by Charles Ottley in 1907 and by Maurice Hankey in 1912.

Campbell-Bannerman became Prime Minister in 1905 and soon shed his doubts concerning the need for defence planning under the pressure of the times. During his premiership, the work notably increased with the creation of subcommittees, both permanent and *ad hoc,* to discuss particular and specialised problems.† This policy was continued under Asquith° who also increased the number of persons who were regularly invited to the meetings, adding Haldane, Morley and Kitchener to the list. As a result of the Committee's proliferation there came to be a wide range of individuals who were aware of the progress of thought on defence matters and who had been concerned, to a greater

* Hankey, *op. cit.,* pp. 48–9 states Balfour was also very concerned not to create an administration which would arouse the jealousies of the older Departments.

† "Campbel-Bannerman took his duties as ex-officio Chairman of this Committee with great seriousness, and through them he was fully apprised, as were all his colleagues who sat on this Committee, of the military conversations with the French and the hypothetical plans which arose out of them." Spender, *op. cit.,* Vol.2, p.326. This refers to 1907.

° Note, e.g. the important Invasion Committee set up in 1912.

or lesser extent, with the examination of detailed problems. These individuals were not confined to a very narrow circle but were drawn as seemed appropriate from politicians whether in power or out of it, officials from civilian and service departments, even business men if their services were required, in fact from persons who can reasonably be described as being "in public life" but where the first two groups rather naturally predominated. These pre-war years, too, marked the beginning of Dominion participation in policy. Imperial Defence Conferences were held in 1909 and 1911, whilst the latter was addressed by Asquith and Grey on the international situation and its implications for imperial defence; Dominion representatives were in addition invited to meetings of the Committee whilst they were in London. Plans for military and naval co-operation in the event of war were made with the Dominion Premiers and their consent to the renewal of the Japanese alliance for a further ten years obtained. From then on, Dominion representatives visiting the country were kept informed of defence developments. A further influence on policy making and consequent restriction on British control of her own affairs had thus begun to be created. All in all therefore there were thus many people who were aware of the trends of military and political thinking.

The General Staff had worked out a scheme for the use, if wished, of a British Expeditionary Force on the Continent. On 3rd December 1908 a scheme for such a force was brought before a sub-committee of the Committee of Imperial Defence which was presided over by the Prime Minister and which included Crewe, Haldane, McKenna, Hardinge and Fisher. Discussion on the use and size of the force continued at sub-committee level and by 23rd March 1909 had resulted in the formulation of two main conclusions. Firstly, that the question of using an expeditionary force at all, or whether it would be better to rely solely on the provision of naval assistance for France was not one which could be pre-determined but was a matter of policy which must be left to the government of the day. Secondly, in view of the possibility of a decision to use such a force, plans must be in readiness and for their formulation the plans of the General Staff were worthy of note.* These conclusions were reported to the full Committee of Imperial Defence on 24th July 1909†.

Could members have known this without also knowing that plans for its deployment depended upon agreement with the French and Belgian General staffs? The disclosure cannot excuse the failure to bring to the Cabinet the French request for military conversations but it is strong evidence that this failure was not deliberate and that the knowledge of their existence was not confined to a small group of politicians who irresponsibly drew an unawakened Great Britain into war.

On 23rd August 1911, in the throes of the Agadir crisis, a special session of the Committee of Imperial Defence was held. This meeting was faced with the possibility of Britain supporting France in a war against Germany and it therefore considered the problems involved in sending a force to the Continent. The ways in which this might most usefully be employed were discussed on the basis of the General Staff's view of German strategy. The possibility of sending six divisions to the Continent was also raised. This meeting revealed that the Admiralty and the War Office did not agree on the best form of help to be provided to France and that the Admiralty had refused to disclose its arrangements for transporting the men to France. The War Office strongly believed in support on land for France whereas the Admiralty believed that the main British effort should be at sea; since the British Expeditionary Force would be of negligible assistance there was little point in preparing plans to transport it. This division of opinion was not allowed to continue for long. The display of isolation by the Navy played into the hands of those who had for long argued the need for a naval general staff and the re-organisation of the top level of the Admiralty. These changes were symbolised by the appointment of Churchill to succeed McKenna as First Lord in October 1911 and when war

* These entailed the use of four divisions and one cavalry division.
† B.D., Volume VII, No. 639.

broke out the Navy was ready to transport more soldiers than it was decided to send.

From a modest start the Committee grew steadily until by 1914 it was the body responsible both for the control and the co-ordination of the two Service departments and for their relation to the civilian administration. It was providing the overall strategic planning for military and naval operations, the co-ordination of war preparations made by the service and affected civilian departments and finally it built up the War Book. This was the order of mobilisation, should war become imminent, to be followed by the war and civilian departments. It was largely because of this prior planning that Great Britain, in 1914, changed from a peace to a war economy with the minimum of disturbance. Valuable as the plans were, however, they had not gone far enough for the extent to which modern war necessitates the mobilisation of all branches of national life had not been foreseen. Thus no adequate arrangements had been made to control the financial system of the country, to meet the voracious demands for munitions of all kinds or to encompass the necessary mobilisation of man power both on the military and civilian fronts. These were problems for which control had to be devised as the nature of the war became more clearly understood. When war came, the organisation of the Committee was at once plunged into the centre of things and it was through its expansion that the increasing government control over the life of the nation was exercised as it came to be used as the nucleus of the Cabinet Secretariat.

CHAPTER 3

OPINIONS AND REALITIES

FROM 1905 onwards, Great Britain became increasingly involved in European crises. Against a background of steadily increasing armaments, each one appeared to bring a general war nearer. The debate on the conduct of foreign policy thus became more anxious and pressing both on the grounds that a continental war would in itself be a condemnation of man's social progress and thus a wrong which Great Britain must do her utmost to prevent and, secondly, that if war should come in Europe it was to Britain's interest to keep out of it. Thus the old problem of the proper objects of British foreign policy was discussed again with renewed force and much emotion focussed on the ententes which superficially could be held to be the cause of British embroilment as the persistent trend of support for France and Russia became manifest. Isolationism has always been an attractive idea with its dream of "no foreign politics" and the limitation of international contacts to matters of trade and social relationships. It seemed so obvious in the years before 1914 that the British interest was indeed in peace and trade from which it would appear to follow that she could gain nothing from participation in war and yet the fact remained that the danger of such a conclusion was growing more acute. It was natural therefore that both the objects of British foreign policy and the methods used to pursue them should be subjected to searching examination. From this process many drew the conclusion that both policy and execution were gravely at fault, not only in moral terms but also in any valid interpretation of the national interest.

The general election of 1906 saw the rise of a new class to political effectiveness and its incorporation in the highest level of government. The Campbell-Bannerman administration had to represent a far wider range of interest and views on social relations, including foreign affairs, made necessary by the rise of a new type of member to power than been customary in the past. The international thinking of the Labour member, or Labour-inclined Liberal, tended to be in very general and undifferentiated terms based on an approach to international problems as an extension of opposing class interests. He was not therefore temperamentally sympathetic to a conception of the national interest conceived in terms of the traditional objects of British foreign policy and executed by men who were, ipso facto, his opponents. Before 1914 this process had not yet crystallised and was complicated by the fact that Labour was not yet a party in its own right, but the seeds of a distinctive Labour foreign policy as opposed to a traditional and conservative one had not only been planted but begun to sprout. Whilst these dissenting views on foreign affairs were often vocal and articulate, they were not as yet co-ordinated and, indeed, were composed of a number of different strands. The nearest approach to an organised movement came with the founding of the Union of Democratic Control in September 1914 which not only brought together persons profoundly dissatisfied with the conduct of British foreign policy, but who also had strong Labour sympathies. This formalised the gap of mutual suspicion between the 'traditionalists' and the 'progressives' by making these viewpoints more closely identifiable with the Conservative and Labour parties. One saw the old gang plunging the country into dubious, class-motivated ventures, the other feared that, if Labour ever became the government of the country, considerations of national security might well be jettisoned in favour of vague generalisations about international peace.*

* The title of an article "Labour's Greatest Menace: The Foreign Office" symbolises the difference of view. See J. Hudson, *Foreign Affairs*, Vol.I, No. 7. The Union of Democratic Control issued a periodical from Nov. 1915. Known firstly as *The U.D.C., it* became *Foreign Affairs* in July, 1919.

One of the strands of the attack on capitalism as an unsatisfactory economic and social system was precisely that it contained within itself the inevitability of war either because of the external struggle for markets or because of the private manufacture of arms. War might thus benefit small sections of the community, notably the governing classes and financial circles, but was obviously opposed to the interests of the mass of the people, whose well- being demanded the recognition of the brotherhood of man and the solidarity of the working classes.* Norman Angell† sought to show that war could not achieve the aims for which it was ostensibly fought, while others pinned the blame for the country's difficulties on the machinations of the evil men in the Foreign Office. These ideas combined with the traditional liberal attitude to foreign affairs with its emphasis upon peace, trade and economy to produce a strong current of pacificist thought. This, it must be pointed out, was not necessarily the same as pacifism in the sense of refusal to fight at all, or most costs, but a wider movement composed of persons who felt that they were more alive to the importance of peace to the country, and who believed they would have been prepared to pay a higher price for it had they been in command of affairs, than the existing government.

This critical view of the country's foreign policy falls into three sections although, of course, these were not distinct in the writings of the time since each one tended to reinforce the others to make one simple, overpowering argument. In so far as it is feasible, a rough attempt at classification has been made, but it is impossible to make this clear cut. These three elements were the disapproval of the objects of foreign policy; the unacceptability of the machine which pursued them, and finally the undemocratic nature of the process whereby the foreign relations of the country were conducted.

The liberal view was well expressed by the *Manchester Guard-*

* See e.g. H. Brailsford, *The War of Steel and Gold.*
† *The Great Illusion.*

ian and the *Economist.* The latter took particular interest in the rising cost of British defence policies. The major expenditure resulted from the ever increasing naval estimates which were particularly burdensome at a time when large plans for social legislation were in the offing. "Granted that Sir Edward Grey is the most personally acceptable Minister who could be chosen to manage our foreign affairs, can we afford him? Can we afford to pay twelve millions a year for the luxury of admiring his perfect dignity, his fine self-control, his parliamentary skill?" asked the *Economist* on 25th November 1911. "The motive and cause, the official and unofficial justification of the enormous additions made in the last three years to our naval expenditure, and consequently to our taxation, have been the quarrels of our diplomatists with the diplomatists of Germany."* Both papers took a broadly similar view of the country's interest in foreign affairs. Great Britain must work for a world based on free trade, the rights of small nationalities and international justice. The right way for her to do this was to be free of any entanglements which necessitated support for other countries pursuing a narrower conception of the national interest; objects which might in any case conflict with these more fundamental principles and with which she had no concern. "Only a position of splendid isolation can leave a nation free to act in an honourable way."† Since Great Britain's alignments were, in fact, with France and Russia, such views tended to be anti-Russian and anti-French. This general approach was supported by a traditional hostility to Russia and, to a lesser extent, France. The ententes were young and memories of hostility to French colonial expansion were older whilst no liberal could accept the morality of an association with Russian autocracy and repression, let alone contemplate fighting for it. The signature of the Anglo–Russian entente which carried the possibility of strengthening the Russian government against internal forces of reform and which appeared, in its provisions, as a typically un-

* The *Economist,* 4th November 1911.
† F. Neilson, *How Diplomats Make War,* 1916, p. 52.

pleasant example of great power politics was thus the occasion for some of this unease to be expressed:

"the course pursued in the present instance of completing a great international instrument, profoundly affecting British interests, entirely behind the back of Parliament, [cannot] be allowed to pass unchallenged. I agree that there is much to be said for some agreement with Russia, though, as a Liberal, the present occasion, when reactionary influences are in the ascendant in Russia, seems to me to have been singularly ill-chosen. . .

"It is becoming evident that the origin of this Agreement is to be found in questions of high European politics – to meet some perhaps remote eventuality . . . But the true interests of England do not lie on the Continent of Europe, except in so far as the situation in Europe may react upon our overseas interests."*

H. N. Brailsford agreed. "The explanation is, no doubt, that we have made sacrifices in Asia in order to win Russian support elsewhere.

"The plain fact is that the Agreement has been concluded to restore the European balance of power or, as some would put it, to isolate Germany. . . had peace been our object we should have sought it rather at Berlin than at St. Petersburg."†

Whilst the French entente had initially been received with greater kindness, the recognition of its political aspects led to severe and constant attacks with the peak of criticism being reached at the time of Agadir. The *Economist* considered that for years the country had been entangled in a form of alliance which had menaced her with war on behalf of French interests. It was time, it thought, for us to disentangle ourselves and to re-establish the concert of Europe.° "Friendships" which fetter a nation's freedom are unnatural compacts" complained Morel,+ but in a situation in which friendship to France is interpreted as hostility to Germany, it is a meaningless cry and from its early

* Mr Lynch, Letter to *The Times,* 10th Sept. 1907.

† H. N. Brailsford, Letter to *The Times,* 10th Sept. 1907.

° 2nd Dec. 1911.

+ E.D. Morel, *Morocco in Diplomacy,* p.207.

days both France and Germany had seen in the entente a wider significance than a limited colonial settlement. Bertrand Russell, who saw the true reason for the British entry into war in 1914 as the need to support France, put this down to the desire of the Foreign Office to support France in a war with Germany and by claiming that Britain had no cause to fight except in self-defence, by implication denied the value of an independent France. During the Morocco affair, the Foreign Office and *The Times* had, he thought, been against the liberal and conciliatory elements in France and the major British and French influences in settling the 1911 crisis had been those of exclusive nationalism. Britain had been readier for war than Germany that year. In short, British actions had encouraged German aggressive policies.* In truth, British interests were those of all mankind and the aim of a democratic foreign policy was not adventure, or the support of other claims to territory, but to further the welfare of democracy at home. Any influence to be exerted in other countries must be to obtain peace and freedom.†

The belief that England had no concern in international politics and that her only interest was to remain at peace underlay not only the dislike of the entente but also the attempt to ensure British neutrality should war come. The *Manchester Guardian* was one paper which had consistently pursued this policy during the years preceding 1914. It voiced its suspicion that special friendships with France and Russia might lead to the support of one combatant rather than another in a European war. "Herein lies the only danger to our peace" since, if war should come, we should be able to state our neutrality in advance.° This policy

---

* Compare this with the directly opposite criticism voiced by *The New Europe,* Dec. 4th, 1916, which castigated Grev's pre-war policy as a "pathetic desire to placate the tiger with bread and milk." (For a note on this periodical see p.234, note *.) See also L. Maxse, *National Review,* July 1918. It was Grey's weakness towards Germany, not his antagonism, which had helped to bring on war.

† B. Russel, *The Foreign Policy of the Entente.*

° 3rd Dec. 1912. Morel took the same line. Speaking at Rock Ferry, Birkenhead, he spoke of the need for Great Britain to be neutral if war came in Europe. See *Manchester Guardian,* 4th Dec. 1912.

continued with increased intensity during the fateful summer days of 1914. "Not only are we neutral now" it wrote on the 28th July "but we could and ought to remain neutral throughout the whole course of the war. It is strange that Sir Edward Grey should not have referred to the fact which is the chief source of our moral authority in Europe. We want peace in Europe but we want England to be and remain at peace even more". It called *The Times* to task for saying that we should be ready to see our friendships tested and maintained this attitude as the crisis continued. On 30th July, it criticised Grey for by-passing all opportunities for saying that the country would remain neutral and also *The Times* "whose influence at great crises in our foreign affairs has almost always been for evil" for taking it for granted that if war was not localised we ought to fight with France and Russia. There was no obligation on Great Britain to see "fair play" between Austria and Serbia and certainly no interest to fight to maintain the balance of power. "Englishmen are not the guardians of Serbian wellbeing or even of the peace of Europe. . . . We have not seen a shred of reason for thinking that the triumph of Germany in a European war in which we have been neutral would injure a single British interest however small whereas the triumph of Russia would create a situation for us really formidable."

The ensuing days saw the attack continued. The effect of the preliminary army preparations would not be to deter Germany and Austria but to stiffen Russia in the determination to resist. "We are running the gravest dangers and that not because honour bids us, or interest counsels, but because a powerful and irresponsible group, some of them political, some official, some holding great rank and influence, have persuaded themselves that it is right." There was in fact "a conspiracy to drag us into war". The government was isolated from public opinion in foreign affairs and indeed considered this a virtue. The conspirators preferred the confidence of certain newspaper editors to that of the representatives of the people who would see that their arguments were false. Intervention was based on three reasons. Firstly the need to maintain the balance of power when it was obvious that a Russian victory could only be inimical to this aim; secondly to protect the neutrality of Belgium although we had no obligation to do so single-handed, and thirdly that we were in honour bound to stand by our friends whereas the responsibility of honour lay towards our own people and the need to keep them at peace since we had no commitment to go to war. England was not in honour bound to go to war; it was only the honour of those who had led France to believe in British support that was involved. The country was a victim of "the plot to drag England into war".*

Norman Angell took the same view. "A nation's first duty is to its own people" he wrote,† "This isolation which will result for us if we keep out of this war is that—for a long time [we shall] be the strongest power in Europe and, by virtue of our strength—its arbiter. The object of the war, he continued, could only be to promote the strength of Russia. This would be a far greater menace than the hegemony of Germany, "highly civilised and mainly given to the arts of trade and commerce". The supremacy of Germany in Europe could not be a menace to Great Britain. Mr J. King, a staunch Parliamentary Liberal, followed him on 3rd August with a plea for British neutrality. Any other course would be a "failure" and a "crime".

The *Economist* added its quota. "In maintaining strict neutrality Mr Asquith and Sir Edward Grey can count upon the support of the Cabinet, the House of Commons, and the nation. So far Great Britain has taken the lead in Europe on behalf of peace.

"It is deplorable that at such a moment Mr Churchill should have given sensational orders to the fleet. Every British interest points irresistibly to the maintenance of strict neutrality. And, of course, by so doing we shall be in a far better position later on – if the worst comes to the worst – to mediate effectively between exhausted combatants."° By the 8th August, it had come

* See e.g. N. Angell, *After All,* p.138 referring to the 'conservative mind'
† *The Times,* 1st August 1914.
° 1st August 1914.

to a rather grudging acceptance of the war as one to defend small nationalities in Europe against aggression and oppression whilst insisting it was not a fight in which populations had either been consulted or in which they had concurred.

To this cast of thought it appeared only too clearly that Great Britain had for years been pursuing a policy disastrous to the true interests of the nation which had ended in the ultimate calamity of war. An explanation was looked for and fairly simply found in the nature of the machine which conducted the foreign affairs of the country and its relationship with the politicians who seemingly represented the electoral will but in reality provided but a democratic facade for the ruling class who had come to believe in the inevitability of war.*

Having demolished the ostensible object of current policy, the critics proceeded to the men in charge. No one impugned the honesty or personal integrity of Grey. The *Economist*† wrote "If his policy seems to creep along the ground, it is nevertheless inspired by a strong sense of the value of continuity and a high-minded determination to fulfill honourably whatever obligations he or his predecessors may have incurred. His integrity is recognised and respected at home and abroad". It was, however, suggested that he was unfitted for the task he had to do. One of the charges against him was that he was insular. Since he had never travelled abroad he could not be expected to understand the point of view of other countries, neither was he prepared to go abroad for conferences and discussions on matters of difficulty.° Nor was Grey a linguist+ and this too was held to cut him off from the ease of contact with diplomatic representatives which was so necessary. Thus said the *Economist* in conclusion "we

* See e.g. N. Angell, *After All,* p.138 referring to the 'conservative mind' in politics which, believing that war was part of man's nature, had fatalistically accepted the fact of war with Germany. See also W. Scawen Blunt, *My Diaries.* Entries for 9th May 1907; 13th Oct., 25th Oct. 1911.

† 25th November 1911.

° See too George, *op. cit.,* Vol.I, p.98 "He had no real understanding of foreigners". One of the most important aspects of the pre-war conduct of foreign policy was its influence upon Lloyd George.

+ See Carnock, p.388, for a very nice illustration.

must recognize and allow for the deficiences and drawbacks which tend to place him at the mercy of his own officials, and make it very difficult for him to estimate at their real value the coloured despatches and partial telegrams on which his policy is based. Nevertheless, it is much easier to find fault with the Foreign Secretary than to find a successor for him".

Then again, Grey did not confide in Parliament. "The House of Commons has never had a Foreign Secretary who told it less or suited it better."* This state of affairs was contrasted with the nineteenth century when both Parliament and people were far better informed about the true state of affairs because of the recognised obligation on statesmen to explain their views. "Under Lord John Russell and Lord Palmerston and Mr. Gladstone the discussion of foreign affairs in the Press, in Parliament, and on the platform was freely encouraged. The great election of 1880 turned on Gladstone's criticisms of the Eastern policy of Lord Beaconsfield. Lord Salisbury and Lord Lansdowne were by no means indisposed to keep the public well informed of what they were doing."† Grey however was far more secretive, and only went to the Commons once a week to answer questions. He did not lay down broad lines of policy as Salisbury had done or take Parliament sufficiently into his confidence.° Even Austen Chamberlain gently chid the government+ "would [it] not be a good thing that the Foreign-Secretary should take the House of Commons in the first instance, and his countrymen at large, in the second, much more into his confidence than he has done in the past. We have passed in recent years through European crises, the full gravity of which was not realised by our people, if realised at all, until after they had passed into history. I ask myself, can you conduct democratic government on those principles".

Such aloofness led to the Commons being unable to develop an informed criticism on foreign affairs and to a tendency to

* The *Economist,* 25th Nov. 1911. See also 4th Nov. 1911.
† The *Economist,* 12th Oct. 1912.
° A. Ponsonby. Speech at Manchester, 2nd Dec. 1912.
+ 8th Feb. 1914 at Birmingham.

look on foreign policy as a secret mystery in which they could take no part.* Thus Parliament was not in a position to counter-balance the baneful influence of the Foreign Office and the whole situation was one which encouraged suspicion and mischievous rumour. Foreign affairs, far from being a mystery, were in fact less difficult than domestic affairs and required no more secrecy. The country had never got round to working out true Liberal principles in foreign affairs.† A similar attitude underlay Morel's demand for a Parliamentary Foreign Affairs Committee. Parliament, complained Morel, had no real control over foreign affairs. The desire to remove them from party controversy had led to the disappearance of any effective Parliamentary debate and to the decay of the sense of its proper responsibility. This process had been helped, he considered, by the fact that the real conflicts on foreign policy lay within one party and not between opposing ones. The split lay between the Liberal Imperialists and the Tories on the one hand and the radical Liberals on the other, and Parliament did not provide the opportunity for the conflict to be expressed.

The nation, he thought, was not entirely faultless for it had contributed to this unhappy situation by ignoring foreign affairs. The Foreign Office was the last stronghold of the aristocracy and the landed gentry in the public service and British democracy had largely neglected it. It had thus created a favourable environment for the growth of autocratic management of the foreign relations of the country. His suggestions for the rectification of this situation included the reform of entry into the Foreign Service; the inability of the executive to conclude a treaty without the consent of Parliament which should have ample opportunity to discuss the details of any international instrument before ratification. The House, he thought, should debate the Foreign Office vote in the same way as the army estimates; that the Foreign Secretary should provide periodic reviews of foreign

* Note the parallel with Lloyd George's criticism that the pre-war Cabinet was never called into genuine consultation on foreign affairs.

† *Manchester Guardian,* 3rd Dec. 1912.

policy; that Parliament should have a foreign affairs committee and that all treaties should be submitted to periodic discussion with a view to their amendment. All such proposals, he claimed, would help to lessen the autocratic position of the Foreign Secretary who was "entirely dependent upon his permanent officials".*

The real strictures, however, were reserved for the Foreign Office. "The seat of the mischief" said the *Economist*† in discussing an accord with Russia over Persia "is to be found in our Foreign Office and its anti-German policy, its anti-German Ambassadors, its anti-German clerks. Until the atmosphere is changed and the Office is reformed we are not very hopeful of improvement." It was not the Cabinet but the Foreign Office which was for war. Because of this anti-German bias, the Foreign Office had gone out of its way to embroil the country in continental rivalries° whereas the *Economist* had always held the view that friendship with one country did not imply friction with another and that there was no quarrel between the peoples of Great Britain and Germany. The Agadir crisis had been one of diplomatists and newspaper writers, not one of real substance between the people+ and in the recent debate in the House of Commons all speakers had expressed themselves as in favour of friendship with Germany.× A policy of continental alliances must be eschewed because it meant the need to support a power even when it acted wrongly. Parliament must insist on a radical revision of foreign policy and a return to older and better traditions.** "If there were no Foreign Office and no ambassadors, a speech like Mr Lloyd George's to the bankers would have been regarded as a most excellent plea for peace and economy."†† Once again,

* E. D. Morel, *Truth and the War,* p.179. See also pp.107–113, and E. Morel, *The Morrow of the War.*
† 20th Jan. 1912.
° 13th July 1912.
+ 9th Sept. 1911.
× 16th Dec. 1911.
** 9th Sept. 1911.
†† 11th Nov. 1911.

it was the Press and the Foreign Office which had blown the matter up into a crisis. "It is merely that the diplomats and a handful of fire-eating officers on either side (with a few snarling and ill-conditioned newspapers) choose to say that Germany and England are and must remain at enmity."* The Foreign Office had evidently been working under French influence for French ends without any proper regard to British interests. It neither understood nor cared about our true commercial interests in Morocco.

E. D. Morel wrote in a similar vein. "The 'man in the street' is apt to suppose that the Foreign Minister of the day incarnates in his person the foreign policy of the country subject to Cabinet approval. That, of course, is a delusion. He only does so nominally. Foreign policy is the work of many—not of one, with very rare exceptions. There are the embassies abroad, and it happens that some one or other of the ambassadors may have different views from those entertained by the Foreign Minister at home on a specific issue. If the latter has no very decided views one way or another, or if he does not keep a tight hold over his mouthpieces abroad, the influences directed from a particular embassy in a certain direction may have the most far-reaching effects upon policy. That, to my own personal knowledge, has occurred within the past four years, in two questions of foreign policy. Then there are the permanent officials at home, some of whom have decided views, and consider themselves the real directors of the nation's foreign policy and not only exercise that influence to the uttermost upon the Foreign Minister of the day, but impose it upon the public (and so, indirectly exercise pressure upon their chief) through social circles and by the medium of journalists *de confiance* with whom they are permanently in touch. It may even be—here again I speak in one such case from personal knowledge—that certain events may be prepared and worked for by members of the Foreign Minister's *entourage* entirely without the latter's knowledge. So that to speak of a

* 25th Nov. 1911.

diplomatic machine is strictly accurate. Among the units composing the machine are to be met with rivalries, private grudges, exaggerated notions of personal prestige and dignity, personal ambitions, and all the concatenation of ills to which ordinary flesh is heir. Among the embassies abroad, promotion may depend, often does depend, upon keeping on good terms with a particular permanent official at home. In that you have the usual inconveniences from which Government Departments can never be free, doubly aggravated in the case of the Foreign Office by the close caste system therein traditionally prevailing which makes of it the glorious preserve of a favoured few, and the lack of any real, effective control from the outside. All Foreign Offices are more or less tarred with the same brush. Some are worse than ours in certain respects (i.e. indiscretion and personal corruption, from the latter of which we are free), but in several cases (notably in the United States and in France) there *is* an effective outside check in the shape of a Parliamentary Committee which can often cut the knot of personal intrigue, or at least expose it, and so prevent further mischief for a time. In our case there is no such corrective."* At times he became really virulent "It was given to me to see behind the veil, and to realise how utterly at the mercy of a Bureaucracy working in darkness and in secrecy, were the peoples, not in Africa only, but of Europe; a Bureaucracy rooted in obsolete traditions, badly informed, out of touch with and supremely indifferent to the human pulse, cynically and openly contemptuous of moral conduct, deeming the finest of arts the art successfully to lie, living in a world walled round by narrow prejudices, and absorbed in the prosecution of rivalries for the attainment of objects bearing not the remotest relation to the well-being or fundamental needs of the masses, whose destinies that Bureaucracy held in the hollow of its hands".†

* E. D. Morel, *Morocco in Diplomacy,* p.86. Although some critics feared that such a committee would lead to even less being divulged to the Commons, see *Manchester Guardian,* 3rd Dec. 1912, report of a meeting in Manchester on foreign policy.

† E. D. Morel, *Truth and the War,* pp.XV–XVI.

Twelve men "are in a position to exercise a decisive influence upon the Department's actions. They are the Foreign Secretary, the Under-Secretaries at the Foreign Office, and the Ambassadors. We may say, therefore, that the Foreign Department of this country is managed, and the foreign relations of this nation are conducted, in all essential respects by twelve gentlemen."*

These gentleman and their assistants came from a closed caste, one of "long lineage and short vision",† thus their objects and desires could not be those of the ordinary citizen. The first requirement for a democratic foreign policy was that our agents "should be in closer touch with the movements of popular thought.° It was indeed a mistake to suppose that Grey or the Cabinet had much responsibility for foreign affairs much less Parliament and people. "There was, moreover, a deliberate conspiracy on the part of certain people to foist a policy on this country which was not that of the people, and which had no connection with Liberalism. It was a conspiracy of the bureaucracy against the conception of Liberal foreign policy and Sir Edward Grey, not being a masterful man and not, perhaps, the industrious man that we sometimes think him, has found those forces too great for him."+ It was fallacious to suppose that Grey initiated policy or that the principle of Cabinet responsibility existed. "The real rulers of the country were the Civil Service and the diplomatic corps. The growing complication of affairs has made it impossible for every member of the Cabinet to know the business of every other member."× An enormously popular quotation was from Carlyle's Latter-Day Pamphlets "That there was but one reform for the Foreign Office – to set a live coal under it". Even *The Times*** delivered itself of a stricture against the professionals "In England men will learn with amazement and incredulity that

---

* E. D. Morel, *Truth and the War,* p.108.

† F. Neilson, *How Diplomatists Make War,* p.79.

° *Manchester Guardian*, 3rd Dec. 1912.

\+ See meeting of Manchester Reform Club and '95 Club reported *Manchester Guardian,* 3rd Dec. 1912.

× op. cit.

** 26th Nov. 1912.

war is possible over the question of a Servian port, or even over the larger issues which are said to lie behind it. Yet that is whither the nations are blindly drifting. Who, then, makes war? The answer is to be found in the Chancelleries of Europe, among the men who have too long played with human lives as pawns in a game of chess, who have become so enmeshed in formulas and the jargon of diplomacy that they have ceased to be conscious of the poignant realities with which they trifle. And thus will war continue to be made, until the great masses who are the sport of professional schemers and dreamers say the word which will bring, not eternal peace, for that is impossible, but a determination that wars shall be fought only in a just and righteous and vital cause".

The newspapers, perhaps naturally, placed great faith in their ability to create a mature and enlightened public opinion if they were given the facts. A great deal of the blame currently put upon the Press for recurrent scares was unfair because the Press as a whole was only given halftruths to report, the "secrets" being kept for a favoured few.* This encouraged irresponsibility on the part of journalists but they would not, in Mr Ponsonby's view,† be able to do much harm if only people were better instructed for it was only the ignorant who could be aroused to passionate excitement.

We can surely say today that this attack was an exaggerated one. Neither Grey nor his permanent officials were war mongers, neither did they support French interests as an end in themselves but because they had come to believe that the independence of France was a vital British need which necessitated the containment of Germany. Thus "The deliberate policy of the encirclement of Germany by British diplomacy"° is not a full or fair assessment of official motives. Neither was Grey the tool of his permanent officials whose desire to turn the ententes into alliances was not satisfied. Under Grey, Great Britain did, in fact, attempt to

* *Manchester Guardian,* 31st Dec. 1912.
† Speech at Manchester, 2nd Dec. 1912.
° C. Trevelyan. *Foreign Affairs,* Vol.II, No. 12, June 1921, p. 192.

fulfil one of her traditional roles as the arbiter of the peace of Europe. For years the Foreign Secretary aimed to perform a balancing act of restraint on France and Russia through leaving them in doubt as to the extent of British support and through using the reality of the ententes as a curb on Germany against an attack on either. The former aspect is a passive one; it was the latter which drove him into activity therefore inevitably his policies appeared from the outside to be anti-German. Nevertheless, there was an ultimate difference of view since Grey was not prepared to pay as high a price for the maintenance of peace as his radical attackers believed they would have done, as his attitude in 1914 clearly shows.

The outbreak of war, and its frightfulness, generated a search for new principles and methods for the conduct of foreign affairs and in this search old ways and old executants were discredited. The Radical attack began this process and was of great importance in influencing the climate of opinion about the nature of foreign affairs and the conduct of foreign policy. In this process it came to be believed that the instruments of secret diplomacy and of Foreign Offices were hindrances to the creation of a peaceful world. "This War has been brought about by secret diplomacy, and diplomatic failure must be stopped, if possible, by the united determination of democracy."*

This was a view which made Grey very cross. "The talk about 'old diplomacy' and 'new diplomacy' is little better than useless chatter. In so far as it leads people to look for safety in new methods, it is a positive hindrance and mischief. It was not the old diplomacy that was to blame for the war."† Nevertheless, for many people it acted as a scapegoat and thus, when attention turned to problems of reconstruction, the responsibility of secret diplomacy for the ills of the world was remembered.

---

* Mr Ponsonby, House of Commons, 23-2-16, *Hansard,* Vol.80, Col.741.
† Grey, *op. cit.,* Vol.II, p.268.

II

The strongest case against the prewar handling of foreign affairs is that which accused the government of neglecting the proper processes of democracy, for here there were sins of omission which greater thought and a more meticulous consideration of constitutional morality could have prevented. For these the government must bear responsibility. Even when these are allowed for, however, one is still left with a genuine problem, for it was not in the last resort the wickedness of the government but the changing circumstances in which Great Britain found herself which made a mockery of her freedom of action and thus of the concept of ultimate decision remaining with the people. On this level, both government and opposition lived, until too late, in a world which had gone.

It has long been accepted that general responsibility for government policy rests with the Cabinet and that in foreign policy a greater freedom of action rests with the executive than in home affairs. Although the control of Parliament, and ultimately the electorate, is recognised yet the need for decision and for compromise with other states results in a control largely depending upon the determination of broad issues of principle upon the basis of which the Foreign Secretary is expected to act. There is thus the perennial problem of the exercise of democratic control in such a way that the executive is not paralysed from taking any action at all, and for the Cabinet to decide what, in any circumstances, belongs properly to the area of general debate and consensus of opinion and what is a matter for executive decision. This absence of any clear, and static, dividing line means that governmental representatives are often faced with very fine decisions. It would seem likely that their temptation is always to err on the side of over caution and this provides a justification for the activities of the constant, awkward, and no doubt very irritating, parliamentarian who can be relied upon to question absolutely everything. Governments will always face the temptation not to tell even if they do not always claim the public interest quite so crudely as did Robert Cecil in 1916 during a debate on foreign affairs "we [i.e. the Government] cannot share that responsibility with the House of Commons or with anybody else—not during the War".*

The principle that, in the last resort, decision must be taken by the community was well understood by Grey who persistently refused to take action which he believed would compromise that freedom on the basic issue of peace or war, where the country's decision might differ from his own. As has been explained in Chapter 1, before his first two months of office were through, he had already been faced with the problem of possible British support to France in a war with Germany and had stated categorically that it was not in his power to commit the country without the assent of Parliament. Such a commitment would in effect be a defensive alliance. This would be "too serious a matter to be kept secret from Parliament. The Government could conclude it without the assent of Parliament, but it would have to published afterwards. No British Government could commit the country to such a serious thing and keep the engagement secret".† His view that the military conversations were valid on a technical level only and did not infringe this basic principle seems curiously unimaginative but it was a judgement which, with whatever doubts, was in effect approved by the Cabinet in 1912 through its sanctioning of these talks. Neither, as has been explained, was the Foreign Office unmindful of its obligation to Parliament.°

It was therefore possible for Grey, in 1914, to stress to Parliament that the decision for war rested with it and not with the government and that in taking that decision it was in no way hampered by any prior commitments made on its behalf. His speech, on 3rd August, was thus not a firm statement that Great Britain would go to war but a reasoned case as to why both honour and interest demanded that she should. "My object has been to explain the view of the Government and to place before

---

* 31–10–16, *Hansard,* Vol.86, Col.1676.
† Grey to Bertie, 31st Jan. 1906. B.D., Vol.III, No.219.
° B.D., Vol.III, No.220(b).

the House the issue and the choice." The supreme decision rested with Parliament and its freedom was in no way hampered by any prior obligations to France beyond that of 2nd August.* Even the Belgian guarante had never been interpreted as absolutely binding in all circumstances. Nevertheless, Great Britain had a long-standing friendship with France, "how far that friendship entails obligation—let every man look into his own heart and his own feelings and construe the extent of the obligation for himself." The dangers arising from the disposition of the fleets were not run by France alone. If Great Britain remained neutral and France had therefore to withdraw from the Mediterranean to protect her coasts, British interests there would be left undefended. As for Belgium, the circumstances were such as, in his opinion, to invite a positive British reaction. To remain outside the war would not mean that Great Britain would not suffer. As a great trading nation, she was bound to be seriously affected by the inevitable disruption of normal commercial ties. Furthermore, she would be able to exert no influence on the combatants because her moral position would have been discredited.

Although Grey, when he went to the Commons, felt fully conscious of the fact that the final decision remained with Parliament and that it was up to him to convince it of the validity of his argument which it was at liberty to reject, others denied that the Cabinet had in fact left Parliament any true freedom of action in view of the implied commitment in the Grey–Cambon letters. Thus in the *Manchester Guardian* of 4th August, 1914, Grey's speech is referred to as a death bed confession which did not atone for his secrecy, for it had been nothing but a mockery to give the House of Commons responsibility at the last moment at a time of great excitement.† The same point was made by the *Morning Post*° during a discussion of the general problem of democratic control. It argued that foreign policy was the domain

* That is to protect the northern coasts of France from German naval attack in view of the naval rationalisation.

† See also Lord Hugh Cecil, *The Times,* 29th April 1916.

° 24th May 1916.

of the king "in theory and in history" and denied that Parliamentary control existed. Grey in 1914 had only made a show of consulting Parliament which approved his policy but "did not lay it down, nor direct it, nor control it." The belief that the government possessed only a cynical regard for Parliamentary responsibility was unfortunately enhanced by Grey, for in his speech he inadvertently omitted the last sentence of the British letter to France. The discovery of this was to Morel the last straw, for he was convinced that it was a deliberate action designed to prevent Parliament realising the cut and dried nature of the military plans. "They stooped to the lowest depths of political dishonesty."*

There is substance in this point that the freedom of action of Parliament was illusory. Is it, however, sufficient to say that Britain was committed because of an exchange of letters of whose existence the country was unaware? At a deeper level the problem of the value of an independent France to Britain still remained; the letters were but its symbol and differences of opinion on this question would still have existed in their absence. In other words, if Grey was giving the House of Commons an empty choice, was this not rather because of the nature of reality than the sins of the government? Again it is true that the idea of Parliament indulging in rational discussion to determine the nature of the British interest once August 1914 had been reached is nonsensical. Such debate should have taken place years before, both in and out of Parliament so that there would already have been a valid public opinion concerning the British interest in a European war. One cannot hold the Liberal government totally responsible for the lack of an informed and critical opinion on foreign affairs but one can point out its contribution in that it failed to provide the necessary succour without which such an opinion could not develop.

Responsibility to Parliament and the public can only operate as an ultimate sanction on government action. By the time decision

* E.D. Morel, *The Secret History of a Great Betrayal*, p.44.

at public level has to be taken, any true freedom of action may have gone and the choice, as in 1914, may not be meaningful. The only real way to prevent the nation simply acting as a rubber stamp at times of great pressure and high excitement, is for there to be a continuous, informed and intelligent interest in foreign affairs on the part of the general public which is felt by the executive during the long years of policy making which precede a crisis. To some extent this is a counsel of perfection but a strong case can be made out for saying that such an interest did not exist in the country before the First World War. It is always difficult to recapture the attitude of mind of a by-gone period or to make valid generalisations about public opinion especially since, with the advantages of hind-sight, the clouds of the gathering international storm as the twentieth century opened can so easily be seen. At the time they were not so obvious. Since 1914, war, or the possibility of war, has not seemed an unnatural thought but prior to that date, a major war fought by civilised nations was, if thought of at all, considered an anachronism. This feeling that war was an outrageous offence accounts for the intensity with which government policy was criticised by the interested few. In general terms, however, international affairs did not press upon the consciousness of the public, or even of the government, to the extent which they have done since, simply because no issue arose which was felt to threaten the very existence of the country. As soon as one such did appear, as in the naval scare of 1909, public opinion soon took a hand. The lack, except at moments of crisis, of any feeling of pressure created a favourable environment for the continuance of the assumption that Great Britain retained a freedom of manoeuvre she no longer had and also for an uncritical attitude towards governmental actions which assumed that, as long as nothing untoward occured, there was no need to bother. Such an attitude encourages leaving the conduct of foreign affairs to a comparatively small number of persons and assumes, often incorrectly, that mistakes in foreign policy can be rectified before having done too much damage.

Freedom of manoeuvre exists in foreign policy in two senses.

Firstly in a general way as when one asserts that British freedom declined with her relative loss of power over a century or more and secondly in a particular situation. Each problem after all has many facets, and its roots in the past. Some of them may never come to fruition whilst others ripen rapidly but each one has a history and foreign policy is likely to have a greater set of choices in dealing with it the earlier it comes to grips with the matter in hand. There are surely very few issues which pose the stark necessity of a fight for survival when they first impinge on international consciousness. In both these ways, British freedom of action had declined by 1914, and in the first sense was so to continue thereafter but she has often approached an international problem with the attitude of mind of a more spacious age.

The isolation of the electorate and the backbencher from the progress of foreign affairs can easily be exaggerated. It is not difficult to think of occasions upon which public opinion has been decisively asserted but this is rather different from the exercise of continual vigilance over a long period of time. It would be foolish to pretend that the creation of a popular interest which is sensible and mature is an easy thing to achieve but it can be argued that a necessary pre-condition for its accomplishment is access to the facts of the case, and this the popular press did not provide in the early years of the century when a new form of journalism was being created. Comparatively little space was devoted to foreign affairs, appeal was to the reader's emotions rather than his intellect, facts gave way to stories of human interest; parliamentary debates were no longer reported to the extent they once had been.* The Liberal government was largely unaware of the need to appeal and explain to a popular opinion outside and different from that expressed in Parliament. The emotional displays of what was contemptuously referred to as the "yellow press" were not counteracted by an attempt at education. The need for "public relations" was not appreciated by the

* R. Ensor, *England* 1870–1914, p.144 and pp.532–6 traces the decline in serious political reporting.

Foreign Secretary. Grey and Asquith limited their contacts with the Press to J. A. Spender of the *Westminster Gazette* and *The Times* maintained regular contact with Foreign Office personnel.* But no formal machinery for giving information to the press as a whole, and in an easily accessible form, at that time existed.

Lack of understanding at a Parliamentary level can also be fairly attributed, at any rate in part, to the inadequacies of the Liberal government and particularly to Grey. The realities of social change were reflected in the changing composition of Parliament† which posed a similar problem of communication for the government which, displaying a lack of adaptation to modern conditions, performed it inadequately. The general elections of 1906 and 1910 not only brought into Parliament a significant number of working class representatives but created Liberal majorities dependent on their votes. Thus 1906 really sounded the death knell of the validity of the distinction between a governing class and the governed. As far as foreign affairs were concerned the former were more at home with the conception of the maintenance of British interests as expressed in such practical objects as the independence of the Low countries, or the prevention of European hegemony but these were unfamiliar ways of thought to the latter whose approach to public affairs was in terms of the brotherhood of the working classes, the oppression of the poor by the rich and the use of the governmental machine as an agent in the class war. The true British interests in foreign affairs were trade and peace and the rest was chimera. The connection between events in Europe and these desirable objects was often not adequately made and it was one which the government could have taken steps to help to make. One must not press the differences in view in pre-war governments too far, but the background, upbringing

* Those who realised this looked upon the Gazette as the nearest approach to an official organ that the country possessed; although in the eyes of the Continent nothing could shake the position of *The Times*.

† 1906 Parliament: Tories 132, Liberals 377, Labour 53. 1910 Parliament: Tories 273, Liberals 275, Labour 40, Irish Nationalists 82.

and the road to power of the members of the Liberal-Imperialist wing were very different from those of humbler origin whose main concern was with domestic reform. It was not easy for those of the older traditions to adapt their ways and habits of thought and in particular the assumption continued to be made that members of parliament naturally understood and accepted the terms of discussion and the objects they embodied. This was no longer necessarily true; both sides needed to make an effort to understand the other. In particular, Grey never realised that a House "rich in inexperienced idealists"* needed to be nursed and educated rather than misled over British policy. His sense of accountability to the House of Commons permitted him to give it but limited attention whilst his weekly response to questions can on more than one occasion be fairly described as equivocal. Thus, on 30th March 1911 Grey was asked if, when he came to office, Great Britain had any obligations, expressed or implied, to assist the French army in certain eventualities. He replied that the extent of the obligation was that expressed or implied in the Anglo–French convention and that there was no other obligation. This was true but the secret articles were as yet unknown. Again in his speech of 27th November 1911, whilst admitting them, he denied the existence of any others. This once again was strictly true but not everyone took his meticulously detached view of the military and naval conversations when they were finally disclosed. They had at this time been continuing in secret for five years. Finally, on 11th June 1914 he was questioned on the subject of naval negotiations with Russia. He replied with such a soporific that his own comment was to be "The answer given is absolutely true. The criticism to which it is open is, that it does not answer the question put to me".†

His speeches, too, tended to avoid the real issues for fear of giving offence abroad and thus did not contribute to, and were not aimed at, the enlightenment of the new backbencher. Grey was, of

* R. Ensor, *England,* p.391.
† Grey, *op. cit.,* Vol.I, p.289.

course, aware of the need to carry the radical wing of the Liberal party with him but he considered this the limit of his explanations and he did little positive in the years before the war to persuade it of the necessity and logic of his actions. To him, this type of persuasion was a disagreeable necessity and not a challenge to be surmounted. Had he been more interested in domestic affairs he might have won radical confidence but he limited himself to the responsibilities of his own office and looked forward to the day when he might honourably retire therefrom. He was thus not in a position to overcome radical distrust.

III

The lead and the initiative in foreign policy during this period thus came from the Cabinet with Parliament falling in behind. The nature of foreign affairs and the form of the British constitution are strong, permanent pressures which dictate this, they were but reinforced by the special parliamentary and political context within which they operated. It is therefore necessary to discuss the concept of Cabinet responsiblity for foreign policy and the extent to which it can be said to have been in control of affairs.

The pre-war Liberal Cabinet represented the different currents of thought combined in the party itself and the need to maintain unity in the Cabinet was a further check upon the unfettered responsibility of the Foreign Secretary. This situation was well illustrated by the series of events immediately preceding the outbreak of war when those who believed it to be a British interest to support France were held back by those who did not. As Grey has written, the Liberal opponents of his foreign policy and especially the Press "made the mistake, as is so often done, of attributing all that they disliked to the influence of one man, not realising that all important telegrams to and from the Foreign Office were circulated every day to the Cabinet, and that it is impossible for any Secretary for Foreign Affairs to continue in his post unless he has the general approval of the Cabinet".* Here Grey was guilty of a certain amount of exaggeration or at the least defined an important telegram more narrowly than most.

The general statement of responsibility at Cabinet level has, however, to be further broken up for not all members of the Cabinet have felt equally responsible in the field of foreign affairs and it has often been the case that a small inner circle has been peculiarly concerned. Much will here depend upon the play of individual personalities, it being generally accepted that the Prime Minister and Foreign Secretary have a more direct and individual responsibility. Who will be added to this nucleus will obviously depend upon the circumstances of the time and the more serious the question, the more likely it is that the whole Cabinet will be involved. Thus Disraeli complained that he had seven different views on the Eastern question in his Cabinet and much of the hesitation in 1914 was due to Grey's recognition of the need to carry the Cabinet with him. He did not believe that the Cabinet would agree to British participation in a European war unless and until Germany invaded Belgium although his own conviction was that it was a British interest to support France. As it was two ministers resigned.

The extent to which this need to carry the Cabinet can act as a check upon individual action must depend upon the acceptance of this liability by each member. The charge has been that Grey did not abide by it to the extent that he ought to have done in that he did not disclose the depth of the relationship with France.

The tradition of the independence of the Foreign Secretary from his colleagues was well established by the vital personalities of the nineteenth century. Palmerston, particularly, but in later years Disraeli, Salisbury, Lansdowne and Grey, to different degrees, upheld this supremacy. The Foreign Minister is not merely the mouthpiece of a collective decision but rather the leader where others follow and, as has already been explained,† Grey found

* Grey, *op. cit.,* Vol.I, p.240.
† See p.89.

this responsibility acceptable whilst remaining aware of the need to act within the framework of Cabinet approval.

The greater importance of the Prime Minister and Foreign Secretary was generally accepted but this does not rule out the possibility of friction between the two. Great Britain was perhaps fortunate from this point of view in the late nineteenth century when the two offices could still be satisfactorily combined by the same person — Lord Salisbury. When they were not so combined, Salisbury was still the dominating figure. After his retirement, Balfour and Lansdowne ran easily in harness and Asquith and Grey seem to have done likewise but that it is a generally uneasy relationship is borne out by Balfour. "It's the rarest thing when the Prime Minister and the Foreign Minister don't clash. That's what makes me so impatient of all this talk about Lloyd George interfering so much. I don't say Lloyd George didn't often do things he had better not have. But you can't expect the P.M. *not* to interfere with Foreign Office business. It's only when you get a combination of two men who see absolutely eye to eye and work in perfect harmony that you can avoid it. Lansdowne and myself were one of the rare cases, — but I could give you any number of instances of the other. — The fact is that the Foreign Office cannot be in a water-tight compartment."*

The predominance of a few members of the Cabinet does not seem to have been seriously challenged until the great debate on responsibility for the war was opened. In retrospect, Lloyd George is scathing of the system and declares that very little time in Cabinet was spent in discussing foreign affairs in the years preceding the outbreak of war and that, in any case, those who were not of the inner coterie were not expected to make any contribution. "We were made to feel that, in these matters, we were reaching our hands towards the mysteries, and that we were too young in the priesthood to presume to enter into the sanctuary reserved for the elect."† But in fairness it must be pointed out,

* B. Dugdale, *Arthur James Balfour,* Vol.II, p.292–3.
† George, *op. cit.,* Vol.I, p.47.

as Lloyd George recognised, that foreign affairs were not the most pressing issues facing the government in the immediate pre-war years. "A Cabinet which was compelled by political and economic exigencies to concentrate its energies on domestic problems left the whole field of foreign affairs to Sir Edward Grey."* Attention was fully absorbed with questions of social reform, of education, of land taxation, the disestablishment of the Welsh church and, above all, Ireland. It is also easy to understand that Lloyd George's ebullient personality would not have taken kindly to exclusion.

It was customary to circulate Foreign Office despatches regularly to Cabinet Ministers but there is evidence that this did not mean that all important despatches went to everyone.† Lloyd George may be going too far when he claims that only the harmless ones were circulated,° but in view of the fact that certain matters were kept from the Cabinet some selective process obviously took place. Ministers had the right to question the Foreign Minister on the basis of the information contained in the despatches in Cabinet meetings and foreign affairs were normally on the agenda.

Prior to 1914, Cabinet meetings were conducted with considerable informality. After consultation with his immediate associates, the Prime Minister issued an agenda. No formal record of discussion was taken, the nearest approach to minutes being the letter written to the king by the Prime Minister to tell him what had been decided. Pre-war Prime Ministers attached great importance to these informal methods as the necessary safeguard for complete freedom of discussion. The great drawback was that there was

---

* George, *op. cit.*, Vol.I, p.98. See also Lichnowsky, *op. cit.*, p.67, who tells us that Grey's influence in foreign policy was almost unlimited. Whilst on important matters he would say "I must consult the Cabinet", it always agreed with him.

† This was a practice with a precedent. "Still they [i.e. the Ministers] liked to believe that they were omniscient and it was a shock to Lord Cadogan, who had a young cousin in the Office when, on his humourously saying at a dinner party "You don't mean to say, Henry, that you see all the secret telegrams," he received the answer "Yes, George, but *you* don't". Tilley and Gaselee, *The Foreign Office*, p.137–8.

° George, *op. cit.*, Vol.I, p.48.

often confusion as to what had actually been decided. "The Cabinet often had the very haziest notion as to what its decisions were" said Curzon in 1918 referring to pre-war lack of organisation.* The door was certainly wide open for this and for ministers to miss items of information which would have concerned them. In any case it was not a system which could stand up to the pressure of war time government with its urgent need to discuss, decide and execute the important policy decisions which were continually occurring.

There were two serious matters which Grey kept from the Cabinet. The first was the Cambon inquiry in January 1906 which, as has already been explained,† was not reported to the Cabinet although an inner circle knew of it. The negligence for this was essentially Grey's. The second was the military conversations° which arose out of the same Grey–Cambon talks. Both Liberal Prime Ministers were doubtful about the wisdom of those talks+ but it occurred to neither that they should be submitted to the Cabinet. Grey claims× that many Ministers must have known what was going on by virtue of their attendance at meetings of the Committee of Imperial Defence and its proliferating committees and to the later reader this rings true, particularly for the period after 1909. Lord Sydenham, of course, contests this argument. Up till September 1907, when he ceased to be Secretary, he states that the conversations were never raised officially at the Committee and "I only heard quite informally what was going on". The points that he believed were studied were that in some circumstances four divisions might be sent to France, the railway facilities and, finally, the position to be assigned to the Expeditionary Force in the French battle line.** Lord Hankey has recently confirmed Sydenham's view that the conversations were only known in the vaguest way, although the Com-

* House of Lords, 19–6–18, *Hansard,* Vol.30, Col.265.
† See p. 28.
° See pp. 32–3.
\+ See p. 33.
× *op. cit.,* Vol.I, p.93. See also above p. 96, note †.
** B.D., Vol.III, No.221.

mittee was informed from time to time of "the plans drawn up by the General Staff as a result of the conversations, but the conversations themselves were never alluded to".* Nevertheless, it was not until October 1912 that the talks were officially revealed to the Cabinet with the consequences that have already been related.

In retrospect, Grey felt both these decisions had been wrong. One cannot but agree with him whilst at the same time recognising that the charges against him of secrecy and lack of consultation need to be put into perspective. The relative simplicity of international affairs had encouraged the independence of the Foreign Minister from all but his immediate colleagues and thus there was no tradition of intimate Cabinet control. The Cabinet was concerned with more pressing issues and was deliberately not organised to exert a tight control over its members. Nevertheless, as Grey was aware, ultimately the Cabinet was the deciding body for British policy and although as Foreign Minister his voice would have the greatest weight, it was still necessary for him to persuade the Cabinet to accept his views as theirs.

* Hankey, *The Supreme Command,* Vol.I, p.63. Apart from the possibility that these authorities are referring to different years, the reconciliation of these views may lie in the fine distinction to be drawn between the conversations and their results. The focus of interest between the politicians and the Secretariat would no doubt be different and the latter, from whom the planning momentum came, was concerned with a range of defence problems and thus less likely to lay particular stress on any one. Probably the facts were there but few bothered about them so that they did not make sufficient impact for their full implication to sink in.

CHAPTER 4

LIBERALS IN WAR TIME

I

With the outbreak of war, the world in which diplomacy had to function underwent significant change. No longer was its purpose that of negotiating settlements of outstanding differences in order to maintain peace but of making a contribution to the over-riding purpose of victory. In a war of great magnitude, this means that many of the traditional values of diplomacy must be jettisoned; no longer can it afford to think of long-term policies but only of short-term expedients; no longer can it consider the legitimate rights of other nations if war-time benefit will result from riding rough-shod over them; above all it cannot afford to wait for the right moment to suggest a settlement or for the acts of persuasion to complete their work. The conception of diplomacy as a method of negotiation in order to achieve the signature of a reasonable compromise, fair as far as possible to all parties and based on thoughtful deliberations is often the antithesis of what must be done in war when the compulsion of necessity over-rules the niceties of international conduct. It was not always easy for the Foreign Service to shed the traditional values for which it stood and the time for painless adjustment was not always present. Neither were the men employed therein always convinced that it was in the national interest so to do.*

---

* See e.g. Carnock, p.427 *et seq.* Arthur Nicolson neither played, nor wished, a part in war-time diplomacy.

At the same time, its job had become more difficult in that the context in which it worked had become more limited and thus the capacity to obtain national ends was similarly restricted. Under such circumstances, and at a time not noted for the generosity of its judgements, the Foreign Service inevitably became a sitting target for criticism which found it easy to ignore the difficulties arising from the clashing interests of Britain, neutrals and allies and to concentrate upon those aspects of the work with which it found itself dissatisfied.

Whilst formal military and naval preparations for war had been carried to an unsuspected pitch of efficiency, in a deeper sense the nation was unready for the struggle which lay ahead whose nature was largely unrecognised. The climate of opinion both politically and publicly was not one geared to the realities of total war and the necessity for full scale planning and mobilisation of the totality of the community's resources and the realisation of what was involved in modern war was but gradual. To add to this was the general expectation that the war would be short with the presumption that Britain's major contribution to it would be through her sea power; whilst the temper of the Asquith government was against taking revolutionary decisions. It is not to be expected, therefore, either that plans could already have been in existence to deal with new and unsuspected problems or that there should immediately have sprung into maturity an attitude of mind anxious and eager to look round for new forms of government. During the whole period of the Asquith premiership the search continued for a satisfactory body to assume the supreme direction of the war. It only gradually became clear that the older forms of peace-time government expressed through the Cabinet system and served by a limited Civil Service were firstly too cumbersome to deal with the pressure of decisions and secondly too constrained to control the necessary mobilisation of the whole community. Thus at a political level the old methods of the peace-time Cabinet at first continued. The leisurely expression of opinions, the postponement of finality of decision for as long as possible, the dislike of over-riding the opinion of colleagues all led to long and inconclusive debates in which the search for unity of opinion was of major importance. Such a process presupposes unlimited time and its undoubted qualities came to be considered a serious drawback in the face of war-time urgencies. Similarly, at an administrative level, decisions for the creation of new machinery were taken under the pressure of immediate events on a somewhat ad hoc and limited basis. Nevertheless, although it was a period of improvisation, developments in the nature of government had already begun to show themselves during the first part of the war; under Lloyd George the process was to gather increasing momentum, but the roots of his system of government lay in the past and were determined by the circumstances of the time as well as by the play of personalities involved. In this change, great inroads were made on the conception of the Foreign Secretary as the main inspirer of decisions and as his position declined at the political level, so his official machine found itself by-passed both in its function of giving advice and in its execution of determined policy.

The change in the balance of responsibility at the political level for the conduct of foreign affairs and the consequent decline in importance of the Foreign Service were not to the liking of the officials concerned. Whilst during the war their necessity was largely accepted they resulted in an outburst of accumulated resentment when the war was over. This, as is well known, took the form of a rejection of Lloyd George both as policy maker and executor but the reasons for this change of status were not entirely personal. The twentieth century had already begun to force a change in the nature of foreign affairs and their handling which the war enormously accentuated. At neither level could they be kept any longer in a water-tight compartment of their own as something distinct from, and unrelated to, domestic policies. Whilst a glimmering of this can be seen in the pre-war problem of trade, it became glaringly obvious during the war when question of shipping, munition supplies, finance, strategy, blockade, manpower and food became national problems with internal and external aspects. It was thus inevitable that the

Foreign Service should become only one amongst several departments whose opinion on a governmental problem was necessary and that it should find that its expertise was not necessarily that aspect of an international problem which was considered the most important. Thus on a purely administrative level the problem of demarcation was bound to become acute and since it was the Foreign Service that was ousted from its traditional position it was natural that it should dislike the change. A process of adjustment to the new world was, in fact, necessary but this was all the more painful since the Foreign Service was peculiarly traditional in its nature and because the continuance of the old criticisms allied with the new complaints concerning its inefficiency at winning war. This apparent supersession, some of it for good reasons, whilst some was less justifiable, was the result of a combination of personal, social and military factors which led to a serious loss of confidence within the service at a time when it had to face the problems of the post-war world.

It was implicitly recognised from the beginning of hostilities that some body smaller than the Cabinet would be needed in order to take the most immediate and pressing decisions associated with the war. The original concept was that a clear distinction could be made between strategy and the control of military and naval policies on the one hand and all other matters of government on the other. The former could be left to a war committee of the Cabinet based on the peace time Committee of Imperial Defence with the full Cabinet continuing responsible for the latter. Thus problems of munitions, of finance and of raising an army remained with the larger body. It soon appeared that this was not a practicable arrangement for war decisions were found to be not, in fact, separable from the normal problems of government and thus the question of the division of responsibility between such an executive body and the whole Cabinet became acute. This problem of relationship was central to the conduct of the war during the whole period of the Asquith administration. The Prime Minister was not prepared to see his war committee supersede his Cabinet which kept the reins of control in its own hands with consequent delays, frustrations and reversed decisions.*

Obviously, at the highest level, politics and strategy meet and in war the fusion is immediate and complete. Thus the war committee found it impossible to separate the political and strategic elements present in its projects as is so clearly seen in its decision to undertake the Dardanelles campaign where military and diplomatic factors were inextricably mixed. At such a time it is difficult, or even impossible, to take a long-term view of foreign policies which tend to become subordinated to immediate military advantages even if it is appreciated that a political day of reckoning will one day come. The secret treaty with Russia on the possession of Constantinople bears witness to this since the decision was compelled for military reasons.† This tendency, inherent in the situation, was accentuated by Grey's own view of the function of war-time diplomacy as subsidiary to military and naval ends. "In war, however, diplomacy is the handmaid of the necessities of the War Office and the Admiralty",° and believing this he did not press the diplomatic objections to the Dardanelles campaign as strongly as he might have done. It was, of course, recognised by him that a victory in the Dardanelles would encourage the Balkan States to join the Allied side but strong objections emanated from Russia's fear as to who would inherit Constantinople. It was known, too, that Russian opinion was not all in favour of the war since the traditional German influence in St Petersburg was still strong and it was thus, to his mind, important that the West should not give a handle to the anti-allied faction in Russia. In order to allay her fears, Great Britain found it necessary to agree to the Russian possession of

---

* But see also Hankey's opinion that Asquith would never have got his colleagues to agree to a War Cabinet on Lloyd George lines. Hankey, *op. cit.*, Vol.I, p.323.

† It was not until after the decision to meet Russia's claim that it was found that the pre-war Committee of Imperial Defence had decided it was not a vital British interest to keep Russia out of Constantinople. Hankey, *op. cit.*, Vol.I, pp.289–90.

° Grey, *op. cit.*, Vol.II, p.166.

Constantinople after the war. In February 1915, Grey prepared the way by his announcement in the Commons that the government was willing Russia should obtain access to the sea. Shortly afterwards the War Council met on 10th March and decided that Russia must be allowed ultimately to acquire Constantinople and this agreement was transmitted to Russia, subject to British compensation elsewhere in the region. This War Council meeting was notable not only for the attendance for Arthur Balfour who had been before, but also for that of Lansdowne and Bonar Law so that leading members of the Opposition might be associated with the decision.

Thus as far as foreign policy was concerned, the traditional balance at Cabinet level was reversed. No longer was the Foreign Secretary the decisive voice in policy making and, taking this view, Grey was prepared to indulge in activities, for example the secret treaties, that he would never otherwise have considered. In view of these circumstances, Grey was no longer an initiator of policy in the sense in which he would have claimed that position before the war. He accepted, as a member of the highest council of war, his share of responsibility for the decisions taken, but these were comprehensive national questions rather than specifically foreign policy ones and he thus claimed no special position or knowledge. In fact the basic war question in the council in the first part of the war was that of strategy and in so far as Grey held specific views he was a Westerner, and never fully convinced of the value of the diversions of Gallipoli, Baghdad and Salonica. There is, however, no reason to suppose that this affected the energy with which he pursued his Balkan policy.

Whilst in general terms Grey was willing that foreign policy considerations should take second place to war-time needs, there remained one aspect of foreign affairs upon which he was adamant and upon which he was not prepared to give ground however much he was attacked. This was the maintenance of the friendliest possible relations with the United States. He held to the view that, with the decline in British power and the growth of American, were Britain to survive at all in the modern world, she must keep Anglo-American relations harmonious.* This was, to Grey, a long-term policy which was as important to the country as winning the war. Thus the blockade was implemented, through Grey's influence, so as to take account as far as possible of American suspectibilities.† The Foreign Office, so recently accused of being pro-French, was now accused of pro-German tendencies because of the way in which it hampered the navy in its vital task.°

The 1914 Cabinet contained 22 members, which was far too many for it to be an effective executive body and from the outbreak of war decisions were in fact taken by a small inner group about whose membership there was neither finality nor formality. Thus on 5th August 1914, a meeting of the Prime Minister, Haldane, Churchill, Grey and the professional advisers decided that the British Expeditionary Force must be despatched at once to France although the full Cabinet met to ratify the matter the following day. In the same way it was only Grey, Kitchener, Churchill and Tyrell who met on the night of 2nd October and agreed that Churchill might go to Antwerp. (The Prime Minister was out of London.) Churchill was very keen to go, Grey being at first reluctant for fear of the complications involved should a prominent member of the government fall into enemy hands. "Finally Kitchener gave an opinion in favour of his going, and then I acquiesced."+ This small body of men was really carrying on the tradition of the inner core of the Cabinet and inevitably represented on the civilian side those Ministers (Asquith, Grey, Haldane and Churchill, with others on occasions) who were most closely associated with the war decision. This council of war superseded the meetings of the Committee of

---

* Hendrick, *op. cit.*, Part 1, pp.364, 366.

† Hankey, *op. cit.*, Vol.I, Ch. 35 shows the extent to which Grey was prepared to subordinate British maritime interests to American views over the question of the freedom of the seas both immediately and as a post war policy. It is clear too how out of sympathy he was with this view point.

° Hendrich, *op. cit.*, Part 1, p.365.

\+ Grey, *op. cit.*, Vol.II, p.80.

Imperial Defence and thus in October 1914, A. J. Balfour, whose creation the Defence Committee so largely was, rejoined its modern counterpart. This he found quite compatible with his party obligations as long as the limited view of its functions held good but as the war entered 1915 and the War Council was drawn inexorably into wider spheres of government policy than strictly naval and military ones he became increasingly worried about his membership.*

This sporadic arrangement continued until the end of November with meetings held as required by the necessities of the situation, but the full Cabinet also meeting frequently. The relations between the two remain somewhat uncertain with Lloyd George claiming that the larger body was but little concerned with naval and military decisions at this stage whereas the Report of the Dardanelles Commission† insists responsibility in theory and mainly in practice still remained with the full Cabinet. It described the system as both "clumsy and inefficient". On 25th November 1914, this inner group was placed on a regular footing being officially designated the War Council. Asquith described the consequent arrangement thus "The proposal, as I understand it, is that there should be a small Committee of the Cabinet, not fewer than three or more than five in number, to deal executively with the conduct of the War.

"It is understood that the Committee will from time to time call to their aid, for the purposes of both discussion and decision, other members of the Cabinet, either because their departments are concerned in the particular matter which is being dealt with or for other special reasons.

"The Cabinet to remain as it is, in numbers and composition.

"The *plenum* of the Cabinet to be kept constantly informed of the decisions and actions of the Committee, and in all questions

---

* Dugdale, *op. cit.,* Vol.II, p.131. As did Law and Lansdowne over their attendance on March 10th, thus Asquith arranged to send them the papers referred to the War Council but not to invite them to any more meetings. Hankey, *op. cit.,* Vol.I, p.289.

† Cd. 8490.

which involve a change or new departure in policy to be consulted before decisive action is taken."*

Although envisaged as a very small body concerned with a limited field of work this conception was steadily departed from as the scope of the war grew. Continuing the pattern of the earlier body there was no fixed personnel and ministers were called to meetings as necessary. The original hard core consisted of six persons (Asquith, Lloyd George, Kitchener, Grey, Churchill and Balfour) together with the professional advisers (Fisher and Wolfe-Murray) and the Secretary (Hankey). Crewe, Haldane, Arthur Wilson, McKenna and Harcourt had been added by 10th March.† The tendency, therefore, whatever the memorandum might say, was for it to supersede the full Cabinet; a development which was increased by the attitude of some members of the Cabinet who preferred not to be told too much. In practice it became the War Council rather than the Cabinet which decided on important matters and in this it did not always wait for the approval of the full Cabinet, although the Prime Minister usually reported its decisions to the Cabinet.° Thus the decision to undertake the Dardanelles expedition was not communicated to the larger body until a day or two before the first bombardment. The Dardanelles Commission found a conflict of evidence as to the extent to which the members of the War Council were in fact clear as to what they had decided and therefore how far the necessary instructions were sent out to departments although Asquith claimed+ that its decisions were always formulated in writing and read out at the meeting "as had always been our practice". The conclusions, he said, were circulated at once to the departments concerned thus any vagueness as to policy could not be attributed to the system. In coming to decisions in the War Council Lloyd George, Grey and Crowe "exercised undoubted and very legitimate influence, and occasionally stated their

* H. H. Asquith, *Memories and Reflections,* Vol.2, p.24.
† Hankey, *op. cit.,* Vol.I, p.237.
° Hankey, *op. cit.,* Vol.I, p.238.
\+ 20–3–17, *Hansard,* Vol.91, Col.1755.

opinions but the main responsibility rested on three members of the Council – namely the Prime Minister, the Secretary of State for War and the First Lord of the Admirality"*. Of these Lord Kitchener "was in reality the leading spirit of the triumvirate which was conducting the war".† It was obviously not clear where the division of responsibility lay otherwise it would hardly have been possible for a War Council, nominally responsible for the executive conduct of the war, to have no meetings during the critical weeks between 19th March and 14th May 1915 and for Asquith to claim as defence that during this period 13 full Cabinets were held, at 11 of which the Dardanelles expedition was discussed.°

In May 1915, the first coalition government was formed and this necessitated the reconstruction of the War Council. Its un-established position in the pattern of government is evidenced by its re-creation under the title of the Dardanelles Committee and the belief that its function would be limited to that operation. In practice this proved impossible because all problems of military, political and domestic policy were inter-locked and thus the Dardanelles Committee in effect took the place of the earlier War Council. The new coalition was never a good team+ and the inner council suffered correspondingly. Intead of having to incorporate the leading personalities of one political party, it now had to find room for a "galaxy of ministerial talent"× and therefore found it more difficult, not simpler, to come to speedy and coherent decisions. At this stage it contained 11 civilian members, Asquith, Lansdowne, Curzon, Kitchener, Balfour, Bonar

* Cd. 8490.

† Cd. 8490. para. 99.

° Hankey, *op. cit.*, Vol.I, pp.238–9, 322–4 claims that this was perfectly possible because Asquith saw the War Council as a body for exploring the larger questions of policy and not for the day to day conduct of the war. It was thus summoned as required, did not meet regularly and once the Dardanelles decision had been taken there was not much for it to discuss. In that case it would seem rather to parallel the Cabinet and to leave the problem of execution uncovered.

+ Hankey, *op. cit.*, Vol.I, p.334.

× Berriedale–Keith, *The Constitution of England from Queen Victoria to George VI*, Vol.1, p.201.

Law, Grey, Crewe, Lloyd George, Churchill and Selborne. Carson was added in August. In the November a further attempt was made to streamline the arrangement by the creation of a War Committee "not less than three, and perhaps not more than five in number". The first meeting on 3rd November had 3 members, the Prime Minister, Kitchener and Balfour; it soon rose to 5 (Grey and Lloyd George) and then to 7 (Bonar Law and McKenna).* On November 11th the Prime Minister told the Commons that its membership at that time was five,† but Kitchener, of course, was normally a member and in practice Grey was always present.° To these men must be added the professionals and in practice other members were called in as necessary so its creation still did not meet the need of a small directing body which many had come to feel was the real necessity. In explaining these changes in the Commons+ Asquith described once again his conception of responsible war-time government. The full Cabinet was to be ultimately responsible for questions of policy and was to be kept fully informed of the decisions and actions of the War Committee. The Cabinet "in all questions which involve a change, or a new departure in policy, should be consulted before decisive action is taken". The War Committee was to be a small body "to whom the strategic conduct of the War is from time to time referred" and which would be capable of taking decisions at short notice but "I am very jealous of the maintenance of collective Cabinet responsibility for large changes and new departures in policy".

This arrangement did not provide the focal point for decisive action which was to be increasingly demanded in the months to come. Had the Dardanelles venture been successful no doubt little criticism would have been expressed, but as it was the critical movement grew in force until it culminated in the overthrow of the Asquith government as the necessary preliminary

* Hankey, *op. cit.,* Vol.II, p.441–2.
† Prime Minister, Balfour, Lloyd George, Bonar Law, McKenna.
° Hankey, *op. cit.,* Vol.II, p.442.
+ 2–11–15. *Hansard,* Vol.75, Col.526.

to the adoption of more energetic methods. *The Times* was in the forefront of the attack. Its serious criticism had begun in August 1915 and was continued with ever increasing virulence. "The promise of a small War Council is being less and less fulfilled."* The conception of a council rather than a committee of a larger body had not materialised although for wartime government a small policy-making body was held to be essential. A Cabinet meeting for two hours twice a week was not a competent body to keep control of a war of infinite complexity and range.† This point was taken up by others in the New Year. It was not clear to outsiders just what powers had, in fact, been delegated to the War Committee and although it was smaller than originally it was still composed of busy administrators who, in the nature of the case, could not devote their whole time and thought to large problems of policy. The idea of a small Cabinet of four persons without administrative responsibilities was put forward° and one, moreover, which would be in continuous session. The publication of the first report of the Dardanelles Commission heightened the criticism. Thus *The Times* described it as "a tragic record of drift, disorganisation, and ultimate disaster, for which the blame in chief must be placed on want of leadership in the head of the government".+

Thus at the political level, the decline in importance of the Foreign Secretary in the inner councils of government had begun before ever Lloyd George took office. Although he continued to attend meetings of the war committee, accompanied by his Permanent Under-Secretary, his was no longer the predominating voice in foreign affairs.× Known to be one of Asquith's intimates he inevitably shared in his leader's declining prestige. Whilst his

* *The Times,* 17th January 1916.

† *The Times History,* p.279.

° See e.g. House of Commons, 15–2–16, *Hansard,* Vol.80, Cols.44, 48; 21–2–16, Vol.80, Col.503, 2–5–16, Vol.81, Cols.2638 *et seq.*

\+ 9th March 1917.

× The same *Times* leader considered that the report of the Dardanelles Commission had shewn Grey appearing "from time to time on the fringe of events, half way between the principal actors and the outer ring of Ministers".

views on the relative importance of military and foreign affairs did not lead him to take a predominant position in Cabinet councils his ill-health made it increasingly difficult for him to devote all his time and energy to his public life. Above all, the failure to obtain more adequate allies in the Balkans was laid particularly at his door.

II

Administrative developments of the period tended to weaken, albeit insensibly at first, the position of the Foreign Service thus creating a parallel to the subordination which was taking place at a political level. The War Council, being to some extent the successor of the Committee of Imperial Defence, had taken over the secretariat of the earlier body which thus came between the Foreign Office and the ultimate political authority. Its system of minuting committee discussion and the circulation of decisions for action to the appropriate departments no doubt contributed to efficiency and with the increased volume and speed of decisions some formalisation of procedure was obviously necessary but at the same time it became a filter through which departmental opinion had to pass and one moreover whose traditions and patterns of work were military and naval and not diplomatic.

It was no longer possible either for relations with the Allies to be handled purely by the Foreign Office as the war progressed. Allied co-ordination was found necessary in wider spheres than the purely diplomatic and in particular in the fields of finance, munitions, supply and strategy. Where joint action was necessary it was natural to use the appropriate specialists. The need for speed in decision also created a tendency for such negotiations to be handled by the politicians with the necessary authority to clinch decisions rather than through accustomed channels needing to refer their negotiations back. The Foreign Office had originally created a War Department out of the traditional Western Department, which was at first headed by Crowe. He, however, soon went to the Trading department which was to grow into the

Ministry of Blockade and the War Department declined in importance as discussions with the allies were increasingly carried on at Ministers' meetings.*

Finance and munitions, under the impetus of the driving force of Lloyd George, soon became subject to a series of allied conferences and the pressures of the time demanded their continuance. Lloyd George's belief in personal contact as an effective method for getting things done led him to condemn the more pedestrian methods of concerting Allied diplomacy. Certainly this was often ill-coordinated, but it is a moot point how far this arose from the immobility of the foreign ministers rather than from a basic unwillingness to subordinate political ambitions to the war-time alliance. Even so, its concert impressed Page "All the while, too, the Allies work closer and closer together. They'll soon be doing even their diplomatic work with neutrals, as a unit",† and on 15th February 1916 Asquith found it possible to claim "During the past three months the most outstanding feature of the general European situation has been the growing intimate relation, co-ordination, concentration and unity of direction and control amongst the Allied Powers, and that change, or development, as I should prefer to call it, applies to diplomacy just as much as it applies to strategy. The distinguished Prime Minister of France, M. Briand, did us the honour to pay us a visit here early in the year, and has since been to Rome where he had, as might have been expected, a most cordial reception. These two visits are to be followed, and followed I hope at an early date, by a general Conference in Paris, at which both the political and strategic aspects of the War will be reviewed generally by all the Allied Powers. We hope that by this growing intimacy . . . we shall counteract . . . the advantage which our enemies . . . in the earlier stages of the War, undoubtedly possessed, fighting . . . on interior lines and with centralised control."°

* Tilley and Gaselee, *op. cit.*, p.178.
† Hendrick, *op. cit.*, Part 2, p.159.
° 15–2–16, *Hansard*, Vol.80, Col.28.

Despite these fine words, full Allied co-operation in many peoples' minds hung fire and Lloyd George in particular became convinced of the need to have some supreme Allied body which could superintend the whole direction of the war and commit the Allies to decisions without the constant need to refer back to national authorities, once broad principles had been agreed.

Meanwhile, the work done by the Foreign Office and properly the responsibility of the Foreign Minister came under heavy criticism. This centred round the handling of the blockade and the failure to win the Balkan States more completely and readily to the Allied side.

In continental wars, Great Britain has traditionally placed major reliance upon the weapon of the blockade. During the years 1914–18 this use of her sea-power caused her great difficulties in her international relationships, led to serious differences of opinion at home and subjected the Foreign Office, as the major instrument of the blockade, to a constant barrage of criticism and complaint. The root cause of these problems lay in the nature of modern war which made any distinction between war goods and non-war goods or between civilian and military destinations increasingly artificial. The pressure of circumstances thus led to increasing interference with traditional trading patterns and, in particular, with neutral trade, and in consequence Great Britain was placed in an insoluble dilemma. On the one hand her own needs dictated ever sterner measures of control over enemy trade, the implications of which were only gradually realised and which led to government interference in economic matters to an extent which had been quite unanticipated. On the other, her desire to preserve her international connections, a recognition that after the war Britain would have to live with those whom she had offended and perhaps ruined and her increasing dependence on imported war supplies, especially from America, made her hesitate to take draconian measures except as a last resort. Whatever action the government took was bound to be displeasing in some quarter.

Morally, Great Britain's position was to some extent compromised by the part she had played at the second Hague Conference in 1907 and its aftermath in London at which her delegates had been instructed to support any proposal which would tend to free neutral commerce from interference and to work for the restriction of contraband lists as far as possible.* Although the resultant Declaration of London had been rejected by the House of Lords, the Foreign Office was closely identified with its principles which could not but work to the detriment of Britain as a belligerent. The department thus came in for much opprobium whilst its blockade activities were from the start prejudiced in the public eye and this factor inhibited their fair assessment.

The hub of the problem lay in the rights of a belligerent to interfere with neutral shipping which traditionally depended on the exercise of an effective blockade or on the carriage, by a neutral ship, of contraband. It is obvious that the neutral country and the belligerent sea power have opposite interests in the interpretation of these rules. The former wishes maximum freedom of movement and a residual definition of contraband; the latter the maximum freedom of control and the widest definition of contraband. The British attitude before the war was more consistent with her needs as a neutral in any future war than as a belligerent. The Declaration of London had concerned itself with three types of cargo in neutral ships. Absolute contraband which was intended to cover goods which could only be used for war; these were liable to capture from a neutral ship if their ultimate destination was enemy, or enemy-occupied territory, even if they were transhipped through a neutral port. Conditional contraband essentially covered goods which could be considered necessary either for war or peace purposes. Food or gold would be two examples. These commodities were only liable to capture if they were destined for the enemy war effort and were going direct to enemy, or enemy-occupied territory. Finally were the free goods which comprised many industrial commodities and raw materials which were not liable to capture at all.

* Cd. 4554.

It does not require much imagination to see why this was so unworkable. Firstly, the definitions were hopelessly out of date for modern, total war because they ignored the value of so many industrial goods to a modern economy and war effort assuming that a valid distinction could be made between war and non-war purposes. The belief that such rules were still valid and meaningful sheds an interesting sidelight on the extent to which the nature of modern war was quite unappreciated by the politicians and the Foreign Office. The Navy and the Committee of Imperial Defence had, on the contrary, been more far-seeing and had displayed considerable interest in the concept of economic pressure as an instrument of war. Secondly, from the British view, was the enormous drawback that Germany could import so much through the neutral ports, particularly of Holland and Scandinavia, even if her own coasts were effectively closed. This indeed she did and the entrepôt trade of ports like Rotterdam shot up by leaps and bounds. The country, in fact, in the early years of the war was only fumbling towards the conception of economic warfare as part of an overall war strategy which would sweep up into it outmoded traditional blockading rules and in consequence she attempted to apply the limited rules of blockade pertaining to limited warfare and a *laissez-faire* economy. "Also, it cannot be too often repeated, that in the autumn of 1914, we were not engaged in an unlimited economic capaign in which every commercial transaction, and every branch of trade, is considered as though it were an economic weapon for use against the enemy. The campaign that was being conducted was still for the interception of contraband."* It was not until the Order in Council of 7th July 1916 which announced the British presumption that vessels going to enemy destinations were carrying enemy goods that the country finally disposed of the toils of the Declaration of London and it was from the middle of 1916 that the new conception of economic warfare became formalised with the adoption of the aim of severing all economic relations between

* A. Bell, *The Blockade of the Central Empires,* p.188.

the central powers and all other countries. Even in the early years, however, when Great Britain was still concerned to execute a blockade policy she never found it possible to abide by the rules of the Declaration of London and it became the job of diplomacy to "secure the maximum of blockade that could be enforced without a rupture with the United States".*

America found herself immediately and gravely concerned not only because of the interruption to her own commerce but because she felt that the rights of small, neutral nations were being ignored in a peculiarly ruthless way. Anglo–American relations in the early years of the war became at times extremely sensitive and required a great deal of attention in order to prevent their serious deterioration. The possibility indeed had to be considered that American opinion might turn actively against the entente powers. Her moralistic fervour led to her becoming the champion of neutral rights and the steady abandonment of the Declaration of London by the allies to suit their own convenience appeared to her as the height of cynicism. At the same time, the genuine disruption of American trade caused national annoyance, and indeed distress since the American economy was depressed in 1914. Thus the latent hostility felt towards Great Britain threatened to erupt. That it did not was due to Grey's conviction of the importance of maintaining a strong American link as a mainstay of enduring British politics; the British government's appreciation of the importance of America as a source of munitions supply; the strong pro Allied sentiments of Walter Page; the very friendly relations existing between him and Sir Edward Grey and the work of the British embassy at Washington.†

A problem of great concern in the early months of the war was the American cotton crop. As an important article of warfare the question was soon raised in the Cabinet whether cotton should be placed on the contraband list. Due to Grey's persuasion, this was not done on the grounds that such action would ruin

* Grey, *op. cit.,* Vol.II, p.103.

† Note Hankey's tribute to Grey and Page, *op. cit.,* Vol.I, p.357.

the American interest and that the risk of American retaliation by the refusal to supply munitions was a serious one. It was not until August 1915 that conditions in the cotton trade had changed sufficiently for it to be listed and during the first year of the war Grey had to suffer considerable misunderstanding from the public and from his colleagues because of his alleged subservience to American trading interests. At the same time he could not possibly prevent American discontent that her commercial problems were not sufficiently considered. Thus Grey was once again under attack from two sides. "I fight Sir Edward about stopping cargoes, literally fight. He yields and promises this or that. This or that doesn't happen or only half happens. I know why. The military ministers balk him. I inquire through the back door and hear that the Admiralty and the War Office of course value American good-will, but they'll take their chances of a quarrel with the United States rather than let copper get to Germany. The cabinet has violent disagreements. But the military men yield as little as possible. It was rumoured the other day that the Prime Minister threatened to resign; and I know that Kitchener's sister told her friends, with tears in her eyes, that the cabinet shamefully hindered her brother."*

The steady extension of the blockade policy meant increasing interference with neutral trade. To the Foreign Office and those who held a restrained view of the limits to which this policy could be pushed, it was a matter of both morality and expediency to pay some attention to neutral rights and thus, rather than acting in too dictatorial a fashion, to try to obtain neutral agreement on imports wherever possible. Too often the neutrals were between the devil and the deep blue sea as far as the blockade was concerned. Naturally they wished to enjoy the extra benefit of handling goods destined for Germany which could no longer reach German ports direct, neither did they wish to refuse German requests and run the risk of being overrun in consequence. On the other hand, they could not afford to displease Great Britain

* Hendrick, *op. cit.*, Part 1, p.365. Dec. 1914.

overmuch since their own essential imports depended upon the goodwill of the British navy. Diplomacy thus attempted to fulfill its time-honoured function of compromise upon the basis of mutual interest between Great Britain and the neutral States. The basis of policy was found in rationing agreements by which a sufficiency of imports was allowed in return for adequate controls on the re-export of goods to Germany. The actual manner of execution varied; in some cases Britain relied upon governmental assurances, in others goods consigned to governments or approved firms were exempt from seizure; in others the dependence of neutral shipping upon British coal and coaling stations throughout the world was judiciously invoked. In the search for such agreements, the Foreign Service became very active in the early years of the war in a field to which it had not hitherto devoted an exceptional amount of attention. In order to fulfill its responsibilities it became necessary for it at last to leave the rarefied fields of diplomacy for the immediate and day to day activity of commercial life, a process which was accentuated by the tendency to form agreements not with states but with trader's associations which had become noticeable by 1915. This development had great advantages in that by making neutral business men partners to the operation of the system it infinitely lessened the strain and difficulty to which the blockade was subjected "in the field", whilst at the same time it enabled many legal controversies concerning the interpretation of the official blockade policy to be by-passed for such non-governmental arrangements "impinged upon no legal doctrine, or rule of policy".* This contact with reality was found by the Foreign Service to be both a salutary and a satisfying experience.†

Such measures began to be seriously applied during 1915 and continued thereafter although it is impossible to claim that the problems of the blockade were ever solved in any final sense; rather was it a case of adapting measures of control to meet a constantly developing situation.

---

* Bell, *op. cit.*, p.403.
† See p. 257 *et seq.*

Meanwhile, it was necessary to control the destination of British exports and the disruption of trading patterns on the Continent sometimes created unexpected opportunities for the development of British trade. This side of the problem was handled by the Board of Trade and, in default of an overall policy, it is not surprising that serious discrepancies arose between the ways in which the two departments handled matters. In the early years of the war, a notable increase in British trade to the European neutrals occurred precisely at the time when the Foreign Office was trying to cut down on any abnormal increases of imports into neutral countries. This it felt, and reasonably so, was seriously damaging to a reputation for honesty abroad and resulted partly from the dichotomy of responsibility in Whitehall. It is, in fact, a neat illustration of the difficulties that may follow from having more than one department concerned in a field of governmental policy and the Board of Trade was becoming extremely active in the handling of overseas trading relations. Thus it was found necessary to despatch a mission to Sweden in 1915 to keep the negotiations on blockade policy open and as friendly as possible in view of Sweden's importance on the supply route to Russia. This was originally intended as a Foreign Office mission* but was altered and "it was not a Foreign Office deputation we sent out ... but ... a team of business men".† The problem of demarcation between the two departments became more serious with the development of economic policy and "Foreigners may therefore be excused, if they believe us guilty of their accusations, for they cannot be expected to understand the real explanation: that two departments of state, with their headquarters in the same thoroughfare, and separated by only a few yards of pavement, were engaged on two opposite endeavours, at a moment of great national danger".° The lack of a coherent economic policy and of a demarcation between the roles of the two departments

---

* R. Vansittart, *op. cit.*, p.145.
† Mr Runciman. 23–12–15, *Hansard,* Vol.77, Col.666.
° Bell, *op.* cit., p. 189.

implied that the blockade was always less than satisfactory. In addition the tolerance of overseas governments, and most particularly the American, was bought by giving the extremists at home, the advocates of the "Blockhead blockade", certain material upon which to develop their criticism. It was not possible to stop all German imports and to devise fully adequate control of the entrepôt trade of Holland and Denmark or of home-produced goods which could be sent to Germany overland.

As the pressure of war necessitated the abandonment of limited contraband lists in favour of a far-reaching economic policy so the role of the Foreign Service in trade was high-lighted. The old question of whether it was incapable of playing a more positive role and if so of whether it should hand over the job to a more competent department was heard again, this time in terms of the extent to which the blockade fell short of one hundred per cent efficacy. Certainly in the light of the changing conception of the nature of economic warfare, the ad hoc and essentially piece-meal machinery created under the Asquith government was generally held to fall short of what was necessary.

The blockade required a large official machinery which had to represent the different, and in the ultimate analysis often opposing, views of the Admiralty, Foreign Office and Board of Trade which met upon the Contraband Committee representing the three departments and chaired by a member of Parliament. It was this committee which was responsible for the fate of individual cargoes. Much criticism centred round its work and the extent to which this was said to be interfered with by the Foreign Office ordering the release of cargoes detained by an irate Navy. The possibility of this was officially denied by Grey who stated that the Contraband Committee was fully responsible for this job and that its decisions were only over-ruled at Cabinet level.* In this he was supported by Mr Pollock the chairman. "It is not a question of the difficulties created by the Foreign Office, but it is the difficulty of proofs and the difficulty of

* 26–1–16., *Hansard,* Vol.78, Col.1316–7.

certainty in Prize Court proceedings."* At the same time, as Grey pointed out, it was the job of the Foreign Office to maintain relations with neutrals who were important as sources of supply and to prevent any 'wrongful' interference with neutral rights and these opposing responsibilities make it unsurprising that Cecil should later admit that there had indeed been friction between the departments when he first became responsible for blockade policy.†

Furthermore, the Foreign Office created a special Contraband Department responsible for dealing with both allies and neutrals on the subject. Problems resulting from the war for British traders were dealt with by the home departments and a special export licensing committee controlled British export trade. This was loosely linked with the Contraband Department. In February 1915, the Cabinet decided to adopt reprisals for German activity at sea and this decision led to the Order in Council of 1st March which implied a very big increase in the scale of work because it was intended to stop all goods entering or leaving Germany. This was to be done partly through the operation of the contraband regulations and partly through the interception of ships coming from or going to a German port or a neutral port if they were carrying goods intended for the enemy or of enemy origin. Contraband goods were, of course, entitled to seizure, non-contraband goods thus intercepted were to be requisitioned or restored to their owners whilst German exports would be requisitioned and sold.

Such an economic boycott presented a major problem for British administration of co-ordinating the work of the different departments involved. This was attempted by the creation in September of the War Trade Advisory Committee under the Marquess of Crewe. Formed by the chairmen of all Committees engaged in contraband work, it was also responsible for advising the Cabinet on questions of blockade policy as they arose out of the work

* 26–1–16, *Hansard,* Vol.78, Col.1341.
† 27–3–17, *Hansard,* Vol.92, Col.248.

of the departments involved and, in particular, advised on the restriction of enemy supplies.*

Although Robert Cecil had been appointed Assistant Under Secretary for Foreign Affairs with a special responsibility for blockade matters in May 1915, the administration remained on an *ad hoc* basis and the ultimate scope and object of economic policy remained undefined. As Cecil himself later admitted all that existed was a series of sub-departments, belonging to various departments, and working more or less together but with no unity.† It was, of course, quite true that there was no prior experience to go on as to the best way of blockading Germany and the problems had to be dealt with as best they could when they arose. Nevertheless by the end of that year there was a general belief that the whole matter needed to be thought out in a more coherent form, more positive machinery created and the blockade tightened. Public discontent, as expressed through meetings and resolutions, was vocal during the ensuing months.

In January 1916, four *Times* leaders were devoted to the inefficiences of the blockade and their relationship to the higher direction of the war was also discussed. It was pointed out that there was a growing conviction in the country that the blockade was ineffective, that there was a notorious division of work between the Admiralty, Foreign Office and Board of Trade and their innumerable committees. In this situation the Foreign Office was largely at fault for it was still wedded to principles which threatened the effective use of sea power in war. The Foreign Office has been "haunted all along by the remembrance of their by-gone blunders ... and the public, rightly or wrongly believe that the cold hand of these ghosts has constantly paralysed the decision of the government and the activities of the Navy".° It

* In addition to being a co-ordinating body it, in fact, carried out considerable executive work as well. Thus it regulated contraband lists, apportioned quantities under the rationing systems, published a black list of merchants known to have dealings with the enemy and from time to time sent missions to neutral countries to advise on the purchase of goods it was anxious to prevent falling into German hands.

† 27–3–17, *Hansard,* Vol.92, Col.247.

° 24–1–16.

urged the declaration of a regular blockade and the further extension of the contraband lists and there would thus be fewer references to the Foreign Office and fewer releases of suspicious cargoes.

A great storm was raised that month by the publication in the *Daily Mail* and the *Morning Post* of large quantities of statistics showing the increase of neutral imports of basic raw materials, including foodstuffs, over peace-time requirements. The controversy raged particularly around the import of wheat and cocoa. Endless play was made on both sides with the significance of these figures and although Grey, in the Commons, and the War Trade Advisory Committee through official publications could shew that the implications of the figures were grossly exaggerated, a general impression remained that the Foreign Office was not pursuing the blockade with the vigour demanded by the circumstances of the time.

The *Economist* on this occasion was broadly in favour of the blockade as it was currently being run since it considered that to deny neutrals reasonable rights would only embarrass Germany a little, carried the danger of making the neutrals unfriendly with the consequence that they might refuse to send their goods to Britain or cease re-exporting to Russia equally with Germany. It strongly condemned the Northcliffe Press for the hullaballo it was making about the blockade "in the conduct of war and of war diplomacy there is a case for common sense".*

The *Morning Post,* however, immediately returned to the attack over the question of cotton products whose import into the Netherlands, Norway and Denmark had increased enormously over prewar. It launched a criticism of the general handling of the blockade. The doctrine of continuous voyage had never been put into effect. Grey thought it was impossible to do so and in his weak-kneed fashion he intended to rely on making agreements with traders in neutral countries.†

The Times complained on 24th January that the explanations

* The *Economist,* 22nd Jan. 1916.
† See e.g. 28th, 31st Jan. 1916.

for the increase in neutral imports were not completely satisfactory whilst on 9th March 1916 the record of the Foreign Office in handling the blockade was described in Parliament as "deplorable" starting from its original acceptance of the Declaration of London and continuing with its slow and dilatory behaviour in enforcing the necessary provisions during the war. The old charge that the Foreign Office and Diplomatic Service knew nothing about trade and commerce because of the aristocratic birth of their members was heard again. It was linked too with the demand for reform in the Consular Service, which, despised by its superior relations, was still too largely composed of unsalaired representatives of foreign nationality who could hardly be expected to have the interests of British traders at heart.* Trading interests too began to realise that the war had led to a disruption of trading patterns which would necessitate positive steps of re-creation and than in this process the sort of help previously given by official machinery was likely to prove inadequate. In March 1916, the Association of Chambers of Commerce passed a resolution stating "That the present Consular arrangements are not of an adequate nature and that steps be taken to reorganise the consular service with a view to providing better facilities for the maintenance and expansion of the trade of the Empire". Mr Ponsonby returned to this particular attack many times in the House and at length wrung from Cecil agreement that it would no longer be possible to act after the war as if trade was of no particular concern to the government. "I agree, generally speaking myself, that great changes will have to be made as the result partly of the changes produced by the War, and partly as the result of the experience which this War has forced upon us. I myself feel that it would no longer do to act as if it was possible to proceed upon the theory that trade is a matter with which Governments have no concern, and that the less they interfere with it the better. That was the theory on which we proceeded for many years ... I have no

* 9-3-16, *Hansard,* Vol.80, Col.1788 *et seq.* Col. Yate especially on this point. Of 111 Consuls and Vice Consuls in Scandinavia and Holland, 83 were unsalaried aliens.

doubt that as part of the change which we shall have to make we shall have to make very considerable changes in our Consular Services."*

To meet this situation, in February 1916, Cecil became responsible for all question of war time trading policy including the blockade and for the co-ordination of the work of the various departments and committees involved. At the same time he became a member of the Cabinet. Thus at long last there was created a focal point for what was proving to be a major weapon of the war.† With the adoption of a more vigorous policy went the need to streamline the machinery involved which was done through the creation of a Ministry of Blockade. This was housed in the Foreign Office, largely staffed by its officials and absorbed the work previously done by the Foreign Office proper and certain specialist departments which had been created but administratively it was quite distinct.°

The Ministry thus consisted of the old Contraband Department which continued its responsibility for the negotiations with neutrals, a War Trade Statistical Department and a War Trade Intelligence Department to provide information bulletins on the basis of the statistics concerning neutral trade; a Foreign Trade Department responsible for the black lists, a Finance Section and a Department dealing with the Restriction of Enemy Supplies. The War Trade Department itself and the Contraband Committee remained outside the Ministry but Crewe's War Trade Advisory Committee provided an effective co-ordinating mechanism. As a result, during 1916, a coherent Ministry was created which was not only concerned with the immediate purpose of blockading Germany but was enabled to co-ordinate commercial activities generally. Although there was recognition that the blockade was more efficiently run after this re-organisation, it remained a point

---

* 9–3–16, *Hansard,* Vol.80, Col.1809

† This was not a change forced upon Grey but one which was recommended by him. See G. Trevelyan, *Grey of Fallodon,* p.308.

° The P.U.S. had no contact with contraband work. Hardinge, *op. cit.,* p.197.

of disagreement throughout the war. Officialdom came increasingly to believe that the negotiation of rationing agreements with neutrals was the most effective method of achieving the necessary objects* but this policy inevitably meant that a bargain had to be struck. There were always critics ready to complain that the terms were unsatisfactory. Under the circumstances criticism was the easier part, for it was simplicity itself to point to the fact that goods were still reaching Germany whereas the maintenance of reasonably good relations with neutrals and the importance of this both at the time and for the future was very much a matter to be taken on trust and was not susceptible to proof.

It was never found possible either to separate the blockade machinery from the Foreign Office as some of the critics wanted. "but there is a general feeling abroad that the blockade so far has been a side-show of the Foreign Office rather than one of the main branches of our war activity."† But the need for constant discussion and negotiation and the necessary use of the Diplomatic Service both to explain policy and to provide much essential information for its determination effectively prevented any other solution. With the fall of the Asquith Government greater recognition was given to the importance of economic matters and although the blockade machinery remained part of its parent body it was established that Cecil, as Minister of Blockade, would have a right of accesss to the War Cabinet direct, and not through the Foreign Office. It does not "in the least mean he is under the Foreign Office as Minister of Blockade".° After two years of teething troubles the way was clear for a freer development both of this important war weapon and of the concept of a governmental economic policy.+

* Cecil, 27–3–17, *Hansard,* Vol.92, Col.259.
† Mr Hewins, 27–3–17, *Hansard,* Vol.92, Col.235.
° Bonar Law, 18–12–16, *Hansard,* Vol.88, Col.1160.
+ See p.251 *et seq.*

III

The setbacks from which British diplomacy suffered in the first years of the war in the Balkans, were undoubtedly damaging to Grey and to the Asquith government as a whole; in addition they helped to throw renewed doubts upon the efficiency of the machine as a proper instrument for the conduct of foreign affairs since it could not achieve the objects considered desirable. The special conference, the special mission as means to clinch a bargain since orthodox diplomacy could not were held up as panaceas. If only Grey had adopted some such special technique how much happier would have been the result. The effect of failure upon Lloyd George was of particular importance for he was strongly of the opinion that decisive action in this area would have enormous effect upon the war and lead to its quicker conclusion. Grey's failure to keep Turkey and Bulgaria out of the war, efforts "which a more strenuous or resourceful Foreign Minister would have converted into success prolonged the War by years, and very nearly caused the defeat of the Allies".* As with most criticism, the attack was partial, singling out of a complex situation but one factor to be deplored. In particular, the relation of the effectiveness of wartime diplomacy to the military situation was overlooked. Thus it was not coincidence that Bulgaria finally determined to join the central powers in October 1915 when the Dardanelles expedition was seen to be unsuccessful and after a disastrous summer on the Russian front or that Rumania joined the Allies in August 1916 in the excitement of the Brusiloff offensive.

The immediate problem for Great Britain was seen to be the necessity to keep Turkey neutral or, secondarily, to delay her entry into the war for as long as possible. For this course there were powerful reasons, not the least of which was the need to maintain an effective supply route to Russia. Future events were to prove the correctness of this reasoning. The military mind was concerned with the use of the Suez Canal especially in the early

---

* George, *op. cit.*, Vol.I, p.96.

weeks of the war when it was necessary to bring Indian troops to the West; the political mind feared the adverse effect on Moslem opinion in the empire should Britain be at war with Turkey; neither wished to see troops diverted to defend Egypt from Turkish attack. Another important consideration was that Allied fighting against Turkey would arouse all of Russia's traditional suspicions of western aggrandisement in an area to which she was peculiarly sensitive with the ensuing danger that Russian participation in the war might falter.

The Turkish government in 1914 was in a state of flux. A number of different groups and personalities were jockeying for power with no clear indication which would finally succeed. This gave both to the European powers the opportunity to back those elements they thought most favourable to them and to the Turks the increased opportunity to play off one power against another. In circumstances of this nature it is a question of which side can offer the more attractive terms and there was little of a concrete nature in the British stock. Furthermore, Anglo–Turkish relations started badly with the requisition of two Turkish battleships which were being built in England and were ready for despatch when the war broke. Excitement in Turkey ran very high and in the face of it British diplomacy was ineffective in that the best offer it was in a position to make was a promise to return the ships after the war if Turkey remained neutral.* Naturally enough, such a suggestion appeared trivial to the Turks who viewed the ships with enormous national pride. On the other side, German influence had been active in Turkey for some time and as the war approached, reports of German troops and supplies entering the country soon began to be received in London. To this disquieting news was added public evidence of German determination through the action of the two warships, the Goeben and Breslau. In August they evaded the British navy and anchored off Constantinople, thus neatly fulfilling the dual role of bribe

* Grey to Mallet, 25th August 1914. State Papers 1915. Correspondence leading to the rupture with Turkey.

and threat. The Turkish response to Allied queries as to their purpose was that the ships were necessary for her own protection and defence and were meant as part of the Turkish navy but the demand that their German crews be repatriated as an earnest of good faith was not met.

It was thus against a steadily deteriorating situation for the Allies that the diplomatic bargaining was carried on. Considerable pressure was exercised by the Allies on Turkey both to maintain her neutrality and in particular to prevent further German infiltration into the country. On 20th August 1914, Turkey presented her terms for neutrality to Great Britain. These were the immediate abolition of the capitulation system; the immediate return of the two Turkish battleships; the renunciation of any interference with the internal affairs of Turkey; the restoration of Western Thrace should Bulgaria join the central powers; the restoration of the Ionian islands taken by Greece in the Balkan wars and that the Allies should undertake to insist that the Triple Alliance respected the capitulation agreement. The next day she followed this up with a request for a written declaration respecting Turkish independence and integrity.

Grey wrote to Mallet on 22nd August giving the British reply. In concert with the French and Russian ambassadors, he was to ask for the repatriation of the German crews; a written assurance for the free passage through the Straits of merchant vessels and that Turkey would fully respect the obligation of neutrality. In the same despatch the Allies agreed to withdraw their extraterritorial jurisdiction as soon as a scheme of judicial administration satisfactory to modern conditions could be set up and to give a joint written guarantee to respect the independence and integrity of Turkey then and in the peace terms.

No real bargaining took place on the basis of these two documents. Mallet continued to reiterate his belief that Turkey would remain neutral whilst at the same time reporting that the Vizier was not really master in his own house and describing the increasingly obvious signs of German influence. By late September he was reporting the gradual worsening of the situation for the Allies.

The Germans were increasingly in control; the Turkish fleet entirely in German hands and the Dardanelles impassable. Nevertheless, a fortnight before the Turkish entry into the war, Mallet still held to the opinion that Turkey would remain neutral and could be bullied and brow-beaten into so doing.

British diplomacy in general and Mallet in particular came in for much criticism over this episode. Mallet was indeed grossly over-optimistic about the Turkish situation and seems not to have appreciated the changing balance of power within the Turkish government with the rise of the pro-German party until very late in the day. On the other hand, had he done so it is questionable if the final result would have been different since allied diplomacy had few cards to play. The note of 25th August gave little and made no attempt to meet Turkish schemes for the recovery of territory which Russia would not have been prepared to countenance. For this Mallet cannot be blamed; the only question is whether had he assessed the situation more accurately the allies would have offered more. Diplomacy on this occasion had to operate within a very limited framework created by the highest common factor of agreement between the Allies, the early German military successes, the inflammation of Turkish public opinion by the action of the Admiralty and the shifting internal Turkish situation. It was not in a position to accomplish a great deal. Mallet nevertheless became the scapegoat for Turkish belligerency and his career was at an end.

"Mallet had his leg badly pulled by the Turks at Constantinople, and sent utterly misleading dispatches to the Foreign Office ... When the F.O. issued the White Paper on the rupture with Turkey, it contained ... so much evidence of Mallet's foolishness that we alluded in a leading article to "the remarkable sedative effect" upon him of the Grand Vizier's assurances."* The quarrel between *The Times* and the Foreign Office which resulted from this comment led to a cessation of relations between them for the next six months. This has been held to have been

* Steed to Bourchier, 12th March, 1915. *The Times History*, p.234.

unfortunate since it meant that Grey was deprived of the information sent in by Bourchier, the knowledgeable *Times* correspondent. Once again it is very questionable how far this made any difference to the negotiations carried out with the Balkan states. Bourchier was biased by his championship of his "beloved Bulgaria" into believing that the possibilities of a Balkan league were there for the having and that the non-fruition of this plan was due to the inadequacies of the British diplomatic representatives in the Balkan capitals.*

Grey's handling of the Balkan States and in particular his inability to re-create a Balkan league was considered his second major failure in the area. Once Turkey had entered the war, a strong current of opinion in the country held that, with suitable encouragement, Balkan antagonisms could be subordinated in return for promises of aggrandisement once the war had been won. This was indeed a tempting view, "if the Allied Powers had taken strong and timely action they could have organised ... a formidable confederation with an army of trained men already tempered in the fires of war."† Lloyd George estimated that an army of over $1\frac{1}{2}$ million men would be put into the field through an alliance of Greeks, Rumanians and Serbs, rising to two million if the Bulgars could be brought to join. Even allowing for over-optimism (Bourchier spoke of one million bayonets) the advantages were obvious.

The difficulties were correspondingly great. Grave divisions existed between the Balkan States particularly since the ending of the Balkan wars, and their mutual antagonisms could only be overcome, if at all, by arrangements between themselves rather than by bribes and threats from an outside power. In any case the Allies had few of either. A European war in which the Balkan area was involved would create for these states a favourable situation to extend their territory at the expense of each other provided they picked the winning side in time. In consequence,

* *op. cit.*, p.235.
† George, *op. cit.*, Vol.I, p.365.

their attitude to the offers put out by both protagonists was dependent mainly upon their assessment of the progress of the war. The larger view, taken by more detached observers, that their interest in co-operation to eject Turkey from Europe was greater than the divisions between them may have fitted well with the entente desire to create a Balkan unit but it was not necessarily the view taken by the states themselves. This provides justification for Grey's attitude that his diplomacy could only be successful in so far as it was backed up by military strength.* The loss of prestige resulting from the failure of the Dardanelles campaign was, to his mind, a vital causative factor of the disasters which shortly followed.

The third general difficulty in the way of this project was the attitude of Russia and her suspicions of western activity in the Balkan area. The hard core of her attitude related to the post-war possession of Constantinople and the fear that as a result of a Balkan campaign the city might fall into hostile hands.† Whilst therefore by the winter of 1914–15, Russia was anxious that her allies create a diversion to relieve Turkish pressure on her, she continually made difficulties over the way in which this should be done. It will be recalled that Grey had grave doubts about the Russian will to remain in the war at this period and thus considered it necessary to meet Russian demands.

British diplomacy was thus hampered in the achievement of its objects by Balkan rivalries, the progress of the war and Russian susceptibilities. It was also hampered in its execution by the delays necessitated by the need to obtain Allied agreement on what was to be proposed to the Balkan states. "It may be imagined how busy the telegraph was and often how futile."° We can, of course, never know whether some one with greater energy and unscrupulousness would have made a better job of the Balkans in view of these most unfavourable circumstances but Grey had to bear

---

* House of Commons, 14–10–15, *Hansard,* Vol.74, Col.1513.
† i.e. Greek or British.
° Grey, *op. cit.,* Vol.II, p.154.

the responsibility for failure however impossible success might truly have been.

Opinions in Greece were divided as to the best way of utilising the war to fulfill the expansionist drive against the Turkish empire and in the months which followed the outbreak of war the swaying struggle between the pro-German and pro-allied parties prevented diplomacy from achieving any solid bargain. On 18th August 1914, Venizelos proposed that Greece should join the Allies, but the British Cabinet, on Grey's advice,* refused the offer two days later. There were strong reasons for this. It was still hoped to retain Turkish neutrality; it was feared that a Greek move would bring Bulgaria in on the side of the central powers and finally Sazanov declared that he "was not ... going to allow Greece to drag Russia into a war with Turkey".† Grey's rejection of the Greek offer thus hardly deserved Lloyd George's scornful dismissal of it as "inscrutable".°

The deadlock in the West, the need to obtain contact with Serbia, and the Russian appeal in December for relief, all combined to make the opening of a second front urgent and as 1914 drew to a close the War Council began to discuss its future military plans. The basic division between Westerners and Easterners began to shape towards the problem of making decisive contact with the central powers and with stalemate in the West the notion of an attack elsewhere became increasingly attractive. A drive against German's allies would, it was argued, relieve the pressure on Russia, bring in the Balkan waverers and maintain a badly needed supply route to Russia. By the end of the year, the military situation for both Russia and Serbia had grown more menacing and thus the Eastern school of thought grew correspondingly stronger. It was reinforced by the formal receipt on 2nd January 1915 of the appeal by Grand Duke Nicolas for a western demonstration against Turkey in order to relieve Russia in the Caucasus, an appeal which was immediately accepted in

* *op. cit.*, p.174.

† Buchanan to Grey, 6th Sept., 1914. Grey, *op. cit.*, Vol.II, p.175.

° George, *op. cit.*, Vol.I, p.390.

principle by the War Office.* After discussion of various projects, by 28th January the Council had finally agreed to the Dardanelles expedition with the ultimate object of capturing Constantinople.

Grey was not altogether happy about this decision for fear of the effect upon the Russian attitude to the war and because he was, in general terms, a Westerner. "The chief mistakes in strategy may, in my opinion, be summarised in two words: "Side-shows". In justice to Kitchener it must be recorded that he disliked them all, and my own particular regret is that I did not resolutely support every resistance he made to them."† On the other hand, he felt it necessary that the Allies should obtain some definite military success as a preliminary to the search for allies. Italy was still on the side-lines, Greece torn by internal dissensions as to which side to support and a Bulgarian attack on Serbia seemed imminent. This situation could only, he felt, be turned in the allies favour by a decisive action in the field. He was finally led to support the Dardanelles campaign by the belief that it would very probably cause revolution in Constantinople° with the possible prize that Turkey would leave the war. Always provided, of course, that Russian suspicions could be kept at bay. "Even as it was, and even without the irritant to Russia of a Greek army *en route* for Constantinople, the British operations against the Dardanelles came near to impairing our relations with Russia.+

Meanwhile, the efforts to re-create the Balkan league against Turkey continued unsuccessfully. Essentially, they foundered on the inability of Serbia and Greece to agree to the cession of territory which would satisfy Bulgaria, and British diplomacy there-

* Cd.8490. Prior to any general discussion at Cabinet level. Hankey, *op. cit.,* Vol.I, p.253.

† Grey, *op. cit.,* Vol.II, p.72.

° Cd. 8490.

+ Grey, *op. cit.,* Vol.II, p.180. Hankey, *op. cit.,* Vol.I, pp.265–71 gives the impression that Grey was rather more keen than this. Grey had previously suggested some attack in the Adriatic to impress Italy, was favourable to an alternative to the Western stalemate and saw the Dardanelles campaign as finally settling the attitude of Bulgaria and the Balkans.

fore had but little to offer the latter by way of concrete advantage. Whilst it could suggest that "the satisfaction of Bulgarian claims" to the Turkish territory in Thrace would be possible, it could only hold out the hope that Serbia would agree to the settlement of the Macedonian question in return for compensation elsewhere.* But Grey felt he could go no further at this stage and Serbia remained recalcitrant. "The Serbian Minister said that the uncontested zone, as interpreted by Bulgaria, was a thing that Serbia never could concede. Serbia would rather stand alone against the shock of an Austro–German offensive."† He pressed again in August and September 1915 as the likelihood of a Bulgarian attack on Serbia increased. But "It was all in vain. The Serbian Minister closed one conversation with me by saying they would all rather die than let Bulgaria have Monastir".°

The early months of the New Year showed clearly how progress in obtaining Balkan allies depended upon military success. The Russian reverses of January were followed by the Bulgarian acceptance of a large German loan; on 9th February Grey reported to the War Council his fear of an attack on Serbia.+ The Council thus agreed to urge on Greece the need for her to help Serbia promising allied assistance in the form of troops and in consequence a joint allied démarche was made in Athens on the 15th February but it was refused.

This inability of diplomacy to bring the Balkan states to heel created feelings of much impatience which tended to assume that if more active steps were taken by the Allies, a solution could be found without much difficulty. Thus on 22nd February, Lloyd George urged that a conference should be held in Greece of the Foreign Ministers of France, Russia, Great Britain, Greece, Rumania and Bulgaria at which a joint Balkan bloc of allies against the central powers might be established. This proposal floundered on Grey's unwillingness to be absent from the Foreign

* Grey to Bax-Ironside, 13th Nov., 1914. Grey, *op. cit.*, Vol.II, p.185.
† Grey to de Graz, 26th July, 1915. G. Trevelyan, *Grey of Fallodon,* p.285.
° Grey, *op. cit.*, Vol.II, p.197.
+ Hankey, *op. cit.*, Vol.I, p.276.

Office for so long. "We missed our chance of organising a confederation that would have decided the War by 1916, and all through lack of enterprise and gumption."* Lloyd George also toyed with the idea of going himself on a round trip to Russia and the Balkans to bring them altogether and into the war on the entente side. Grey was opposed to that too.†

The favourable start to the Dardanelles campaign brought a more hopeful situation in the Balkans. Bulgaria did not join the central powers; Greece offered troops for Gallipoli; Italy made a tentative approach to the Allies. The hopes thus engendered, however, were short-lived. In early March Venezelos was ousted and the pro-German party was temporarily in the ascendency whilst Russia vetoed the Greek condition of an entry into Constantinople. To make assurance doubly sure, a definite Russian claim to Constantinople and certain areas of South-Eastern Europe was submitted on 4th March. It was this claim which the War Council accepted on the 10th in return for British compensation.

By April, matters in the Dardanelles were going badly. Greece refused the offer of Smyrna in return for an immediate attack on Turkey. On 7th May, Serbia was offered the eventual cession of Bosnia–Herzegovina with access to the Adriatic and this was followed by an offer to Bulgaria on 29th. If she would attack Turkey she would be allowed immediate occupation of Turkey in Europe up to the Enos-Midia line and certain post-war gains in Macedonia subject to Serbia's willingness to be content with territory from the empire. Serbia, however, refused to agree and it was not until 14th September that the Entente finally decided to dispense with Serbian consent and to make a formal, final offer to Bulgaria. By now, however, the Dardanelles campaign had clearly failed and on 22nd September Bulgarian mobilisation was ordered. Diplomacy could do no more.

It thus became increasingly important to attack elsewhere to

* George, *op. cit.*, Vol.I, p.416.

† Asquith, *Memories and Reflections*, Vol.2, p.64.

attempt to restore badly shaken allied prestige, to prevent a link up between Germany and Turkey and, finally, to send aid to Serbia. Thus the idea of a landing at Salonica was resurrected. The ability to carry this out in good form depended upon an invitation from Greece but she was still shilly-shallying between the two sides of combatants. The difficulties faced by diplomacy are well illustrated by the culmination of Greek indecisiveness on September 28th when two telegrams were received in London. The first thanked the Allies for the offer of troops but declined them; the second insisted that the wire should be ignored.* During the next few days the fate of the whole project hung in the balance whilst there appeared doubt as to whether Bulgaria might after all accept the latest entente offer or Greece refuse a welcome to the troops. Final action was precipitated by Russia breaking off diplomatic relations with Bulgaria and the Allies began to land on 5th October under formal Greek protest. Grey felt strongly that such action was wrong but was overruled by his less squeamish colleagues. That very day Venezelos fell once more; the pro-German party was on top again and the obligation to Serbia repudiated. The British offer of Cyprus to Greece in return for help for Serbia was refused. By the end of the autumn Serbia was overrun; no effective help could be got to her, the remaining Allied objects in the area were defeated; the Allied troops were locked up in the Balkans and a situation of utmost embarrassment created from which French requirements prevented a withdrawal.

This unpleasant fiasco created a field day for the critics. Grey's declared policy of working for Balkan unity had tumbled about his ears. His own reasoning was always that only military success, which could ensure large gains to the Balkan states, could possibly overcome the disadvantages resulting from the fact that their quarrels were essentially with each other. The reasoning of his critics rested on the argument that he should have had no scruples in forcing Greece and Serbia to buy off the Bulgars with solid

---

* Hankey, *op. cit.*, Vol.I, p.419.

gains that would not depend upon the outcome of a European war. There were two objections to this course, one ethical and one practical. "To guarantee to Bulgaria, by the use of force in the last resort, possession of territories in Macedonia and Thrace now occupied respectively by Serbia, which is fighting with us as an Ally, and by Greece, which has displayed a not unfriendly neutrality, constitutes a proceeding for which no defence can easily be framed."* This moral reluctance found little favour. British foreign policy had been "a policy of self-deception. It was a policy partly dictated by a belief that all men are activated by copy-book motives and principles and partly due to the indolence and the timidity which will not face unpleasant facts."† The other difficulty was practical. Short of military operations against Greece to force a way to Serbia the Allies had no bargaining counters to force unity on the Balkan States. If Serbia was to be overrun anyway it was of no advantage to her to placate Bulgaria. This of course was one reason why a landing of significant size in the Balkans was considered so important by those who wished to see a more dynamic policy pursued in the region and for the absence of this Grey cannot be held particularly responsible. He can however be said to have had scruples; he was not a convinced easterner; he was afraid of the effect such activities might have on Russia and his health was failing badly during 1915. It was thus perhaps inevitable that he did not give the appearance of great enthusiasm for Balkan diplomacy and with the policy failure in the area his reputation suffered a severe blow. Page, in describing the prevailing mood of public opinion in December 1915, wrote "even Sir Edward's scalp isn't safe when they suspect that he wants to be lenient in that matter. They keep trying to drive him out on two counts 1) he lets goods out of Germany for the United States 'and thereby handicaps the fleet;' and 2) he failed in the Balkans. Sir Edward is too much of a gentleman for this business of rough-riding over all neutral right and for bribing

* Grey to Bertie, 7th July 1915. Grey, *op. cit.*, Vol.II, p.200.
† Amery. 2-11-15. *Hansard*, Vol.75, Col.595.

these Balkan bandits."* An opinion echoed by Hankey when he writes that Grey was too fastidious a man for war.†

"Not only in the case of Bulgaria ... but originally in the case of Turkey, and now in the case of Greece, the diplomacy of the Foreign Office has been most lamentable and disastrous to the country."° Nothing had been done, complained Mr Lynch, to counteract the German wooing of Bulgaria "I know we have Ministers, but the whole diplomatic service suffers from being chosen from too narrow an area, and high positions and titles are considered instead of ability".+ Grey was more than ever considered to be a failure and the Foreign Office with him. "His record during this War has been a record of disaster. ... The main point is this, that he has not the quality ... of a great diplomatist ... He ... has unfortunately what I may call the insular mind. ... He is one of the great failures of this War."× " 'He can't play for shucks'.... He knows very little about foreign affairs to begin with. He has none of the peculiar personal qualities which are essential – neither the finesse of the French diplomatist, nor the subtlety of the Italian, nor the plastic sympathy, the sense of life of the Slav, nor the bold straight directness of the American."** Britain's unique position and advantages in the Balkans had been "frittered away in the last few months, largely as the result of inattention, half-heartedness and the want of a definite policy".†† The *Morning Post*°° wrote in the same strain. Under the heading "A Word to the Foreign Office" it claimed that "The failure [in the Near East] is complete and ignominious. A Department whose foible is omniscience, and which has demanded an absolute immunity from criticism or comment as the only condition under which the Minister for Foreign Affairs and his

* Hendrick, *op. cit.*, Part 2, p.103.
† Hankey, *op. cit.*, Vol.I, pp.184–5.
° Mr Cooper, 23–12–15, *Hansard,* Vol.77, Cols. 730–1.
\+ 11–11–15, *Hansard,* Vol.75, Col.1367.
× Mr Lynch on 12–2–16, *Hansard,* Vol.80, Col.544.
** Mr Lynch on 19–10–16, *Hansard,* Vol.86, Col.899–900.
†† *The Times,* 9th October 1915.
°° 9th October 1915.

staff of permanent officials could possibly be expected to achieve their subtle and delicate tasks, has accomplished and crowned a series of blunders which would have been remarkable in a Parish Council". It was obvious that Bulgaria was the key to the Balkan situation; that Ferdinand was only concerned to sell himself to the highest bidder. If the Foreign Office didn't know this it had no excuse for there were plenty who did. It had been out-manoeuvred on every point.

Pre-war policy in the Near East had been to give away British interests in order to placate Germany and the country had constantly been assured that relations with Germany could not be better. Secrecy prevented the country knowing otherwise. "Last year, the result of diplomacy, secrecy and misrepresentation combined was, briefly, war. What was the first action of the Foreign Office? To fasten upon the Navy the discredited and illegal provisions of the Declaration of London." This document was drawn up deliberately by German jurists to hamper British sea-power. Then orders were given not to allow the navy to arrest German and Austrian reservists going home to be called up. Cotton was not declared contraband and along with many other goods, e.g. magnetic iron ore, was being imported into Germany.

Grey had now announced that he was ready after the war to discuss "the freedom of the seas". That is to say, he was prepared to consider the surrender of Britain's major weapon. Apparently too, the Foreign Office was now considering the use of an international tribunal instead of our own Prize Courts. The "old conspiracy, which framed the Declaration of London, is still active". If it should go through, Grey must resign for the security of the nation. "The record of the Foreign Office is sufficiently dubious as it is. It may be that the series of unparalleled blunders is simply due to incompetence. If it is not incompetence, what is it?"

IV

War is not a favourable time for the development of democratic processes and the maladjustments between constitutional theory and the expectations of public and Parliament on the one hand and harsh reality on the other deepened the suspicion in which the handling of foreign affairs was now held. A considerable amount of this was simply the expression of anxiety because the war was going badly but a contribution was made by the unimaginative nature of the government's approach to the whole problem of news and information and its unwillingness to allow the free discussion of war-time policies. Before the war, the Liberal government can fairly be charged with a failure of public relations and this failure was perpetuated albeit with more excuse. Furthermore, it was not until later in the war that the importance of public morale and the use of propaganda as a war weapon both at home and abroad came to be appreciated; in the early years there was a tendency to clamp down on the dissemination of all information and to let the minimum of news be published. In consequence the gap between government and people and government and Parliament increased during the first two years of the war through lack of any positive attempt to carry opinion along with authority. Under such circumstances, the worst interpretation was always likely to be put upon governmental action and suspicions, already planted before the war, to flower.

The outbreak of war saw the creation of a Press Bureau for the control of information at home. This organisation, together with the rigid views of Lord Kitchener concerning the role of newspaper correspondents at the front, combined to produce a very strict censorship of news indeed. It was only gradually realised that the control thereby exercised was excessive and in the early part of the war the existence of the Bureau, the fear engendered by the Official Secrets Act and the general belief that the government disliked any public discussion of foreign policy, all combined to make the press feel hamstrung. It was not until 13th December 1915 that censorship by the Press Bureau on behalf of the Foreign Office was suspended; thereafter it depended upon unofficial contact and discussion with correspondents on publication problems until in 1916 a modest News Department was created in the Foreign Office to provide an official channel of communication. The press thus found it more difficult to fulfill its role as a debating arena* and its decline in effectiveness was associated with the loss of the power of Parliament to provide a sanction on governmental action. Thus, at the Prime Minister's request, there was no Commons debate on the deteriorating situation in the Balkans and Grey's short announcement thereon on 14th October 1915 did not meet the growing dissatisfaction with the conduct of the war, and the secrecy with which it was surrounded. Carson's resignation that same month increased parliamentary disquiet and although the Lords found an opportunity to express some of this unease on 26th October 1915, strong pressure continued to be exercised by the government to prevent parliamentary discussion or criticism in the Commons. Finally the government gave way and a debate was initiated on 2nd November but the general discontent continued in the ensuing months. Parliament had become ineffective and knew it.

The dilemma of knowing where to draw the line between governmental and Parliamentary responsibility had become more cruel for governmental latitude could more justifiably be claimed for the prosecution of the public interest yet such action, taken for war purposes, might well affect the nature of the peace where, it could surely be argued, the country's representatives were entitled to a greater say. The problem was shown over the Dardanelles campaign when suspicions were freely voiced that its object was to "obtain Constantinople for Russia". Whilst this was an unfair way of putting it, it was nevertheless true that Russia was going to get Constantinople after the war and the governmental refusal to comment did nothing to allay a serious misinter-

* See e.g. The *Morning Post*, 9th, 15th October 1915; the *Economist*, 16th October 1915.

pretation. In a similar way, Parliament was most upset by Grey's interview in May 1916 with the Chicago Daily News in which he discussed his ideas for the necessary basis for peace. This was a matter which had never been seriously debated in Parliament and therefore it was held that Grey had no right to speak for the nation on such an important topic but that he had neglected his proper responsibilities to speak first to Parliament which was still the ultimately supreme body. Thus when Cecil appeared to repudiate any suggestion that the House of Commons was at all responsible for foreign policy (although later he vigorously denied that this was what he had meant) he had but put into words what many members feared was happening, particularly in relation to the conduct of foreign affairs.* Under such circumstances government action when it was less than perfect inevitably attracted criticism, valid and exaggerated, and in addition served as a focus for suppressed views and anxieties about the way the war was going. In so far as foreign affairs were concerned too often the assumption underlying the argument of the critics was that diplomacy was all powerful. This is never so and during the war its limitations were increased through the need to operate in a situation which provided the minimum of flexibility. It is difficult to avoid the conclusion that the resentments due to a demonstrated allied impotence at the Dardanelles and Salonica were projected onto that part of the conduct of the war which was most vulnerable, namely allied diplomacy. It was far too simple to assert that the "tragedy of the Dardanelles . . . is largely due to the failure of our diplomacy".† Neither was allowance made for the fact that there were allies whose wishes and foibles had also to be considered and the handicap that this imposed must again be stressed. "I remember, on one occasion, saying to France and Russia that, with the military situation so adverse, it was of no use to make offers at Sophia; but I did not adhere to this line. There was nothing except dignity to be lost by trying at Sophia and we all

* See page 118. Also *Hansard,* 7–11–16, especially Mr Lambert and Col. Gretton, Vol.87, Cols.148 *et seq.*

† Mr Outhwaite, 23–12–15., *Hansard,* Vol.77, Col.722.

tried. The more desperate the situation, the more frantic grew the promises. Let it not be supposed, however, that while there was agitation there was speed. All the Allied Foreign Ministers were active in making proposals, but someone had an objection to make everything that was proposed, and the Allied Ministers at Sophia had to wait till they all received joint instructions."* This sorry activity, with its negative result, is an example of diplomacy at its most impotent and whilst it may have been necessary to make the attempt the resulting loss of dignity was not solely at Sophia.

V

By the time of the fall of the Asquith government, the Foreign Service had become widely discredited. "There is undoubtedly throughout the country a growingly profound distrust of Foreign Office policy."† The diplomat has always been a figure to be viewed with some degree of suspicion; poor Henry Wootton was only expressing an opinion of wide currency. The shock of the outbreak of war triggered off a search for the causes in which the temptation to find a scapegoat was irresistible. This built upon the pre-war Radical criticisms and concluded that the instruments of secret diplomacy and of Foreign Offices were hindrances to the creation of a peaceful world. Furthermore, Grey's anti-German policy was a "potent cause of the terrible catastrophe" that had befallen the country.°

In this there was some confusion between ends and means. On the ultimate aim of peace there was unanimity between the Foreign Office and the country; but opinions differed on the way to maintain it, on the price which Britain should pay for it and on the nature of the national interest should a European war occur. All these were proper subjects of political debate.

In determining what policy to pursue at any given moment, the

* Grey, *op. cit.,* Vol.II, p.198.
† Col. Gretton, 7-11-16, *Hansard,* Vol.87, Col.155.
° C. H. Norman, *Britain and the War,* p.2.

Cabinet of course considered the opinion of the Foreign Office. The giving of advice was now part of the *raison d'être* of its existence, but it did not necessarily follow that the Cabinet slavishly followed that advice or that when it took action disapproved by its critics it was because the Foreign Office was in control. Such an argument was to degrade an eminent Cabinet to a level of no importance. Nevertheless there was a certain distance between the Foreign Secretary and his colleagues and one would expect this to throw him into closer contact with his expert advisers than might otherwise have been the case. These men were open to the attack of being persons "saturated in the diplomatic tradition", of treating countries as pawns and whose attitude to ordinary members of Parliament was too often one of contempt.* With the outbreak of war, the criticism of the handling of foreign affairs was in effect given a trump card in that Great Britain had been able neither to maintain European peace nor to contact out of a European war. It was thus inevitable that British policy should be discussed from the new point of its responsibility for the war, and if this was held to be considerable then the Foreign Office as the maker, real or presumed, of policy was a body working against the national interest. "The great danger of England is the Foreign Office . . . and much more the Foreign Office than the Foreign Minister."† In addition the Foreign Service as the executant of policy could also be held to be at fault. The traditional claim of the diplomat that he was a factor working for the maintenance of peace, if true, was a responsibility in which he had failed "The aim of diplomacy also is the maintenance of peace. If it fails, there is better reason for believing that its failure is due to a faulty method and an outworn tradition than there is for attributing its breakdown to uncontrollable forces imbued with irrepressibily hostile intentions"°. To this criticism the Foreign Office had no effective reply.

* A. Ponsonby, *Democracy and Diplomacy,* p.47.

† Candid, *Quarterly Review,* November 1915.

° A. Ponsonby, *op. cit.,* p.7. A more extreme view suggested that "a completely false idea has crept in that diplomacy is synonymous with peace". F. Neilson, *How Diplomats Make War,* p.13.

The elevation of the Foreign Service to the unenviable position of the villain of the piece was helped by more long-term changes which were taking place which contributed to the opinion that it held a position out of all importance to its proper role. The growth of popular democracy meant that suspicions would increase as long as the men employed were drawn from that section of society branded as the out of date holders of power and whose interests were held to be divergent from those of the majority of their countrymen. Thus it could be charged that the objects of "the devil's engine of secret diplomacy"* were not national in the large sense of the word, but governmental and thus considered in official circles in terms of how they were likely to affect the interest of a narrow group rather than the community at large. Being sincerely convinced that the governing class was England they would inevitably put the interests of the part before the whole. "The wonderful combination of severely conventional thought, seventeenth century traditions of procedure, and sublime disregard for the urge of modern political forces which characterised the official machine, combined with a complete indifference towards, and ceaseless ignorance of, anything connected with the social, industrial, economic, or other determining conditions of the very important people concerning whose affairs the official machine was, in the eyes of the British nation, the Government's one authoritative source of information."† This type of diplomatic machine was both consequence and cause of the fact that the control of foreign affairs was still in the hands of a small section of the community. Some believed that financial interests were here of great importance, working behind the scenes "with endless ramifications and untraceable international links, working, not for the public good but for the immediate interests of particular individuals."° Even without this sinister interpretation, however, the "caste", embracing both political and official heads remained

* *Daily News,* 17th June 1916.

† H. Grenfell, Behind the Veil of Diplomacy, *Foreign Affairs,* Vol.I, No.11. May 1920.

° A Ponsonby, *op. cit.,* p.107.

as an entity clearly distinct from the mass of the nation. "L'esprit de bureau" was carefully cultivated in the Foreign Office and regardless of national interests. "In the days of recognised Whig supremacy the formula of the Foreign Office was: If you cannot find a Russell, take an Eliot; if an Eliot is not to be had, take a Grey; if a Grey is unavailable, secure a Leveson-Gower. Changing the names, the same rule applied to the Tories. The tradition holds good to this hour. Fitzmaurice, Grey, Cecil, Balfour."* Such people were bound to be considered out of touch with popular thought both at home and abroad yet the involvement of the whole nation in war inevitably increased the need for a foreign policy felt to express the totality of the national interest. Whilst it was true that the man in the street knew little about foreign affairs this was not entirely his fault since little of the necessary material for his education was provided by press, Foreign Secretary or Foreign Office. "To the man in the street foreign policy has too long been an affair of mystery, but there is no reason why this should be the case . . . But if you wish to have a voice . . . you must shoulder your responsibilities, devote some of your time to the study and examination of foreign politics . . . the great internal enemy [is] the steady growth, with all its attendant abuses, of the power of the Bureaucracy."† But "There can be no "free peoples", and there can be no "free negotiations" between "free peoples", so long as international relations are conducted behind closed doors, and so long as nations are committed blindfold to combinations, policies and schemes of which they are allowed to know nothing."° Equally, it was admitted, it was up to the citizen to study and consider foreign affairs otherwise he would never be able to control the Foreign Office and see that its policies

* H. Hyndman, British Policy and the Rights of the People, *The New Europe*, Vol.1, No.11 28th Dec. 1916. Though some went further, see e.g. F. Neilson, *op.cit.* who thought Castlereagh, Canning and Goderich had all been figureheads, here today and gone tomorrow, whilst the machine went stolidly on.

† From an address by Sir Robert Kennedy, published in *The U.D.C.*, May, 1916.

° *The U.D.C.*, 11th April, 1916.

accorded with true British interests. Since his opinion was not sought except at moments of crisis and patriotic excitement he could not be expected to provide a sane and commonsense restraint on policies which were determined largely in isolation from him. His reaction was neither necessarily pacific nor right.

Looking back on the handling of foreign affairs from the middle of the war, men saw that the traditional check of Parliament had been absent. Less and less time had been devoted to foreign affairs;* few Labour members were knowledgeable about them; no one on the Front Opposition bench, barring Mr Balfour, had any special claim to competence therein. The tradition had developed that foreign affairs were properly above the arena of party politics and whatever the advantages the principle of continuity may have in one's dealings with other countries, at home it must encourage the acceptance of policy rather than its critical appraisal. In the years before 1914 this doctrine became well established; a process which was helped by the fact that differences in views on foreign affairs lay, not between parties, but within one. It was thus more difficult than might otherwise have been the case to get policy questions debated.

The other major failure of democratic control was thought to be at Cabinet level. It was recognised that in the nature of the case the Foreign Secretary stood in rather a different position vis-a-vis his colleagues than other members of the Cabinet because of the nature of his work. Whilst they were concerned with the administration of agreed Parliamentary policy he was concerned with negotiation with other sovereign states, with the protection of British subjects abroad and necessary assistance to British commercial interests. He was bound therefore to be in an isolated position but the large size of the modern Cabinet and the pressure of other governmental work as the scope of governmental responsibilities increased, meant that it remained in comparative ignorance of international developments until, once again, a crisis

* See Select Committee on House of Commons Procedure (378), esp. questions 1703 *et seq.*, 2279 *et seq.*, 2870 *et seq.*

had arisen. There was thus no procedure for an effective check at any level of policy making and diplomacy operated in a rarefied atmosphere in which it could obtain an undue prominence.

The charge that Foreign Offices were to some extent to blame for the outbreak of war became deeply embedded in inter-war thinking: "Or were we all – British, French, Germans, Russians, Austrians alike, the victims of intriguing Governments, the sport of lying politicians, puppets in the grip of dark and sinister forces, pawns in the hands of a dishonest and incompetent diplomacy?" wrote E. D. Morel in 1920.*

In addition to its failure to prevent war the Foreign Service now appeared to be no good at winning it and broadly for the same reasons. Its composition could not reflect the true interests of the nation and its techniques were unsuitable for the needs of the time. The hunt was up. As Vansittart was later to discover "the Press would always blame the Foreign Office for the faults of the politicians".† With the increased speed of decision making and the growth of the war machine, both the Foreign Minister and the Foreign Office lost their pre-eminence in the field of external relations. Thus a convenient moment seemed to have arrived for a clean sweep of the methods of the past. We do not want, said Mr Ponsonby, the "same old rusty machine of diplomacy to be used in the same clumsy way".° In the new Europe peace would depend upon the satisfaction of the legitimate interests of all and this would entail a knowledge of the continent not to be found in diplomatic despatches. "Democracy will not allow war." The *Economist* had frequently made the same point. Skilful diplomacy, it held, needs men not trained in "the small talk of the drawing-room, but in a knowledge of national prejudices and characteristics, of social movements and racial prejudices and of business interests".+ "The common interest of civilised democracies cannot be advanced by a secret diplomacy out of

---

* *Ten Years of Secret Diplomacy*, Preface to the 6th edition.
† *op. cit.*, p.440.
° 24–5–16, *Hansard*, Vol.82, Col.2181.
\+ 16th Oct., 1915.

touch with democratic sentiment."* The climate of opinion was thus ripe for the new methods of personal diplomacy in which Lloyd George so strongly believed. The stately old-fashioned method whereby the Foreign Minister stayed at home, fed by his office and his ambassadors with information and using his staff or the foreign diplomats in London to execute his policy was decried as cumbersome and too slow-moving for effectiveness. The belief in personal contacts between those with "a mandate from the people" who would thereby be in a better position to achieve results, and that speedily, was ready to be brought to the centre of the stage.

* *The Morrow of the War,* The Union of Democratic Control.

CHAPTER 5

NEW MEN AND NEW WAYS

I

After two inconclusive years of battle there were no signs of victory. The easy optimism which had once assumed that "it would be all over by Christmas" had long since vanished into oblivion as the war deepened into a grim, unending struggle whose ultimate purposes too often appeared obscure. Whilst some clung to the vision of ultimate victory there were to be times ahead when the prospect of an indefinite stalemate appeared the best that might be hoped for. The war weariness which this engendered settled over the public mind in all belligerent countries and gave rise to social and industrial unrest with which governments were forced to deal. The malaise was reflected at higher levels where the belief in the impossibility of a decisive victory developed into coherent suggestions for a negotiated peace.

The new British government however was committed to the policy of victory and this provided the context within which all problems had to be seen and to which all other considerations had to be subordinated. Since 1917 was the year in which British fortunes touched their lowest ebb, this made for a period in which planning was essentially for the short-term. It was necessary to keep the civilian population war-minded, or to prevent a quick German victory, or to devise a means of breaking the stalemate on the Western front, or to persuade the Russians to continue to fight, or to find a means to harness the American war effort;

in fact to pursue the manifold activities pressing upon a belligerent government. Political developments and the handling of external affairs fall into place against a back-cloth of these desperate circumstances together with the over-riding assumption of the necessity to win the war. It is against this standard that Lloyd George's unorthodoxy must be judged.

In December 1916, he became Prime Minister of a government which was to prove a successful organism for the winning of the war but which, in the course of so doing, became freed from those checks upon its actions which it is the function of the democratic process to provide. The link between the general community and the Cabinet became more tenuous as the main focus of interest for the government became the means of winning the war to the detriment of its relationship with Parliament; whilst the more subtle restraint on executive action created by the need to carry a considerable body of opinion at Cabinet level was likewise lessened. As long as this could be justified by war-time necessity, disapproval of such a method of conducting the nation's affairs remained at a minimum; with the achievement of victory discontent could no longer be suppressed. During 1917 however it was limited to sporadic outbreaks* against the War Committee and its proliferating Secretariat which focussed the loss of status experienced by Parliament as the Prime Minister neglected it in his pre-occupation with the war and drew some of his closest associates from extra-Parliamentary circles. In fact, the Prime Minister's Parliamentary position was inherently insecure, being dependent upon a majority largely drawn from another party which it was Bonar Law's task to discipline. In the wings were the Asquithian Liberals whose bitter animosity only awaited a suitable opportunity for eruption, a moment which it found in the Maurice debate of 1918. In addition to this lurking opposition and often associated with it, was the antagonism of the military machine. If ever the magic of his genius or the loyalty of his sup-

* e.g. House of Commons, Feb. 12–13, 1917. *Hansard,* Vol.90, e.g. Cols.362, 480; 8–3–17, Vol.91, Cols.602 *et seq.* 19–2–18, Vol.103, e.g. Col.2216.

porters faltered then Lloyd George's position could be destroyed overnight. The need to retain Parliamentary confidence did not, however, prevent the Prime Minister's thoughts developing on lines far removed from the practice of British political life, for his proposal at the end of 1918 to abandon the Cabinet altogether and to govern the country by a triumvirate is an indication of the extent to which his views had departed from normal governmental method.*

This, however, is to anticipate. The widespread dissatisfaction during 1916 with the higher conduct of the war implied that Lloyd George's creation of a War Cabinet, meeting daily and consisting of persons without departmental responsibility, was one to commend itself to many. This body consisted originally of five people,† of whom Bonar Law alone, as Leader of the House of Commons, had outside responsibilities.° It was up to him to retain the confidence of the Commons in the Cabinet for which purpose Lloyd George could not be spared. This War Cabinet survived until November 1919 when the Prime Minister reverted to a peace-time Cabinet of 20 members.

The basic intention of this directorate was to concentrate executive action in a very few hands, thereby providing a focal point for all fundamental decisions and which, through the creation of more effective methods of work, could secure clarity of decision and speed of execution. In practice, as indeed was recognized in theory, the War Cabinet needed to consider the views of other members of the government responsible for departmental affairs and it was thus the intention that they should be called to meetings of the War Cabinet as appropriate. This very often happened.

---

* His reasoning depended upon the need for the Prime Minister and his senior colleagues to be so much in Paris that he could see no purpose in keeping up the sham of responsibility to Parliament. See A. Chamberlain, *Down the Years,* p.139 *et seq.*

† Lloyd George, Curzon, Milner, Bonar Law and Henderson. To these Smuts was added in June 1917, Carson in July, and Barnes replaced Henderson in August. In January 1918, Carson resigned and in April A. Chamberlain replaced Milner.

° "Doing outside sentry duty". Lloyd George, 19–12–16, *Hansard,* Vol.88, Col.1342.

In the year Dec. 1916–17, 248 persons, other than members, attended meetings of the War Cabinet;* in 1918, 278 in addition to the representatives of the Secretariat.† In particular the Foreign Secretary, or his representative, attended the greater number, together with the Permanent Under-Secretary.° At the same time the War Cabinet found it helpful to create a number of standing committees of which the most important were chaired by Cabinet members and it would be absurd, therefore, to suggest that Lloyd George's government was cut off from a wide range of persons who had a contribution to make to war decisions,+ and it may be that Hardinge is right to say that the main difference lay in Lloyd George's greater powers of direction than those possessed by Asquith× rather than in the actual structure of the war-making body. Lord Riddell's War Diary** shows too that the object of sparing the members of the Cabinet so that they could in fact devote themselves to long-term thinking about the war was not always achieved. Greater concentration of decision, however desirable, naturally meant a very heavy burden on those who had to carry it whilst basic policy making could not be entirely divorced from lesser, or from executive action, since these are the elements out of which fundamental decision is made. "The Cabinet is drowned in paper"†† and it is difficult to see how it could have been otherwise. Even this smaller Committee was shown not always to be sufficiently effective and in the summer of 1917, Milner is to be found urging the need for yet another smaller group to study big, strategic issues especially in view of the Russian collapse and the entry of America into the war. This

---

* Cd.9005, p.2.

† Cmd.325, p.5.

° Of 500 meetings of the War Cabinet under the second Coalition Government, Balfour attended over 300 and Cecil represented him at over 100 more. Dugdale, *op. cit.,* Vol.II, p.241–2.

\+ See Hankey's view that the Prime Minister never intentionally took a decision in the absence of the appropriate Cabinet Minister, *op. cit.,* Vol.II, p.580.

× Hardinge, *op. cit.,* p.205.

** E.g. p.261.

†† J. Davies, *The Prime Minister's Secretariat,* p.51.

advice was followed and the Prime Minister with Milner, Smuts and Curzon, together with Hankey as secretary, formed a Committee for this purpose, whilst the formation of committees dealing with broad, though subsidiary topics, continued throughout the following year.* With all the qualifications, however, it still remains a system of which Lloyd George was the heart and thus his views on the conduct of governmental affairs and the play of his personality on events cannot be ignored.

The past had shewn that Lloyd George was indeed a man to get things done. Once his imagination had been fired he devoted himself heart and soul to the execution of the desired object driving himself and others at great speed towards the goal. The implementation of the 1911 insurance schemes; the financial measures he adopted in 1914; the organisation of the munitions supply all stood as monuments to his capacity and energy alike. Once he had come to believe in the necessity of the war, he was able to view it as a crusade of the forces of light against those of darkness and thus to prosecute it with that vigour which comes from the conviction of right. The development of his attitude towards the war led to him becoming the first public spokesman clearly in favour of the defeat of the enemy rather than the negotiated peace. This view point received formulation by him in September 1916 in the "knock-out blow" interview; a policy which he came increasingly to represent in the allied discussions on war aims during 1917. One of his many gifts was to express his imaginative conception in eager and vivid terms of enormous appeal to the general public and it is thus not surprising that in 1916 he had been playing with the idea of leaving the Asquith government in order to devote himself to rousing the country to the magnitude of the job on hand so that it would be willing to make far greater efforts in order to complete it. His appreciation of the importance of civilian morale no doubt lay in part behind his penchant for the press Lords who wielded an instru-

* E. Wrench, *Alfred, Lord Milner,* p.335.

ment daily in touch with the mass of the population on whom, rather than on Parliament, victory would depend.*

His vigour and energy were thus now to be concentrated on the one supreme object and to those natural innate abilities, "a touch of genius – . . . the kind that acts as an electric light flashed in the dark",† was added an extraordinary impatience with the shortcomings and mistakes of the British government during the first two years of the war upon whose policies his verdict could in each case be summed up as "too little and too late". Had the West supplied Russia adequately with munitions the Russians would never have collapsed; had the futility of attempting victory on the Western front been appreciated sufficient resources could have been diverted to open a satisfactory second front against the enemy where he was weakest; had the government appreciated the real nature of total war the problems of the mobilisation of the labour force, of conscription, of munitions supply would have fallen into their proper place. This perhaps was one of the greatest differences between Lloyd George and other British leaders, for he possessed in far greater degree the capacity to see the war whole. Others saw single problems of military strategy, of shipping, of Allied co-ordination, of supply of men for the forces; in Lloyd George they were fused into a single enormous problem in which at home the total community

---

* Thomas Jones has left a vivid portrait of Lloyd George's gifts which by implication delineate his defects.

"Lloyd George's gifts amounted to genius, and his speeches moved men with the spell of a magician. He was exceptional in the greater degree of originality he possessed, in the greater intensity of his passion, and, in time of war, in his concentration and resourcefulness. He was a masterful executive who chose able lieutenants, distributed responsibility, and exacted service to the utmost limit. . . . He was a swift improviser. His mind resembled a signalman's in a busy station, Clapham Junction, for example, with steam and electric trains travelling at speeds to the coast, to the country, to London. He pulled the levers and the traffic moved in Westminster, in Whitehall, in Fleet Street, in party offices, in town and village halls, in polling booths. His friends were few, his instruments many, his acquaintances legion, his inventions innumerable, and his political curiosity inexhaustible. Basically he was a hard realist, with no illusions about men or movements." Thomas Jones, *A Diary with Letters,* pp. xxix–xxx.

† Hendrick, *op. cit.,* Part 2, p.259.

would need to be submerged into the war effort and abroad each ally would have to be subordinated to the common needs of the alliance. This belief in the importance of the support of the general bulk of the working population led him to introduce a Labour representative into the War Cabinet behind whom such forces could rally, despite the fact that Labour representation in Parliament was still comparatively small* whilst one of his major tasks in 1917 and 1918 was to attempt to achieve greater unity of effort among the Allies.

His reaction against the imperfections of the past and his vision of the needs of the war thus led him to a positive view of the conduct of governmental affairs in which he was to ride roughshod over traditional susceptibilities, a process which was to give rise to an accumulation of resentments. The need for speed in decision led him to view the carrying of Parliament with him as of secondary importance; the need for the co-ordination of allied effort in the field to collision with the military; the need to co-ordinate all branches of the war effort to the subordination of departmental machinery to the central secretariat; the use of the new weapons of economic and psychological warfare to the creation of new instruments and the use of non-civil service personnel. In these essays the Foreign Office was perhaps particularly affected since so much of the war effort in fact impinged upon its traditional spheres of work whilst it seems likely that the Prime Minister's general distrust of the Foreign Office and the past handling of foreign affairs made him the readier to look for alternative methods of conducting the country's business. His dislike of experts and their traditional methods of work led him to condemn both their opinions and the formalities of diplomatic procedure. This is nowhere better illustrated than in his view of the Allied conference as a method of getting things done in

* In 1916, of a Parliament of 670 members, 42 were Labour. When Lloyd George became Prime Minister the Labour Party by a vote of 18–11 decided to support Lloyd George although there was strong feeling inclined towards the Asquith section of the Liberal party. J. Davies, *The Prime Minister's Secretariat*, pp.16–23.

contrast to that of his former chief. In the spring of 1916 Asquith attended an Allied conference at Paris "thirty people of six or seven nationalities sitting round a table and emitting a good deal of gas: however, no harm was done, and we all parted good friends".* Whereas Lloyd George could state "After six months of negotiation by cable and three days of conferring face to face we realised that better results were achieved by means of a few hours' business-like discussion . . . than by reams of correspondence. Misconceptions and misunderstandings were cleared away in a second which otherwise might take weeks to ferment into mischief, and it was our conclusion that these conferences might with profit to the cause of the Allies be extended to other spheres of co-operation".†

It is within his attempt to create a unified policy that Lloyd George's interference with diplomatic appointments falls into place. The replacement of Bertie by Derby at Paris, the supersession of Spring Rice by Northcliffe and later, officially, by Reading at Washington, and the near recall of Buchanan in favour of Henderson in Russia were all actions in which motives and reasons were complex and which could in consequence be variously interpreted. What can be said with certainty is that none were actions taken with foreign affairs and diplomatic considerations solely in mind and to that extent were bound to annoy the Foreign Service with its more specialist, professional view. Thus at War Cabinet level the role of foreign affairs, far from being conceived of as a distinctive entity as in pre-war days was clearly subordinated to the main object of the prosecution of the war in which the strings of all policy were to be concentrated in a few hands of which the Prime Minister's were to be pre-eminent. In consequence, Lloyd George needed a man as Foreign Secretary who was prepared to accept this conception and his somewhat unorthodox methods of conducting foreign affairs. He found him in Arthur Balfour. Lloyd George had not been alone in thinking that the Admiralty

* C. Petrie, *The Powers behind the Prime Ministers,* p.94. See also H. Asquith, *op. cit.,* Vol.2, p.120.

† 15-2-15, *Hansard,* Vol.69, Col.918.

was not Balfour's spiritual home and the episode of the Jutland communiqué shewed that the philosopher's gifts are not necessarily apposite to the handling of civilian morale in war time. Whilst Balfour's detached aloofness from life fitted him for the analysis of long-term issues and the discussion of basic policy, it cut him off from a knowledge of the common man and the mainspring of his actions. To remove him from an office which, as the shipping situation grew more desperate, required the initiation of new measures, albeit over the opposition of the Sea Lords, was wise. Temperamentally Balfour was not a man of action as his tenure of the Admiralty indicated; rather than take the initiative and impel some decisive action at sea he preferred to sit back and wait upon the slow results of the policy of attrition pursued through a tightened blockade.* Furthermore, he was not a person to view his new situation in terms of his own personal prestige or who would insist upon the preservation of outward forms in order to preserve the proper dignity of his office. In this respect he was no Curzon.† Quite apart from general patriotic motives to serve where necessary, Balfour had come to believe in the need for a greater unity of political decision and that Lloyd George was a proper person to have control of it. 'A free hand for the little man' for the purpose of winning the war and the necessity to put up with what this might imply underlay Balfour's tenure of the Foreign Office; "the spirit of consistent loyalty not so much to the trusted leader as to the irreplaceable person".° In broad terms too Balfour favoured the conception of the single, all-embracing command as a war-time necessity. "One of the fundamental difficulties of the situation is that the distinctions between what are respectively political reasons and military reasons for any given policy are practically arbitrary, . . . and those who have ultimately to decide must take both sets of reasons into

---

* Dugdale, *op. cit.*, Vol.II, p.148.

† But he shewed human weakness in being hurt by Lloyd George's insistence he should leave the Admiralty which no amount of insistence that he was the right man for the Foreign Office could quite alleviate.

° Dugdale, *op. cit.*, Vol.II, p.240.

account."* His willingness to accept informal relations as a means of contact with the Prime Minister was helped bv the friendly relations that he always preserved with him. Although not officially a member of the War Cabinet it was recognised that he could "come when he liked" and, as has been shewn, he very often did. It is the opinion of his biographer that despite his relaxed attitude to method Balfour would not have tolerated any significant decline in the importance of his office in its proper sphere.† This may well be true but it must be remembered firstly that foreign affairs were only one among many matters clamouring for attention from the Prime Minister during the war; it was from the Peace Conference onwards that he became increasingly preoccupied with them; secondly that all could accept the basic thesis of war-time necessity to which Balfour strongly held and that his temperament was one to incline him to take the last stand rather than the first. The great issues of foreign relations in 1917, apart from the immediate prosecution of the war, were relations with America and Russia. Balfour's share in the former was conspicuously successful whilst the consequences of the Russian revolution escaped Balfour and the Foreign Office along with most other members of official circles. In this matter there were no "experts".

The appointment of Balfour to the Foreign Office aroused a certain amount of criticism but Lloyd George knew what he was doing. He had already expressed to Asquith his opinion that Balfour was not the man for the Admiralty having "neither the energy, initiative, nor the administrative gifts requisite for the position ... at such a critical moment"° but he considered him "an ideal man for the Foreign Office and to assist the Cabinet on

---

* Dugdale, *op. cit.*, Vol.II, p.237. Balfour to Cecil, 12th Sept. 1917.

† *op. cit.*, p.241. An illustration from another source would not perhaps be inappropriate here. When Northcliffe returned to Britain from America for a short visit in the summer of 1917, he suggested that his brother might take over from him, Wiseman wrote the Foreign Office "I learn Northcliffe – is arranging for Lord Rothermere to take his place whilst absent". – "Whom" enquired Balfour "is Lord Northcliffe arranging this with?" See R. Pound and G. Harmsworth, *Northcliffe*, p.580.

° George, *op. cit.*, Vol.II. p.998.

big issues."* To Dawson, who expressed disquiet, Lloyd George was frank "Balfour was an easy man to work with and would allow him without friction to do a great deal especially as regards America".† It was important, too, to cement Unionist opinion behind the Lloyd George régime and the appointment of Balfour to a major post was here an important factor.

II

The calling of the Imperial War Conferences and the creation of an Imperial War Cabinet brought a further diffusion of political discussion at the highest levels of policy and thus helped to weaken the tightly-knit pre-war arrangements and channels of responsibility. At the end of 1916, it was announced that such a conference was shortly to be held in order to associate the Dominions with the progress of the war and to provide the opportunity for a discussion of further action. There were also to be a number of meetings with the Cabinet whereby the representatives from overseas would be initiated into the day to day problems of wartime policy. In consequence the Prime Ministers and specialist colleagues from Australia, New Zealand, Canada, Newfoundland and South Africa, together with the Secretary of State for India and two representatives from the princely states, converged on London in March 1917 for a series of discussions.

The agenda for the conference appears to have been settled largely by discussions between Lloyd George, Hankey, Kerr and Milner° and related to the war effort, the terms of peace and general post war problems. It was also envisaged that policy statements by the appropriate British ministers should be made on strategy, politics, economics and the various international agreements perforce entered into concerning the post-war settlement. Allied desires on territorial and economic changes, in so

* *op. cit.*, p.1017.
† E. Wrench, *G. Dawson and Our Times,* p.144.
° George, *op. cit.,* Vol.IV. p.1742.

far as known, were to be explained and it was anticipated that the question of some overall international organisation was likely to be raised.

In consequence of these meetings the principle of the autonomy of the Dominions was proclaimed but with the recognition of their right for the future to a share in the discussion of foreign policy and the general discussion of imperial affairs or matters which impinged upon them in a continuing Imperial War Cabinet. It was also arranged for two committees of the conference to be created, one to be chaired by Lord Curzon and one by Lord Milner which should concern themselves respectively with the territorial and economic problems of the peace.* The Curzon committee was chiefly notable for the formulation of the demand that the German and Turkish colonies captured or occupied during the war should be retained and the report was accepted by the War Cabinet as an indication of policy subject to possibility and to the demands of the Allies; Arthur Henderson dissenting.†

Milner's committee ranged more widely. Whilst it considered that the Paris resolutions° were no longer applicable, it still considered that the allies would be entitled to refuse Germany equality of treatment after the war and to demand severe indemnities. A tentative discussion of a League of Nations held that further discussion with the allies and America was necessary and that perhaps some system of resort to a Conference for political settlement could be agreed upon by the signatories of the Peace Treaties.+ Considerable discussion in the Imperial War Cabinet followed on the broad themes of disarmament, a League of Nations and arbitration. Further meetings were held in the summer of 1918 at which methods of formalising the right of the Dominions to approach the Prime Minister on matters of im-

---

* *The Times History,* p.323 considers it "probable" Balfour was concerned with the territorial committee.

† George, *op. cit.,* Vol.IV, p.1750.

° See below, pp. 253–5.

\+ Milner's personal views on the peace settlement would seem to have been very tentative at the time. *The Times History,* pp.327–330.

portance were evolved. Overtaken by the ending of the war, the Imperial War Cabinet met yet again in November to discuss many of the problems of the peace.

At the political level, therefore, one is perhaps entitled to inquire what remained of the traditional theory and practice concerning the conduct of foreign affairs. Cabinet accountability to Parliament had become far more tenuous although it had still further yet to go. Within the Cabinet the pre-eminence of the Foreign Secretary was self-evidently in abeyance whilst the introduction of Dominion representatives into the pattern of policy making brought quite a new influence to bear.

III

The streamlining of the political body to take all essential governmental decisions had administrative consequences also. The creation of the Cabinet Secretariat was but a logical outcome of the centripetal tendency now at work and for which the Secretariat of the Committee on Imperial Defence was a ready-made instrument already in existence at the heart of the governmental machine. It became the responsibility of this office to circulate an agenda for the meetings of the War Cabinet and to keep minutes thereof; to ensure that appropriate departments were informed of decisions and received the necessary instructions for action and to obtain from departments the information necessary for War Cabinet decisions. The existing staff nucleus was extended by the addition of a number of civilians drawn both from the civil service and the outside world.

In theory, therefore, the main problem of the Asquith government had been solved for there was now in existence a body small enough to come to decisions and to co-ordinate the war effort in all directions and a method both of ensuring that those decisions were agreed upon in a sufficiently clear cut and precise form for there to be no doubt as to what they were and to serve as a basis for action and also to see that the traditional departments performed their part of the whole.* In practice, this clear outline was blurred through the necessary attendance of many other persons at Cabinet meetings and through the size of the task of wielding the totality of governmental business into a coherent whole which could readily be encompassed. Perhaps the most than can really be claimed is that Lloyd George's methods made sufficient impact upon the problems facing the country for the machine to lurch to victory but in the inevitable untidiness and hurly burly of the storm there was much to criticise in the arrangements he devised. "War is a very slow business. . . . It seems to consist of one chaos after another"† remarked Northcliffe. Lloyd George's government helped to keep the confusion within reasonable limits.

In addition to such formalised central machinery, the Prime Minister created an enlarged personal staff upon which he relied both for advice and for the execution of his will. The "Garden Suburb" consisted essentially of five persons: Professor Adams from Oxford, Waldorf Astor, the owner of the Observer, David Davies the Parliamentary Secretary to the Prime Minister, Philip Kerr of considerable imperial knowledge and experience and Joseph Davies as statistician. In 1917, David Davies left as a result of a disagreement with the Prime Minister over Northcliffe's appointment to head a war mission to America and was replaced by Cecil Harmsworth.

The idea of a personal staff for the Prime Minister was not new, but this was one of considerably enlarged size consisting of advisers each one of whom was expected to be an expert in a group of subjects.° Its duties were but broadly defined being "to assist the Prime Minister in the discharge of the heavy responsibilities which fall upon him under the War Cabinet system"+

* But it was not the duty of the Secretary of the War Cabinet to offer advice to the Cabinet on matters of policy. Bonar Law, 18–6–17; *Hansard*, Vol.94, Col.1422.

† R. Pound and G. Harmsworth *Northcliffe*, p.594.

° Davies, *The Prime Minister's Secretariat*, p.62–3.

+ Report of the War Cabinet for 1917.

thus providing it with the widest possible mandate should it be that the Prime Minister wished to exploit it. Lloyd George's personal inclination was always for the informal and unorthodox and it is thus unsurprising that he should have furnished himself with this personal prop upon which he felt a greater security in relying than upon traditional methods of support. The officially defined duty gives us a clue to the impossibility of the situation which Lloyd George had created for himself in that the enhanced position of the Prime Minister in a Cabinet itself wielding increased power threw a burden on his shoulders which one man could not carry. It was essential to find some form of relief and for this he turned to his personal secretariat which provided him with the intimate support, advice and following which the impersonal civil service could never have supplied. Here was a small group of people, responsible only to the Prime Minister, giving devoted unpaid service and keeping a watchful eye over all the main spheres of the war effort, ready to bring to his notice any situation which might need attention, to provide him with advice and ideas on any subject at short notice, a group of people who constantly had the ear of the man while others did not.

In such a situation, it becomes impossible to distinguish those occasions upon which the Garden Suburb was simply an adjunct of the Prime Minister from those when it is more properly described as his alter ego.

It was inevitable that such administrative arrangements should contain the possibility of resentment by the older established departments although it is necessary to distinguish the reactions to the Secretariat from those to the Garden Suburb. The Foreign Office, with its tradition of independence and separateness from other government departments, was one whose feelings were likely to be particularly hurt by its subordination to an upstart body with no particular experience in foreign affairs. The arguments in favour of the War Cabinet machinery, however, were persuasive and in the early years of the new régime the Foreign Office, together with the other departments, was prepared to accept the system as a necessary war sacrifice.* Whilst regretting the departure of the Asquith–Grey combination, the need for a new broom which would not be too civilised to make war was generally understood and it was accepted that Lloyd George possessed the necessary dynamism which the situation demanded. At the same time from a professional point of view he was considered both ignorant of foreign affairs and excessively confident of his ability to handle them† but the dangers of this combination did not become apparent immediately and during the critical stages of his Premiership the Foreign Office was prepared to accord the new man and the new system a certain indulgence. Later, however, the War Cabinet Secretariat spread to absorb other functions which were looked on more askance. The sittings of the Imperial War Cabinet were served by it, the Supreme War Council received an off-shoot from it at Versailles which by a natural transition transferred itself into the core of the British secretariat at the Paris Peace conference. As Hankey "progressively became secretary of everything that mattered"° the less there was left for anybody else.

The tolerance of the Secretariat as a necessary adjunct of an emergency situation was not, however, extended to the Garden Suburb whose increasing importance to the Prime Minister and general position as "court favourite" was bitterly resented. "That was the way in which foreign affairs and diplomacy were carried on at this time by Lloyd George with a Secretariat, nicknamed the Downing Street Kindergarten, run by Philip Kerr, a charming young man, one of the Editors of the *Round Table*, but with no practical experience of Foreign Affairs."+ It had apparently become the responsibility of the suburb to "contribute ideas"× and the implication that in foreign affairs the traditional advisers

* Hankey, *op. cit.*, Vol.II, p.833.

† Hardinge, *op. cit.*, p.205. Vansittart, *op. cit.*, pp.163–4.

° Vansittart, *op. cit.*, p.164. See also Hankey, *op. cit.*, Vol.II, p.589 on the enlargement of the Secretariat.

\+ Hardinge, *op. cit.*, p.214.

× Hankey, *op. cit.*, Vol.II, p.590; see also *Hansard*, Vol..90, Col.362, 12–2–17. Its function was to convey "thought waves from the outside public".

had not got any and could be bettered by a man whose experience had lain elsewhere was deeply hurtful. "The Garden Suburb Group" were never officially linked with the War Cabinet Secretariat. Like the Foreign Office and other Departments we regarded them at first with some suspicion, which proved not unfounded because they had contacts with the press, which we did not".*

It was not the civil service alone which disliked the system. The *Nation*† allowed itself to be the vehicle for the view that the function of the suburb was "to protect a powerful Chief from the interference of ordinary politicians, including Ministers and the heads of public departments". In addition it was rapidly to assimilate popular ideas and present them to its chief with the assistance of the "dominating daily papers" interspersed with the responsibility to suggest "great and original ideas" based on an imperialist ideology. The Editor supported.° He considered that Lloyd George aimed to depress, not to exalt, Parliament from which he had ostentatiously disassociated himself. The links with the people were weakened and the calling of an extra-Parliamentary conference to settle the issues of the peace and questions of taxation destroyed them further. Now there was a double screen of bureaucrats between the Prime Minister and the heads of Departments which "transmits to them the decrees of the Upper Five". Furthermore there is "a little body of illuminati, whose residence is in the Prime Minister's garden, and their business to cultivate the Prime Minister's mind". There they existed dreaming up large, unthought-out schemes of action, no longer tested by the criticism and debate of the House of Commons. The seat of power was now the New Bureaucracy. In sum the Foreign Office had been ousted from its position as the main source of advice and the main channel of execution for foreign affairs and the usurpation of its functions had led to a position in which "normally Philip Kerr . . . could be counted on to keep [the Foreign

* Letter Hankey to James Butler quoted in Butler, *Lord Lothian,* p.64.
† In a bitterly sarcastic article "All in a Garden Fair" on 24–2–17.
° *The New Bureaucracy.*

Office] informed".* Pettiness, personal factors and lack of consideration arising from pressure of work merely enhanced the possibilities of confusion inherent in the administrative arrangements themselves which had been improvised to meet a vital emergency and in consequence the necessary clarification of function had not occured. It is easy to laugh at red tape and the "usual channels" and to grow impatient at the slowness they so often seem to imply, but to abandon them for ad hoc methods devised on the spur of the moment, whilst perhaps initially quicker, may have other disadvantages. What had started off as a method of bringing order out of chaos in which the professional interests of the departments would be given due, though not undue, scope, degenerated into one which elevated "systematic incoherence"† into a principle of government. Patriotism, the complaisance of Balfour, the liaison work of Hankey all helped to keep the resentments dormant during the war. Whilst hibernating, they nevertheless accumulated and festered. Furthermore, it was not until the peace when, obviously enough, foreign affairs became an all-absorbing function of government that the full potentialities of personal rule by Lloyd George were realised. By the time that the Secretariat had become responsible for staffing international conferences and for League of Nations business, and the Treasury had accepted reparations, Lloyd George indulging in his penchant for diplomacy by conference, Curzon complaining of the "second Foreign Office" of whose actions his own department knew nothing, not only had the responsibility for the handling of foreign affairs become thoroughly blurred but the morale of the Foreign Office had sunk very low indeed. One authority° detects a considerable loss of morale within the ser-

* Davies *op. cit.*, pp.xix–xx. These feelings were not, of course confined to the Foreign Office for other departments also found their established competences eroded. The long-term dangers in the situation apparently did not escape the notice of the suburb itself for it appears that Adams held the view that civil service departments were powerful enough to destroy anyone, including the Prime Minister. Davies, *op. cit.*, p.102.

† Lord Percy of Newcastle, *Some Memories,* p.34.

° Lord Percy, Foreign Office Reform, *The New Europe,* 1st May 1919.

vice under Asquith because of the lack of political direction but it was the War Cabinet system of Lloyd George which largely sapped its vitality and sense of responsibility. He claims that the Foreign Office increasingly came to feel that it had no adequate channels of communication with the Cabinet, that it was "imperfectly acquainted" with the Prime Minister's intentions and that it was never certain the advice it gave reached the Cabinet in its proper form. Under such circumstances it became more and more a rubber stamp in which the new life of the department, born of its economic work, was rapidly stifled. The seeds of this development are to be found in the complex of influences at work as the country desperately thrashed round to find a way to win the war.

IV

The need to create an effective centre for the web of the British war effort was paralleled by a comparable problem in the realms of allied policy making. Unsurprisingly, the effort at solution led to similar results through the suppression of the traditional methods of dealing with foreign affairs which were found to be no longer adequate. It is obvious that the extension of governmental activities into unaccustomed spheres and the total mobilisation of effort brought the necessity for allied contacts between specialists on a scale which was beyond that of the Foreign Office to control. Of more importance however was the fact that national affairs could no longer be divided into water-tight compartments corresponding to the orthodox areas of civil service responsibility, and the machinery which was created at home expressed the recognition that this was now so. It became a major object of policy under Lloyd George to attempt a similar achievement for the allies.

It was the military machine which proved the least amenable to the process of stream-lining the machinery for waging war. This is understandable since its operations aroused the most violent passions and fears. It would seem clear that politics and strategy, far from being divorced, are but two aspects of the national interest and that between them there must be considerable mutual inter-action if the community hopes to achieve a policy which is both politically acceptable and strategically possible. Ultimately a war is fought for political objectives but the manner in which it is fought will affect the possibility of obtaining them until, in the extreme case, a badly fought war may lose them altogether. It seems impossible, therefore, to accept altogether the Asquithian view that once broad principles have been determined it is best to allow the military to get on with the job alone. Conversely, military considerations will affect political aims as has already been illustrated by the way in which the military decision to attack the Dardanelles led to the abandonment of a long-standing political objective. It becomes a nice question which political decisions should provide the framework for military action and which should be subordinated to the needs of war whilst if the total of political issues so subordinated reaches considerable proportions then major, long-term decisions may in practice have been taken through the inability to look beyond the immediate military advantage. Far from one consideration providing a framework for the other, at the top the two must fuse. Furthermore, now that war could no longer be treated solely as a matter of armies it had become even more impossible to hand over its conduct to the military. By implication this had been recognized by Sir William Robertson in a paper submitted to the Cabinet in the latter part of 1917. "Further, the question of the Entente outlasting Germany to such an extent as to be able to dictate terms of peace to her is obviously affected by many political, social and economic conditions of the different Entente countries with which I am imperfectly acquainted, . . . Of no less importance are the naval and shipping situations, as to which also I can express no opinion . . . If we were engaged in a war in which the British Army alone was fighting a single belligerent, and in which considerations other than those of a purely military nature were of little or no account, the General Staff ought to be able to give an opinion with reasonable accuracy.

But nothing resembling these conditions obtains in the present stupendous struggle, which is not a war merely of armies, but of some 20 or more nations, and draws into its vortex every branch of national life."*

In practice, therefore, at the highest level politics and strategy must meet and the actual fighting operations are but one part of a war plan in the broadest sense. The multiplicity of factors involved must also affect what at first sight appears to be a strategic problem properly left to the military. Those who advocated attacking Germany elsewhere than on the Western front were not thinking purely in military terms but of the possibility of capitalising the conflicting interests of the Balkan powers; or the disaffection in Austria–Hungary. The fusion of diplomatic, military, economic and social factors must, in the end, be the responsibility of the politician but the difficult decision of how much weight to give to the opinion of the specialists remains. In the case of military advice the problem is peculiarly acute since the expertise of the profession is surrounded by greater mystery than that of the other arms of State. Civilians are thus more likely to be conscious of their ignorance, more susceptible to charges of amateurishness and in consequence more hesitant in making their views felt. Since an army is not actively employed except at a time of crisis when the risks of neglecting its advice are particularly grave, it is a bold man who is prepared to throw away expert advice when such action may result in consequences of an appalling nature for which he, the politician, must bear ultimate responsibility.

The struggle between Lloyd George and the generals was not only the bitter personal feud which is so often pictured for it represented a far more profound conflict of view and indeed can be seen as the parallel in the military sphere of the suppression in the political field of the Asquithian concept of war making. In this case, however, the struggle was more prolonged and bitter

* George, *op. cit.*, Vol.IV, pp.2345–6.

and in the chronology of events it is not possible to separate three issues which after the passage of time appear more clearly to be distinct. Firstly it contained the need to treat the war as a whole rather than as a collection of independent national ones between which some lucky co-ordination might be achieved. Of this need, Lloyd George was profoundly convinced. Secondly it contained a conflict of view on strategy in which those who believed in the continuing struggle in the West were opposed with equal vehemence by those who wished to attack the enemy elsewhere. Here once again, Lloyd George's passionate adherence to a more imaginative strategy was at variance with the opinion of powerful military advisers. The propagation of these two policies led him into violent collision with Robertson and Haig to whom both concepts were anti-pathetic. Finally the dispute provided one more centre for political opposition to Lloyd George. As the generals gained powerful support in the country and with the desperation engendered by the war in 1917 increasing public anxieties, the danger of his political position increased. It therefore became very difficult to consider the proposal for an effective Allied body for control of the war on its merits and its fruition was hampered by the emotions aroused by the more vivid personal conflict.

The tendency to supersede more formal methods of communication by personal meetings of opposite numbers from the alliance had already begun under the Asquith government. The Prime Minister, and his immediate colleagues, and the military chiefs had experienced a number of Allied conferences to discuss the general conduct of the war. Since the emphasis in these meetings was on strategy it was perhaps natural that they should have been serviced by the Secretariat of the War Council; in so far as strategy implied political decision then by a natural process those who were in attendance at the conference were of more immediate consequence than those who were not. The somewhat intermittent basis and unbusinesslike procedure of these early conferences did not commend them in all eyes. By June 1915, Hankey had become concerned over relations with the Allies and the inadequacy of the procedures in use for discussing policy with them.* The Calais conference of the following month brought home to him even more forcibly the lack of any proper secretarial arrangements† and the need for the adoption on an Allied scale of some procedure approaching that which had been adopted at home. The Paris Conference of November thus saw agreement on the necessity for more business-like methods of conduct. It was left to Hankey to compose their first draft and the procedures were finally agreed by the Prime Ministers of France and Great Britain in January 1916.° This memorandum was an attempt to adapt the machinery of the Committee of Imperial Defence to the circumstances of Inter-Allied conference. It contained five points. Allied Prime Ministers were to constitute a standing committee of an advisory character and all conclusions were to be subject to governmental approval. Other representatives required for the discussion could attend as appropriate. Thirdly, whenever possible, the committee was to be preceded by a meeting of the military and naval staffs and any other departments as necessary so that the political heads might have available to them the latest departmental thinking. All conclusions of the conference were to be formulated and finally each government was to nominate a Secretary-Liaison Officer who would provide the secretarial side of the conference and act as a permanent link.+

The next twelve months saw a number of Franco-British conferences largely concerned with the Balkans and characterised by the inability of France and Great Britain to agree on the need for a withdrawal from Salonica. The disarray in Allied policy-making was due not only to the lack of any forceful political

---

* Hankey, *op. cit.*, Vol.I, pp.346–7.

† *op. cit.*, pp.348–351. He castigates its bad organisation, its lack of minuting and coherent formulation of policy.

° Hankey, *op. cit.*, Vol.II, p.451.

\+ It is interesting that Hankey had suggested a permanent secretariat but Briand would not accept this. Furthermore, the Quai D'Orsay resented what was arranged but the Foreign Office gave "no such difficulty". A member of the service, George Clerk, was used on the secretarial side. *op. cit.*, Vol.II, pp.451–2.

direction during this period but also to the tendency for political and military planning to be carried on as two distinct operations. Thus the incorporation of military plans into an overall political operation was often difficult, if not impossible, because when the time for political discussion had arrived the military were too deeply committed. It was to overcome this difficulty that the Hankey memorandum had suggested a military meeting immediately prior to the political conference. There was, however, a further problem within the context of military planning itself, for it was still the case that each nation determined its own policy which, when finally worked out, was submitted to the Allies for mutual approbation and, at the most, minor amendation. Coordination meant little more in practice than a common agreement on the timing of offensives and although the principle of an Inter-Allied Council of War had been agreed in December 1915 in practice this had meant little for the determination of a true joint strategy. Although on paper the highest direction of the war had improved, in practice it was not yet working satisfactorily.

Lloyd George was another who found in these arrangements increasing cause for dissatisfaction. By the time he entered Downing Street he had become the proponent of three major ideas; each one of which was unacceptable to the country's chief military advisers. These ideas were interlinked. The first was his conception of strategy for the years ahead. Lloyd George had never been a Westerner but had persistently advocated the importance of sending as much material as possible to Russia in order to maintain the Eastern front and also of an attack upon the central powers through the Balkans. He had consistently contended that such action would contain enormous political advantages in rallying the Balkan States as well as forming a military attack upon the enemy where he was weakest, namely on the decaying empire of Austria–Hungary. This opinion was reinforced as the war went on. The static trench warfare of the Western front and the seeming impossibility of an effective break-through thereon, allied with the severe loss of life for little gain, increased both his conviction that other methods of warfare were needed and that the generals who were obsessed with the Western front were to be mistrusted. After two years of war his confidence in the value of military advice was small. He, therefore, required some supreme directorate for the direction of the war effort which would provide continuing political supervision and bring into the discussion all the non-military factors which generals so often missed. Such a supreme directorate would at last be able to view allied strategy as a coherent whole rather than as the piecemeal addition of separate military plans. The three areas in which he particularly saw the need for comprehensive strategy were the Western front in order to supersede isolated attacks by the French and British armies, the co-ordination of the Western and the Italian fronts and finally of the West as a whole and Russia. Quite obviously, such overall planning required strong, positive supra-national direction on both the political and the military plane and this proposal constitutes the second strand of his policy. In this way too, he hoped to overcome the selfishness of each military chief whom he considered was only prepared to work hard at his own plans and "When the Generals were forced by Governments to attempt other methods like the Dardanelles and Gallipoli, they did it so half-heartedly as to make failure a certainty."* Whilst it may well be that Lloyd George hoped to obtain greater support for his own strategic views, the argument for supra-national planning was in fact much stronger. The third main object was to obtain unity of command on the Western front itself and as long as this theatre of war remained the most important and the view prevailed that it was here that the war would be lost or won, then this object maintained its importance.

"The real weakness of Allied strategy was that it never existed."† Instead of one war there were six separate ones. Furthermore, although in theory it was for the statesmen to view the

* George, *op. cit.*, Vol.IV, p.2334.
† *op. cit.*, p.2347.

war as a whole, in practice the opinion of the generals in the field carried most weight. "Governments were at the mercy of the Commanders-in-Chief."* But to change them would not be sufficient; the only answer was an alteration in the "whole method of conduct of Allied strategy"† through the creation of an authoritative Inter-Allied body.

V

It was the events of the autumn of 1916 that crystallised Lloyd George's determination to change the system of planning for the war. The military conferences of the past year showed clearly that the generals remained as determined as ever to keep essential control of their own armies. Although they were willing to concert their plans they were not willing to subordinate themselves to a unified command with overall control of forces irrespective of nationality and in which activities on different fronts would be seen as part of a strategic plan. As Secretary of State for War, Lloyd George was well placed to study military opinion and was not impressed with what he saw. By late October he had determined to try to get some further steps taken to obtain proper co-ordination of Allied policies° and a private discussion between a few of the more important politicians was followed by a meeting of the War Committee on 3rd November 1916. Here it was agreed to urge a political conference of France, Great Britain and Italy, to be followed if necessary by a mission to Russia in order to bring all the Allied plans into line. The essential purpose of this meeting would be to lay down the main lines of the Allied war effort for the coming year and since this was viewed essentially as a political task the meeting, it was hoped, would be confined to statesmen in the first instance.

---

* *op. cit.*, p.2342.
† *op. cit.*, p.2343.
° George, *op. cit.*, Vol.II, p.903.

Furthermore, it was to be kept small in order to facilitate ease of working.

Whilst this broad outline proved acceptable to the allies, the decision ran into a difference of opinion over the follow-up consultation of Russia and as a result of the delay thus caused the conference took place not before, but simultaneously with, a military conference which had previously been arranged. In consequence it proved a set-back to Lloyd George's ambition for he had intended a general review of the war situation and a formulation by the heads of governments of a broad plan which the military could then be asked to fulfill. In fact, the concurrent meeting of the generals resulted in the development of military projects divorced from any political context which, since they committed the politicians to accept the attack in the West as the most important, was bound to be considered by Lloyd George as a further disaster.*

At the political conference Great Britain was represented by the Prime Minister and Lloyd George, accompanied by Hankey and the Ambassador to France, Lord Bertie. Considerable time was taken up by a long and inconclusive discussion on the necessary ultimate subordination of the generals to the political authority but no machinery to ensure that this occurred resulted. The proposal for a conference in Russia was approved.†

Looked at from Lloyd George's point of view, therefore, the conference had little or no merit. There had been no examination of strategy in the light of politics, no consideration of a Balkan offensive but a commitment to a large scale campaign in the West; no method of unifying political and military planning resulted and no plans made to co-ordinate strategic effort with

* It would appear to have been in France that his conviction on the need for a changed War Cabinet at home which could enforce its decisions finally crystallised in a conversation with Hankey in which the two men found themselves in agreement on its necessity.

† Later the War Committee decided that the British Mission should be headed by Grey and Austen Chamberlain assisted by Sir Henry Wilson, Layton (Munitions), Revelstoke (Finance) Kygell (Artillery). In the event of course, Lord Milner went in charge.

Russia. It appeared to him to be "little better than a complete farce".*

When Lloyd George entered upon his Premiership he was thus acutely dissatisfied upon a number of most important issues. His determination to carry his ideas led him into acute disagreement with those whose views were genuinely different or whose interests would be adversely affected by its consequences. His conflict with his military advisers over strategy objectives, the project for standing machinery to formulate them and the proposal for unity of command all attracted the political distrust so many felt for him and the animosity of certain sections of the press of which Lord Northcliffe was the most powerful representative.

A most urgent task facing the new Prime Minister was to hold a really effective Allied conference through which support for his ideas might be obtained. His speech to the House of Commons on assumption of office† stressed his belief that there "must be some means of arriving at quicker and readier decisions, and of carrying them out" as between the Allies and "more real consultation between the men who matter in the direction of affairs". To this objective he devoted his formidable energy. A period of intensive preparation preceded his departure for Italy in January 1917. Accompanied by Milner, Robertson and Hankey he was determined to obtain positive results and to this end declared to the conference his view that the primary problem for the Allies was the co-ordination of effort and the pooling of resources. The enemy, argued Lloyd George, with fewer resources was yet able to make better use of them because of his centralised control and until the Allies could overcome their disorganised arrangements they would suffer a serious disadvantage. Whilst his arguments were persuasive, the victory the British Prime Minister won on

* George, *op. cit.*, Vol.II, pp.958–9. One minor but interesting administrative innovation was that it was the first conference at which the British delegation was prepared beforehand with definite conclusions for the utilisation by the conference at the appropriate moment. A practice which continued. Hankey, *op. cit.*, Vol.II, p.559.

† 19–12–16, *Hansard*, Vol.88, Col.1356.

this occasion was a hollow one for the conference formally resolved to accept the principle but by arranging no practical steps for its implementation, determined also that it should be frustrated. His second effort was devoted to persuading the conference to agree to a major attack upon the Italian front. This beat itself out on the united opposition of the military advisers and the Allies departed yet more firmly committed to the Western spring offensives.

Certain isolated decisions of considerable importance were however taken by the conference. It had always been intended that a second session should be held in Petrograd to round off the discussions amongst the Allies and to integrate eastern and western plans, and a formal decision to send a strong mission to Russia for this purpose was taken at Rome.* The policy to adopt towards Greece in the light of the danger of an attack by the Greek royalist army was decided; a decision to improve the overland supply routes to the Balkans to relieve scarce shipping space proved its worth very shortly afterwards; a special naval and shipping conference was arranged to take place in London in order to co-ordinate the use of allied resources at sea. Nevertheless, despite Lloyd George's later public pronouncement that "it was the most business-like conference I have ever attended", on the major problems it was a disappointment to him for it had not succeeded in creating a cohesive body from which could grow the living plant of united action.

In default of a major second front, Lloyd George decided, with misgiving, to back the project of General Nivelle for an attack in the West which was held to contain the promise of a more hopeful result than previous offensives. It was a plan which necessitated British subordination in the field for the duration of the attack and was therefore bound to arouse considerable opposition in British circles. Thus, in falling in with this proposal, Lloyd George was losing one of his objectives but gaining

* The possibility of a Russian collapse was also considered by Lloyd George. Hankey, *op. cit.*, Vol.II, p.609.

another which, if it proved to lead on to more permanent unity of command, would be an advantage well worth having.

On his return from Rome, Lloyd George ran into considerable divergence of view in the War Cabinet on the desirability of the spring offensive in the West but it was eventually determined to support the Nivelle plan and for this purpose, but this purpose alone, to place Haig under French orders. In retrospect, this meeting of the War Cabinet* was notable for the absence of both Lord Derby, the Secretary of State for War and Sir William Robertson, the Chief of the Imperial General Staff, and in consequence the bitterness that the decision aroused and the fears that it was but the preliminary step towards a permanent arrangement were enhanced.

February 26th brought an Allied conference at Calais where the smouldering resentments of the British military vis-a-vis the French burst into flame. Lloyd George raised the question of unity of command and Nivelle was asked to produce a statement on its operation. His plan when formulated, not only infuriated the British military representatives, but went a good deal further than the War Cabinet had envisaged. It was left to Hankey to produce a formula satisfactory to both sides whereby the general direction of the particular campaign lay with the French whilst the British preparations and plans of operation were to conform to the general strategical plans of the French subject to an appeal to the British government as a last emergency.

The failure of the Nivelle offensive also destroyed any possibility of cementing unified command at this stage but the mounting horrors of the western front, and his increasing sense of their futility, compelled the Prime Minister forward to achieve his goal of a more reasonable strategy. For this purpose, Lloyd George began to enlist the support of America and France but this was not simple since both countries inclined also to the need for a Generalissimo and the British opposition to such an appoint-

* 24th February 1917.

ment was sufficiently strong to engender the fear of the fall of the British government.*

On 3rd September Lloyd George wrote a private letter to President Wilson.† "*the comparative failure of the Allies in* 1917 *is also in some measure due to defects in their mutual arrangements for conducting the War.*"

"As compared with the enemy the fundamental weakness of the Allies is that the direction of their military operations lacks real unity... The direction of the War on their side has remained in the hands of four separate Governments and four separate General Staffs. ... The defects of this system have not been lost sight of. From time to time of late with greatly increased frequency there have been International Conferences to discuss the Allied war-plans. But up to the present these Conferences have done little more than attempt to synchronise what are in reality four separate plans of campaign. *There has never been an Allied Body which had knowledge of the resources of all the Allies and which could prepare a single co-ordinated plan for utilising those resources in the most decisive manner, and at the most decisive points, looking at the front of the Central Powers as a whole and taking into account their political, economic and diplomatic as well as their military weaknesses.*

"*At the forthcoming Conferences,* which will assemble as soon as the results of the present offensives have become clear, *I shall urge the imperative importance of establishing more effective unity in the Allied strategy*". Furthermore "I feel that we are bound to study the position, especially with the view of determin-

---

* R.S. Baker, *Woodrow Wilson: Life and Letters.* Vol.7, pp.372–3. House to Wilson, Nov. 23rd 1917.

See also *The Intimate Papers of Col. House,* edited by Charles Seymour, Vol.3, p.218, hereafter House.

† Hankey, *op. cit.,* Vol.II, pp.694–5 speaks of letters drafted by Kerr and himself at the end of August for Reading to take to Wilson. The subjects covered were the inadequate military management of the war, the Prime Minister's dislike of the Western front policy and his desire to knock out Austria and Turkey, and a scheme for an Allied Council and General Staff in Paris to direct the war. Hankey states 'it was dropped for the moment' but is obviously closely related to the letter the Prime Minister sent.

ing whether there is not an alternative plan of campaign. For some time past, it has seemed to me that we ought to consider very carefully whether we cannot achieve decisive results by concentrating first against Germany's allies ... *In my opinion it will be necessary to establish some kind of Allied Joint Council, with permanent military and probably naval and economic staffs attached to work out the plans for the Allies, for submission to the several Governments concerned ...*

"there are, in my opinion, very strong reasons why the United States should consider whether they ought not to be represented at the Conference of the Allies. To begin with, I think the presence of a representative of the United States at the Conference which will determine the future strategy of the War, would be of the utmost value to the Allied cause ... I believe that we are suffering today from the grooves and traditions which have grown up during the War, ... I believe that the presence ... of independent minds, bringing fresh views, unbiased by previous methods and previous opinions, might be of immense value in helping us to free ourselves from the ruts of the past."*

In addition to the attempt to solicit Wilson's powerful backing, Lloyd George wrote to M. Painlevé on the same lines. Already he had given the Frenchman a secret assurance that he would work to get the Western forces under a French Commander in Chief.† Now he wrote to stress the urgency of an interallied body for strategic planning which could produce a coordinated plan taking into account all the resources of the Allies.°

Meanwhile at home the idea of a Supreme Council was beginning to take a definite shape whilst the Italian disaster at Caporetto made everyone more ready to agree to bring Allied unity a little nearer. Thus on 2nd November the War Cabinet, knowing of French agreement to the principle of Inter-Allied planning, resolved to accept the idea of a supreme Allied Council to consist of the Prime Minister and one other politician which would meet

* George, *op. cit.*, Vol.IV. p.2348 *et seq.*
† Letter of 25–9–17. H. Nicolson, *King George V*, p.320.
° 30th October 1917. George, *op. cit.*, Vol.IV, pp 2385–9.

at frequent intervals and possess a permanent advisory military staff on which Sir Henry Wilson would be the British member.

In view of the serious state of affairs on the Italian front the Cabinet agreed that Lloyd George should go at once to Italy.* On the journey, the Prime Minister discussed the details of the plan with M. Painlevé and a final draft was published from the Rapallo conference on 10th November. A Supreme War Council was created for the Western fronts composed of two political representatives (the Prime Minister and a colleague from each allied country) which was to meet at least once a month. The job of the Council was defined as to watch over the general conduct of the war and to prepare recommendations for the decision of governments, to keep itself informed of their execution and to report thereon. Whilst military plans would continue to be drawn up by the respective military authorities they would be submitted to the Council to ensure their concordance and the Council, if necessary, would be able to recommend changes. The Council was given a permanent military committee, Foch, Wilson and Cadorna, whose exclusive function was to be to act as a technical adviser to the Council and which would be entitled to receive from governments all the information and documents relating to the war which would enable it to discharge this function effectively. The General Staffs and Military Commands were to remain responsible to their own governments. Finally, the organisation was established at Versailles† and round this nucleus developed a considerable secretariat with both a political and military side.

This agreement provided the possibility of an organic fusion of the Allied war-making capacity but it did not automatically imply it. The Supreme War Council was not as yet an executive body and its capacity to become one depended upon the use of the machinery in order that its mandate to watch over the whole conduct of the war might become dynamic. Neither had the

* George, *op. cit.*, Vol.IV, p.2390.
† *op. cit.*, pp. 2393–4.

agreement provided for common execution of strategy for the military commands remained under separate responsibilities thus allowing for infinite delays and difficulties in carrying out common policy. In the pursuit of Lloyd George's objectives, the arrangement still only represented a limited step forward in which perhaps the biggest gain was the provision of an alternative channel of military advice to counter-balance the Haig–Robertson combination.

The British Prime Minister's capacity to implement this agreement was dependent upon the degree of support he could find at home where opposition to the proposal was considerable and fomented by the personal aspect which the struggle had now taken. It was known that the Asquithian Liberals were preparing to attack him in Parliament and that support from the Irish members and a considerable section of the Tory party would be forthcoming. Attacks on the Rapallo scheme were published both in the Liberal press and in *The Times* whilst even members of his own government were disturbed. Lord Robert Cecil wrote to Arthur Balfour "Further reflection ... has made me more distrustful than ever of the Supreme War Council. Taken with the Paris speech* there can be very little doubt that one of the purposes which the P.M. had in view was to enable him to overrule the C.I.G.S. and other advocates of the Western front".† Balfour in reply was only mildly enthusiastic but suggested that the system should be given a chance to work. The present arrangement, he considered, was unsatisfactory but the alternative of a single Commander-in-Chief for all the armies would be no better.° He had, however, "nothing to do with the contrivance of the Versailles plan".+

The danger that the major principle of Allied unity would be swamped by indignation at the military proposals and that the urgent need for co-ordination of Allied planning would once

---

* Made by Lloyd George on his way home. See pp. 217–18.
† Balfour papers, quoted Beaverbrook, *Men and Power,* p.195–6.
° Dugdale, *op. cit.,* Vol.II, pp.238–9. Balfour to Cecil, Nov. 19th.
+ *op. cit.,* p.239. Note of conversation with Robertson.

more be frustrated was very real. According to his memoirs, Lloyd George was under no illusions concerning the danger of his political situation but he was sufficiently convinced of the importance of the plan to put it to the test preferring to be beaten than to continue responsible for a policy in which he had no confidence.* He attempted to rally all support. The creation of the Council was announced by M. Painlevé at a luncheon in Paris on November 12th. Lloyd George delivered a fighting speech "As my colleagues here know very well, there have been many attempts made to achieve strategic unity. Conferences have been annually held to concert united action for the campaign of the coming year. Great Generals came from many lands to Paris with carefully and skilfully prepared plans for their own fronts. In the absence of a genuine Inter-Allied Council of men responsible as much for one part of the battlefield as for another there was a sensitiveness, a delicacy about even tendering advice, letting alone support for any sector other than that for which the Generals were themselves directly responsible. But there had to be an appearance of a strategic whole, so they all sat at the same table and metaphorically, took thread and needle, sewed these plans together, and produced them to a subsequent civilian conference as one great strategic piece; and it was solemnly proclaimed to the world the following morning that the unity of the Allies was complete.

"That unity, in so far as strategy went, was pure make-believe; and make-believe may live through a generation of peace – it cannot survive a week of war. It was a collection of completely independent schemes pieced together. *Stitching is not strategy.* So it came to pass that when these plans were worked out in the terrible realities of war, the stitches came out and disintegration was complete."† He went on to summarise past disasters and the promise of the future if unity of control was tried. He quoted American press opinion on the influence of lack of Allied

* George, *op. cit.,* Vol.IV, p.2396.
† George, *op. cit.,* Vol.IV. pp.2397–8.

co-ordination on the lack of Allied success and that the object now was to see that the Council "is a fact and not a fraud".

The Paris speech created a great furore at home. Certainly by implication it was a scathing criticism of the conduct of the war as hitherto envisaged. To some extent it encouraged the impression that Lloyd George was engaged in a personal struggle with the military to the exclusion of all else. For this he was criticised in measured terms by *The Times* on 14th November which claimed that he had gone too far. It could not be proved, and indeed would be unlikely, that military setbacks had been solely due to the lack of allied unity and the speech had given an "unfortunate impression of wasted effort up till now" which could only dishearten everybody. But on the major principle of Allied control instead of haphazard conferences *The Times* was behind him.* The Americans, too, came to his assistance. On 16th November, Wilson sent House his approbation of moves for greater Allied unity "we not only accede to the plan for a single war council but insist on it, but think it does not go far enough".† Two days later, House gave out a statement to the British press. The "Government of the United States considers that unity of plan and control between all the Allies and the United States is essential in order to achieve a just and permanent peace . . . this unity must be accomplished if the great resources of the United States are to be used to the best advantage, and [President Wilson] requests Colonel House to confer with the heads of the Allied Governments with a view to achieving the closest possible co-operation. . . . Colonel House [will] attend the first meeting of the Supreme War Council with Colonel Bliss . . . as Military Adviser."° It is to be noted that the statement did not specifically endorse the Rapallo scheme which still left the execution of Allied plans in national hands but nevertheless provided strong sup-

* A few days later the Prime Minister was to explain his speech as a deliberate indiscretion designed to galvanise public opinion into acceptance of the urgency of the situation and the need to take steps to solve it.

† R. S. Baker, *Woodrow Wilson: Life and Letters*, Vol.7, p.361.

° *The Times*, 19th Nov., 1917.

port for Lloyd George's case. That he was anxious for it is evident "The Prime Minister was constantly urging me to say something to help the situation [i.e. the political crisis occasioned by the Paris speech]. This I refused to do until I had heard from you. The statement I gave out purposely refrained from approving the Prime Minister's plan, but merely stated the necessity for military unity".* The fact that America was behind Lloyd George made it difficult for his critics to be very effective and, indeed, since no one could deny the importance of the principle the opposition to the Rapallo agreement was hamstrung from the start. The attack in Parliament was divided. On the one side were those who saw the plan simply as an unworthy attack upon the generals, and who argued that if the government wanted to change its military advisers it should do so in an honourable way but on the other were those who believed that the agreement did not go far enough and that an executive agency was required just as had been found at home. Lloyd George presented the middle course. Whilst there was to be no Generalissimo and no body with executive responsibilities for the moment, it was nevertheless necessary to arrange for the continuous oversight of the war. This of necessity, he argued, had to be both political and military since there was a vast sphere in which these subjects could not be divided. Although nominally there already existed a pooling of information and mutual discussion in practice this had meant little. Whilst it was intended that final decisions would still remain with governments the Allies would now be able to press more strongly for each partner to fall in with an overall scheme. In short, it was intended to provide that focal point for Allied effort which had hitherto been lacking.

Acceptance of the arrangement was a near thing. "Lloyd George said that his government was saved only by the adhesion, at the last moment, of the British crisis, of President Wilson to the Agreement of Rapallo."† Even so, unity of command on the

* House to Wilson, 20th Nov. Baker, *op. cit.*, Vol.7, p.366.
† House, *op. cit.*, Vol.3, p.260. Comment of General Bliss.

field had not yet been achieved despite pressure from both the Americans and the French that this be introduced. Lloyd George's political difficulties still remained. "Any Government that proposed it would be overthrown" wrote Colonel House.* There were, in fact, still three steps to go before a true Generalissimo was appointed and once again it was crisis in the field which made the arrangement acceptable. Under the shock of the German offensive of March 1918, Foch obtained firstly the responsibility to co-ordinate the action of the Allied armies on the Western front, then the strategic direction of military operations whilst each commander retained the right of appeal to his own government if he thought the safety of his own army was endangered and, finally, on 24th April 1918, Foch became Commander-in-Chief of the Allied armies.

On 1st December 1917 the Supreme War Council agreed that governments should furnisth it with all that informatin of a general political and departmental character available for the war discussions of their own Cabinets or War Committees. This material was to include the decisions of such Cabinets relating to matters connected with the conduct of the war. The governments agreed furthermore to instruct their Ministries of War, of Marine and Shipping, their Foreign Offices, their departments dealing with Munitions, Aviation, Manpower, Food and Finance to make available to the Supreme War Council the fullest information at their disposal. In order to handle all this material, each section of the Supreme War Council created a permanent secretarial staff of its own from which was organised a joint secretarial bureau for the "production and distribution of the notices, agenda, protocols and *procès verbaux* of the meetings of the Supreme War Council and for such other collective business as it may be found desirable to entrust to it".†

Here then was another section of the war effort for which a

---

* *op. cit.,* Vol.3, p.257, 23rd Nov., 1917.
† House *op. cit.,* Vol.3, p.295. This carries the full draft.

secretariat was required. As early as October, the far-seeing Hankey had realised the way in which the wind was blowing and had drawn his conclusion of the need for a secretariat on the model of, and strongly linked with, that of the War Cabinet. By 1st November 1917 he had even got so far as to draft its rules.* In consequence he was enabled to impose the British pattern of work upon the allies through his production, at the very first meetings of the Council, of his draft plan† which meant that he could "get the thing run on our lines, and [ensure] a high standard of execution". By the New Year, the Inter-Allied secretariat had been set up, the British section, under Storrs and Amery, being drawn from the War Cabinet Office. In February 1918, it was further agreed that the Supreme War Council might execute decisions on the Western front without reference to governments. Inter-allied decision making, supported by an adequate staff to give it effectiveness, had at last become a reality.

Thus for the remainder of the war the Allies had achieved a formal method of co-ordinating their highest policies. The extent to which formal methods of conducting foreign affairs had been submerged is perhaps indicated by Hankey's laconic comment that the Council was a body which could study all "matters affecting the external relations of the Allies".° As thoughts began to turn to the problems of the peace, the standing international machinery which it necessitated could even be envisaged as the model for the international secretariat of the future. Because it was so convenient a forum, the Supreme War Council was bound to be used for a great deal of Inter-Allied discussion whilst the march of events dictated that its focus of interest should be increasingly political. For many months the problems posed by the collapse of Russia and her demands for peace had formed a large and anxious part of the correspondence between the Allies and America and the opening of peace negotiations between Russia and Germany precipitated a crisis for the West. It is unsurpris-

* Hankey, *op. cit.,* Vol.II, p.718.
† *op. cit.,* p.733.
° *op. cit.,* p.721.

ing therefore that the Russian problem, the possibilities of Western assistance to her and the decision for intervention should have formed a dominating theme at so many of the Council's meetings. With the collapse of Germany later in the year it was a natural transition which brought the Council and its secretariat to Paris as the peacemakers.

CHAPTER 6

PROPAGANDA AND ECONOMIC WARFARE

I

Meanwhile, the work of government steadily increased as it became necessary to mobilise ever widening areas of the life of the community. In consequence, it became harder to designate the content of "foreign affairs" which were properly the province of the Foreign Service; they were increasingly becoming matters of finance, of commerce, of labour or propaganda in which the service could claim no special competence whilst other departments very often could. Two developments in particular had especial relevance to the handling of foreign affairs, namely the recognition of the importance of the economic factor in modern warfare and the development of propaganda techniques. The first case is illustrated by the development of the blockade which began as an internal matter for the Foreign Office to handle amongst its many other duties and which developed into a coherent economic policy towards the enemy carried out by a largely independent department and which incubated thoughts concerning post-war international economic policy whose execution was not thought of exclusively in Foreign Office terms. A parallel situation was to develop over the creation of the Ministry of Information and the development of propaganda.

The importance of propaganda as a weapon of war was not appreciated in 1914 and its full explotation had not been achieved by the time the war came to an end. Few were conscious of the extent to which both civilian and service morale affect the waging of modern war and the growing realisation of the possibilities of propaganda was matched both by a moral distaste for the element of manipulation such a weapon involved and by an ignorance of the principles upon which the service should be operated. Thus the need to maintain civilian morale and whether this was better done by concealing unpleasant war news or admitting it; the necessity to define the purposes for which the country was at war and the impossibility of pleasing everybody in the process; the putting of a case to neutrals and the form this should take according to the views and sentiments of the country concerned; the possibility of undermining the enemy will to resist; all these were matters which only gradually became apparent. As has already been noticed, Grey had little conception of the importance of the possibilities inherent in an appeal to public opinion and it is thus not surprising that the first activities in this direction were largely unofficial and the concern of patriotic bodies devoted to the encouragement of such worthy objects as voluntary recruitment or the discussion of war aims at home. In so far as the foreign side was at all developed, it largely originated in the *ad hoc* efforts of individual enthusiasts, and in consequence official backing for these attempts was variable. Thus, for example, there was Mr Guest who specialised in smuggling leaflets into Holland, Scandinavia and Switzerland and thence, on occasion, into Germany and Austria–Hungary. There was also Mr Gilbert Parker who appealed to American opinion largely by mailing material to selected American citizens: whilst the War Office experimented with balloons to carry leaflets over the enemy lines on those fortunate occasions when the wind was in the right direction. 1914 also saw the first fumbling steps taken by the Foreign Office to create a propaganda machine through the creation of the War Propaganda Bureau under Mr Masterman of the *Daily News* who operated from Wellington House. A great deal of unnecessary mystery surrounded his existence and the work he did. Much of it was published anonymously and without official indentification thus helping to encourage the view that nothing effective was being done. Criticism mounted of the lack of attention given to the problem of putting Britain's case overseas and especially perhaps to the United States.*

At the same time, the Foreign Office was required to supply information concerning the war to its diplomats abroad for further dissemination, whilst the foreign correspondents in London and representatives of the home Press also required political news. It was soon found necessary for the Under-Secretary of State for Foreign Affairs to make himself available daily in order to meet the press and the general increase in the flow of information passing through the Foreign Office eventually compelled it to establish a special News Department which, by 1916, had absorbed Wellington House and established rather firmer contact with the independent operators. Apart from the work of Masterman, however, the overriding conception was largely passive† relying on the provision of material from which the reader could draw his own conclusions. It was the mishandling by the Admiralty of the news of the Battle of Jutland which drove home the lesson that the manner of presenting information was after all of great importance but persistence of the traditional view is well illustrated by an exasperated entry in Lord Bertie's diary as late as October 1917.° Buchan, with a room at the Foreign Office, "is going to do what he can to disseminate in France information to our advantage".

The change of government provided an impetus towards the greater co-ordination of machinery and the provision of a more purposeful object. "When a line of policy has been laid down, acutal propaganda operations may be begun, but not before"+

* See e.g. House of Commons, Sept.–Nov. 1915. *Hansard,* Vol.74, e.g. Cols.284–7, 508–20, 1000. Vol.75, e.g. Cols.569, 602, 1596. 22–3–16, *Hansard,* Vol.81, e.g. Col.237. 23–8–16, Vol.85, Col.2749. See Chapter 7 for the opposing views of Spring Rice and Northcliffe on propaganda to the United States.

† A similar situation existed in the Service Ministries which were themselves responsible for the release of news appertaining to the actual fighting.

° *Diary of Lord Bertie of Thame,* Vol.2, p.203.

+ Sir Campbell Stuart, *Secrets of Crewe House,* p.2.

and thus was posed the necessity of a clearer definition of war aims as a preliminary to action. This was all the more apposite since 1917 was a year of widespread war weariness in which the possibilities of a negotiated peace were everywhere discussed; thus whilst the existence of a propaganda machine created a pressure upon the government to formalise its war objects, it was also important that a government committed to a policy of "victory first" should develop a mechanism to convince the public at home and abroad of the rightness of its cause.

In the early weeks of 1917, John Buchan became the head of a Department of Information established to co-ordinate the work of the various offices concerned with publicity.* Buchan was to be directly responsible to the War Cabinet in the person of Carson. By this arrangement, a considerable amount of propaganda work was brought more closely together although its links with the Foreign Office, out of whose early efforts so much of it had grown, remained.

This new department became responsible for four main branches. First of all Wellington House continued to produce books and pamphlets for world-wide distribution; secondly a films and wireless department operated under Mr Mair. This had had a history very similar to that of the first section being originally very distinct from the Foreign Office but later brought more obviously under its control. The Political Intelligence Department performed a dual rôle. Concerned with the collection of information put out in the newspapers of foreign countries and the distribution thereof to the government, appropriate departments and the Press; it continued also to perform for the Foreign Office its function of thought, analysis and planning which became of increasing significance as attention turned to the problems of peace.† Finally there was a News Department which again had developed out of earlier efforts of the Foreign Office.

---

* *The Times,* 21st February 1917.

† This department was carried on the Foreign Office vote and, perhaps significantly, had a high proportion of outsiders, e.g. Lewis Namier, Arnold Toynbee, Alfred Zimmern.

This whole organisation had an advisory committee to assist it staffed by persons with newspaper experience of whom the most dynamic was Lord Northcliffe.

Despite such re-organisation the control of news of all forms remained something of a hotch-potch and during 1917 the movement for greater weight to be attached to propaganda, both at home and abroad, gained ground. *The Times* pointed out that it was very difficult to know exactly the nature of Carson's responsibility because of the great secrecy with which the reorganisation of this work had been surrounded. There had never been any real question of a new Department or a new approach to the problem of propaganda for Buchan's appointment had merely been to co-ordinate what had already been done. Buchan's own work at the Foreign Office "of which so much was hoped" had lapsed into a mere section and whilst it had done excellent work, this had been nothing like what had originally been intended.* In this it is perhaps permissible to detect the hand of Steed but Lloyd George agreed that the time had come for a more dynamic use to be made of this new weapon. "On the other hand, our propaganda has been a conspicuous failure," he wrote to the king. "Propaganda at home and abroad is becoming increasingly important"† and in the first months of 1918, following Carson's resignation from the War Cabinet, he created a Ministry of Information under Lord Beaverbrook who thus became responsible for propaganda.

The field divided naturally into several areas. At home lay the responsibility to maintain civilian opinion and to encourage people to maintain production, to accept hardships and to believe in the war. For this purpose it was necessary to consider not only what news should be released to the press together with the manner of its presentation to the public but also what other methods might be employed to maintain morale through travelling exhibitions, film shows and the like. A similar need

* 20th September 1917.
† Quoted Beaverbrook, *Men and Power*, p.275.

existed for the troops to whose fighting capacity the propaganda arm might expect to make a comparable contribution. Overseas, the job was vast, for services to the neutrals, to allies and the empire and to the enemy each needed separate thought and techniques.* Naturally, and rightly, Beaverbrook saw the task as one which necessitated strong and intimate contacts with broad groups of people in which the main links would be the modes of mass communication developed in the twentieth century. Of these by far and away the most important was the press. News had to be given to the home press that it might be enabled to support the war effort, foreign correspondents be convinced of British determination and the magnitude of her endeavours, newspaper men be brought to Britain to see realities for themselves, educative missions be sent abroad to publicise the Allied cause.

The existence of a free and independent press is ultimately incompatible with the purposes of propaganda and this was a tradition rightly prized. Even though the necessity for a propaganda machine was now more widely accepted, an aura of mistrust continued to surround the whole conception. In particular some critics considered that the moral basis of the British cause was so self-evident that it did not require the support of any dubious technique, whilst others feared that it would be impossible to prevent the degeneration of propaganda for broad, national objects, which could perhaps be accepted as a war-time necessity, into propaganda for narrower and baser governmental purposes. Indeed, it was considered that the situation was even more deadly for it was possible to argue that to maintain the prestige of the government was in itself a furtherance of the national interest under war-time conditions and no one would be able to say at what point this championship passed the permitted line. Such fears were but increased by the widespread dislike of Lloyd George's choice of personnel for Beaverbrook soon acquired both Northcliffe and Rothermere as colleagues thus giving the appear-

* Northcliffe, not Beaverbrook, was responsible for propaganda to the enemy. See p.233.

ance that either the Prime Minister, or the press, had the other in thrall. Although the Press Lords were required to have severed themselves from close running of their newspapers, it was feared that it would be asking too much of the newspapers concerned to exercise their proper function of informed criticism of governmental actions if their owners were participating therein. Whilst it would be difficult enough to ensure that the divorce between the proprietor and his newspaper was made absolute, it would be beyond the bounds of possibility for the public to be expected to believe in it. What was far more likely was that the newspapers would simply become vehicles of government opinion and be used as a means of achieving government ends through launching criticism in the press on policies and personalities thus making it easier for the government to get its own way irrespective of the merits of the case. It would also be possible for undue influence to be exerted the other way round and for the press Lords to compel the government to adopt their views on how to win the war. It was a case in which protestations of innocence would never be believed for appearances would lend plausibility to such charges and it would be impossible to rebut suspicion.

Closely allied to such general concern was the complaint that the rise of the press was associated with the decline of the House of Commons as the watchdog on behalf of the community. No longer was Parliament looked upon as the vehicle for the expression of public opinion and the guardian of the public interest against the Cabinet, for the old forms of control had openly been jettisoned. Parliament was no longer in a position to put any effective pressure on the government. This the press could do but it could hardly be accepted as an adequate substitute since the newspapers were bound to view their function in a somewhat different light.

It is difficult not to suspect that the complaints were made more vocal because of the strong dislike evoked by the very mention of Lord Northcliffe whose irresponsible ways were considered to make him particularly unfitted to act as a guardian of the public interest. A man whose reputation assumed that he was telling either more or less than the truth but never the genuine article in between could not be a success in the propaganda field for anything he put out would be suspect from the start. A jumble of faked stories could do the British cause no good. If the Ministry of Information was to become responsible for launching statements on policy to the world, then the possibility of their propagating the views of Northcliffe rather than the government could not be overlooked.*

The new Ministry of Information had thus neither strong outside backing nor, as events were to show, much acceptability in Whitehall. Its creation provided a focus for much of the latent hostility towards the Prime Minister and his methods of government, whilst it also attracted the resentment of an older department which saw the usurpation of its traditional responsibilities through the development on a grander scale of what it had previously been doing in a smaller way. As long as the Foreign Office retained some form of loose supervision over the various propaganda activities which impinged upon foreign relations no acute problem could arise; but the creation of a new department posed the dilemma that whilst effective operations depended upon the retention of departmental good will in order that it might be fed with necessary raw material, the vigorous pursuit of its duties by the Ministry was bound to raise problems of demarcation which might prejudice that very intimacy it was so necessary to retain.

The bald statement in the report of the War Cabinet for 1918 that the Ministry of Information was from the start concerned with the regular dissemination of reliable news in foreign countries and of making Britain's war purposes more widely known does not do justice to this problem.†

Although Balfour's general attitude was that of a "free hand" for the Prime Minister, he cannot have welcomed the appoint-

---

* See especially Commons debate 11–31–8, *Hansard*, Vol.104, Col.73 *et seq*. It is a nice point whether this in fact did happen.

† Cmd, 325, p.35.

ment of Beaverbrook* any more than his colleagues Lord Robert Cecil or Lord Hardinge. On the one hand stood the still powerful representatives of an aristocratic tradition and on the other the pushful, self-made Canadian. Constant friction arose between the two departments. Appointed in February, Beaverbrook was ready to resign in June. "... The Ministry of Information is the Ministry of Publicity abroad. Its object is to state the British case to the world. Its business is to study popular opinion abroad and to influence it through all possible channels. But since our appeal lies not to the diplomatic representatives of Foreign countries but to the public opinion of those countries, our methods must be different from those of the Foreign Office. We have a diplomacy of our own to conduct – a popular diplomacy – and for this we must have our own special organisation.

"... The Foreign Office has, however, both in principle and practice refused to recognise this duty of the new Ministry from its very inception. It says in effect that the doctrine of popular diplomacy implied the setting up of a Second Foreign Office at home with a new set of representatives abroad and a policy possibly divergent from that of the Foreign Secretary. The consequence of this clash of views between the two departments has been friction and delay and for the Ministry which I represent an intolerable clog on its operations. Of the various missions I have tried to send abroad, missions to be headed by people of the status of Ministers, all save one have been blocked ...

"It seems to me that only two things can be done. One is to abolish the Ministry of Information as a separate Ministry and make Foreign Propaganda a section of the Foreign Office: the other is to authorise the Ministry to operate abroad on equal terms with the Foreign Office, consulting and as far as possible accepting its views but with power to take its own line of action.

---

* Who firmly states "Balfour was my enemy", see Beaverbrook, *op. cit.*, p.276. See also *op. cit.*, p.289 for his views of Foreign Office obstruction of his work.

"Nothing less than this last course in my opinion will meet the urgent needs of the situation and since I cannot make my view prevail, I must with sincere regret place my resignation in your hands and ask you to act immediately."*

Although the matter was smoothed over temporarily, constant diplomacy to keep the friction from coming to a head appears to have been necessary. Even Northcliffe is to be found at work in a conciliatory capacity. On 7th July 1918, he wrote to C.J. Phillips of the Foreign Office to try to get material for Beaverbrook to use in his propaganda to Japan, pointing out how well he was doing vis-a-vis Canada and America. He also tackled Balfour, insisting upon the excellent work being done by the Ministry of Information although its head "is not a particularly tactful man". On 12th July he was back at it again "Propaganda is advertising and diplomacy is no more likely to understand advertising than advertising is to understand diplomacy". The same day he approached the Prime Minister in an attempt to smooth out a dispute which in his view was lengthening the war.†

One publicised clash occurred over the use of the Balfour Declaration for propaganda purposes. This document had been issued in November 1917 but its policy remained unpalatable to certain sections of Jewish opinion and Beaverbrook found himself subjected to some pressure not to make too much of the declaration as a policy directive. To this pressure he succumbed to the extent of querying the matter with the Prime Minister. Lloyd George is reported to have hedged in reply.°

This action was sharply criticised by Balfour.

Dear Beaverbrook,

The policy of His Majesty's Government in Palestine is that laid down by the Foreign Secretary in his last

---

* Quoted F. Owen, *Tempestuous Journey,* pp.483–4.

† This paragraph is based on R. Pound and G. Harmsworth, *Northcliffe,* pp.652–3.

° Beaverbrook, *op. cit.,* p.292.

speech. Until it is altered officially, it is in no way affected by conversations between Sir Charles Henry and the Prime Minister.

Yours sincerely,

Arthur James Balfour*

Balfour was evidently seriously concerned about departmental demarcation and the possibility of losing responsibility to the Ministry of Information. On 12th July 1918† he informed the Prime Minister that "We should end by having two Ministers responsible to the Cabinet for Foreign Policy, each having its own officers," and laid down procedures which in his view were necessary in order to ensure that policy-making remained where constitutionally it had been laid. A further note of 22nd August° pressed home the need for "an immediate decision as to the distribution of functions of the Foreign Office and the Ministry of Information". It appears clear that Balfour's tolerance of encroachment upon his department was not unlimited.

During the same month of February 1918, Northcliffe became Director of Propaganda in Enemy Countries+. Unlike his press confrère, however, he did not accept Ministerial responsibility preferring to exercise his jurisdiction through the chairmanship of an Advisory guiding commitee. Campbell-Stuart became responsible for the actual organisation of the department, Seton-Watson and Wickham Steed directed the Austro-Hungarian section of the work and H. G. Wells, later replaced by Hamilton-Fyffe, the German. Mr C. J. Phillips of the Foreign Office acted as liaison officer. Whilst this department drew its finance through the Ministry of Information, it was in no way subordinate to it in policy matters and rapidly developed a life of its own in its chosen field. Whilst Beaverbrook accepted responsibility for

* *op. cit.*, pp.292–3.

† *The Times History,* p.365 footnote.

° Beaverbrook, *op. cit.,* p.293.

\+ At apparently Tyrell's suggestion. H. W. Steed, *Through Thirty Years*, Vol.II, p.186.

propaganda to the allies, neutrals and Turkey, Northcliffe's team devoted itself to Germany, Austria–Hungary and Bulgaria.

The decision to utilise propaganda consciously and deliberately as a weapon of war inevitably meant the need for a crystallisation of war aims in order to determine what propaganda was going to be about. In this way, it became one influence determining the nature of the peace, forcing the consideration of policy upon a government which up till then had tended to shirk the difficulties involved. It thus became of considerable importance that Northcliffe relied heavily upon Wickham Steed, who had strong and definite views upon the nature of the new Europe which was to rise from the ashes of the old.* Neither did the potentiality of the new department in the field of foreign affairs escape the notice of other people who worked in it. "Your department can be either a little bureau for scattering handbills among the enemy troops or it can over-stride the Foreign Office" wrote H. G. Wells to Northcliffe.† Before deciding to take the job, Northcliffe discussed the matter with Steed who advised acceptance provided he was given a free hand in framing and executing policies subject to government approval.° The latitude thus obtained was used with considerable effectiveness. Immediately on Northcliffe's acceptance of office, Steed produced a memorandum based upon the view that propaganda should be concentrated in the first instance upon Austria–Hungary as the weaker partner in the alliance, through the encouragement of the nationalities within the empire rather than through the attempt to detach her from Germany. The principle was further elaborated in a letter to the Foreign Office on February 24th

---

* Along with R. Seton Watson, Thomas Masaryk, G. P. Gooch, H. M. Hyndman, Sir Arthur Evans, Dr Ronald Burrows, he was concerned with the founding and running of *'The New Europe'* to serve the needs of the Balkan peoples and especially the nationalities of Austria–Hungary by providing a forum for their views. The first issue, in Oct. 1916, was dedicated to 'La Victoire Integrale' namely the reconstruction of Europe on the basis of nationality and the rights of minorities.

See also R. Seton–Watson, *Masaryk in England.*

† Pound and Harmsworth, *op. cit.,* p.641.

° Steed, *op. cit.,* p.186 *et seq.*

which illustrates the process of pressure at work upon the government. "I feel that I must be placed in possession of knowledge of the policy of the Allies as to the Dual Monarchy."* This memorandum urged that the nationalities should be encouraged through the promise of freedom on the basis of consent by the governed with the ultimate aim of building up a non-German Confederation of central European and Danubian States. Whilst it was denied that this policy was specifically anti-Habsburg since the ruling house might be driven to help in the transformation of Austria–Hungary and was not anti-Catholic; the document accepted that it nevertheless implied a radical transformation of the Kingdom which it was intended to effect through the encouragement of the anti-German majority in the empire for which purpose national organisations could readily be utilised. The policy implied also the need to encourage Italy to continue to soft pedal the Treaty of London.†

Arthur Balfour's reply of 26th, whilst approving the propaganda proposals suggested that perhaps no final policy decision need yet be taken. The Cabinet was the only body, he thought, which could really decide policy towards Austria–Hungary. In his opinion encouragement to the anti-German elements in the Empire might lead to the government seeking a separate peace and to it modifying its domestic policy. Thus whether the West was seeking the dismemberment of the Empire or not was immaterial for its propaganda policy which in either case would be to support the nationalities. This answer did not satisfy Wickham Steed who provided a further draft for Northcliffe's reply of the following day. It was urgent to start propaganda to the Slavs at once in order to weaken the offensive which the Italians considered imminent. It was a suitable opportunity to get Inter-Allied agreement on the policy to be followed since allied propaganda experts were converging on London. It was essential that it

* Stuart, *op. cit.*, p.29.

† Steed at the time was playing an active role in bringing together the Italians and South Slavs; efforts which were to bear shortlived fruit in the "Pact of Rome" in April.

should be established whether Britain intended to appeal to the court or the nationalities lest propaganda issued immediately should later be opposed by a policy declaration from the government. For this reason the War Cabinet was urged not to delay a decision. It was also suggested that a public declaration on behalf of the nationalities by the allies and also by President Wilson. if at all possible, would enormously facilitate the department's task. Whilst no written reply came to this letter, the matter was discussed at the War Cabinet and a verbal ruling given that the policy of appealing to the nationalities be followed, provided no actual promise of independence was made. Although Steed felt that the Cabinet was still sitting on the fence he decided to do what he could within this context.*

The immediate stumbling bloc to a policy of appealing to the nationalities was the Treaty of London by which Italian gains made mockery of South Slav aspirations to independence and of the principle of democratic self-government. It therefore became of first importance that harmony should be obtained between these interests. An agreement of principle had been reached by the Italians and Slavs† in the early weeks of 1918 by which they had agreed to settle the territorial controversies between them amicably on the basis of the principle of nationality, the rights of people to decide their own destiny and the guarantee of the rights of minorities. Further negotiations culminated in the Congress of Oppressed Nationalities in April which publicly reaffirmed these principles in the "Pact of Rome." This document recognized the right to existence and statehood of the nationalities Italian, Polish, Rumanian, Czech and Southern Slav. It declared the Austro–Hungarian monarchy to be an instrument of German domination and a fundamental obstacle to these rights and accepted the need for a common struggle against common oppressors. Special attention was paid in the declaration to the thorny problem of conflicting interests between the Italians and

---

* See Steed, *op. cit.*, pp.187–191.
† See Stuart, *op. cit.*, p.24.

Slavs in the recognition that the unity and independence of Yugoslavia was necessary to Italy and that of Italy to Yugoslavia. A mutual pledge to see such ends attained was made whilst these two national groups agreed to settle any differences between them on the basis of the principles of nationality and self-determination and to respect minority rights.

Meanwhile at home, Northcliffe and Steed were determined not to let the momentum slacken. An Inter-Allied conference was held in London where the discussion ranged widely over the nature and possibilities of propaganda. On a more practical level, the meeting decided to create an Inter-Allied propaganda commission, with representatives of the oppressed natonalities, which should be based in Italy from whence it could attempt to disaffect enemy troops. The Conference further agreed that Steed should visit Italy to assist in the creation of this machine and participate in the Congress negotiations. His departure was marred by the last minute refusal of Balfour, at Italian instigation, to allow first Seton-Watson, and later Granville Barker, to accompany him. Although they joined him later, it appeared to Steed to be a deliberate blow, either at propaganda altogether, or at effective propaganda against Austria–Hungary.*

Whilst in Italy, Steed became aware of the fears of the Italian Military staff of the forthcoming offensive and its belief that only authoritative declarations of national independence by the Allies would have much effect in weakening the enemy will. An urgent wire to Northcliffe led to Cabinet consent to such declarations for the Czechs, Poles, South Slavs and Rumanians despite the hesitant policy of a few weeks earlier which had forbidden Northcliffe to go so far. Further reinforcement for the policy came from Lansing on 29th May who gave his official blessing to the aspirations for independence† but the joint governmental statement from France, Italy and Britain on 3rd June was robbed of much

* Steed, *op. cit.*, Vol.II, pp.197–203. It is clear he suspected 'pro-Austrian' influence in high places.

† Steed, *op. cit.*, p.213, "the nationalistic aspirations of the Czechoslovaks and Yugoslavs for freedom have the earnest sympathy of this Government".

of its effectiveness through Italian reluctance to stick to the principle which had been so hardly won from her. Whilst the declaration accepted the need for a united and independent Poland with access to the sea, it merely expressed its sympathy with the national aspirations of the Czech and Yugoslav peoples and the discrepancy did not pass unnoticed. It was not fully made good by Lansing's further statement of 29th June declaring United States support for Slav liberation, "all branches of the Slav race should be completely freed from German and Austrian rule".* Considered as a principle it is increasingly evident that allied policy was veering towards "constructive liberation"† in the empire. In practice, the application of this principle was less clear cut if only because Italian objections prevented its full exploitation by the propaganda machine but, as an influence upon the British government to adopt a particular line of policy, the men responsible for propaganda were clearly devoted towards an attempt to commit Great Britain to the championship of a peace settlement which would incorporate the principle of nationality.

II

Propaganda against Germany posed an even starker problem of definition concerning the nature of the war for it raised the issue of whether it was to be considered as a moral struggle leading to a new world where war would no longer be thinkable and in which a reformed Germany might have an honoured and respected place or as a traditional struggle which could decently be brought to an end on the basis of a bargain when both sides had had enough. The former view increasingly looked upon the war as a crusade which must continue until satisfactory evidence of a purified Germany was forthcoming. If this meant unconditional surrender, so be it. The latter, tired of the seemingly endless and pointless struggle, thought of a negotiated peace.

* Steed, *op. cit.*, p.215.
† Stuart, *op. cit.*, p.46.

It so happened that opinion within the propaganda machine lay on the side of those who viewed the struggle in ideological or moral terms. "The fight for democracy" and the "rule of law" and "the principle of nationality" were ranged against 'Prussian militarism' which necessitated the ostracism of Germany until it was clear that she had purged herself and had "atoned" for the wrong she had done to the international comity. The need to explain such phrases in concrete terms that could be used as an appeal to the Germans also served to explain to the British themselves what they were fighting for.

Emboldened by the success Crewe House had achieved on the Austrian front, on 16th May 1918.* Lloyd George asked Northcliffe if it would be possible for him to attempt a similar attack on the morale of German troops. The memorandum on policy towards Germany was on this occasion the work of H.G. Wells and it can be seen how he in turn utilised his opportunity to put forward his own views on the nature of the peace with Germany and the creation of the League of Nations.

The Wells document stressed the need for a clear, allied policy as the basis of propaganda to Germany, previous attempts to influence the enemy having suffered, in his view, from a looseness of definition which had made them meaningless to the Germans. He suggested that the real allied aim was to establish world peace of such a nature that the resumption of war would in future be precluded and thus the first objective of propaganda would be to delineate the world settlement that would be entailed together with the German place within it. Wells considered it essential that the Germans be convinced of the determination of the Allies to continue the war until she was prepared to accept the Allied peace settlement. Thus she would have to be told that the Allies were prepared to deepen and extend their solidarity and to pool their resources in an ever intensified effort. More precisely, he suggested that since the Germans were susceptible to systematic statements a definite counterpart to the dream of Mittel-Europa

* Stuart, *op. cit.*, p.50.

be provided for them and that in order to do this there was a great need to study and lay down the lines of a practical League of Free Nations of which the alliance would form the nucleus and from which enemies could be exluded until they had rejected their predatory rulers. It could be shown that the Allies were not against the people who, if they could show their will to co-operate, would be welcomed in the new world created to express the principle of self-determination and which would guarantee justice and fair play. If, however, they were not prepared to reject the barbarism of their rulers, it must be made clear they would have nothing to look forward to but permanent ruin. Thus the primary war aim of the Allies was in fact to "change Germany" and here the interests of the German people and the Allies coincided. To do this properly, a definite statement of Allied war aims was essential as a framework for propaganda work "A full statement of the war aims of the Allies is vitally necessary." The world was anxious to know what was going to happen after the war and what sort of peace the Allies were seeking, whilst their capacity to determine the nature of the peace should capitalise the enormous desire outside the central powers for a peaceful world. War aims should increasingly be concerned with ways and means of doing this and with the creation of a League of Free Nations to ensure it.

Wells continued by setting out his own ideas on representation and urging the need of decision on them.

He accepted the ideal of a universal organisation including Germany "purged of her military aggressiveness" which would include some form of Congress to amend and develop International Law, control arms, control expansion and deal with problems of international economics. Both Great Britain and France he considered now ready to limit their sovereignity for the sake of peace and to accept their imperial responsibilities as a trust which would lead to ultimate independence. At any rate at first, the five or six great Powers* should have a greater voice.

---

* United States, Great Britain, France, Germany, Japan and, doubtfully, Austria-Hungary.

The institution of a League would preclude any annexations or military adventures without a mandate from it. It would become the guardian of all unsettled regions and promote developments in derelict areas whether it worked directly or through a mandatory.

With regard to the territorial settlement, the Allies were honour bound to France over Alsace–Lorraine and the incorporation of Italian-speaking peoples of the empire into Italy would be a necessary part of world pacification. But of far more importance than the transfer of territory from one state to another was that the practical ascendancy of German Imperialism over the resources of Eastern Europe should cease and that her African empire should be transformed under some international arrangement.

A great stress is to be found in this document on disarmament and the general need for economic reconstruction, as an international effort to bypass revenge, hostility and to contribute to economic welfare. In this, German co-operation would be essential but it would be useless to expect it from any but a changed Germany. Wherever possible therefore the appeal must be to the ordinary German and his potential reasonableness whilst fighting "Junker Germany" until defeated.*

This line of argument was closely followed by Steed's articles in *The Times.* "It is essential that any step towards the realisation of the somewhat ill-defined ideal expressed by the phrase "a League of Nations" should start from the premise that an effective League of Allied Nations already exists and is tending constantly to grow and to become a more efficient instrument for the defence of justice and right. While it is clear that the complete attainment of this ideal must involve the eventual inclusion in it of States and peoples now hostile, it is equally clear that their inclusion is inconceivable until they have been compelled, by the force of Allied arms, the weight of Allied economic pressure, and the inherent moral strength of the Allied cause, to renounce their insensate dreams of world domination, to bring forth fruits meet

* This document is quoted in full in Stuart, *op. cit.*, pp.61–81.

for repentance and to qualify for readmission to the comity of civilised peoples. The Allied war aims and the Allied peace terms are not vindictive, but just. They aim at building up on sure foundations a system of ordered and world-wide freedom that shall supersede and render impossible any hegemony of militarist *Kultur*. A true Allied peace offensive would make this fundamental fact known to enemy nations, and would cause them to reflect upon the wickedness and the folly of courting utter ruin for the sake of the obsolete dreams of predatory dynasties."* "The German people need to understand two main truths. The first is that while the Allied conception of a League of Nations contemplates ultimately the inclusion in it of a regenerate Germany, it contemplates also the maintenance of an absolute economic ban upon Germany and her vassals until they have relinquished, clearly and convincingly, their present political and military institutions and the dreams that still inspire them. The second is that the longer the war lasts the deeper will be the detestation of everything German in Allied countries and the heavier the moral and economic handicap under which all Germans will labour, even it they qualify for readmission into the society of civilised peoples."†

Mr Wells' memorandum formed the basis for a letter sent by Northcliffe to Balfour in which the need for an authoritative statement of war aims was explained and the general lines of the approach to Germany detailed. Propaganda to Germany must be in harmony with the settled aims of the Allies. "The object of all propaganda is to weaken the will of the enemy to war and victory" and this could be done through the nature of Allied war aims and their thorough explanation to the enemy. If they were presented in suitable form, our war aims might well help to strengthen any opposition which existed inside Germany. The knowledge gleaned of conditions in Germany seemed to show that the German people were extremely anxious for an ending of the

* 17th May 1918.
† 30th May 1918.

war and that they were experiencing both greater suffering and war weariness than Allied populations. Up till now they had accepted the view of their leaders that the only way to a speedy victory was through military success but this belief could be destroyed through impressing upon them that the Allies had an immutable will to continue the war at whatever cost and that, military victory or no, they would continue to experience a ruthless, commercial blockade. Economic ruin would face Germany if she continued with her avowed aim to subject other free nations to German domination but she could avoid this fate if the German people would accept the allied scheme for a "new organisation of the world". Hitherto, continued Northcliffe, war aims had been defined too loosely to be comprehensible to the Germans and there had been apparent inconsistencies of which they had been quick to take advantage. It was in fact possible for German writers to misrepresent allied war aims as imperialistic whereas the real object after defeating Germany was, he assumed, the establishment of a world peace which, as far as possible, would preclude war. Any particular aims, such as the restoration of Belgium would need to be put forwards as part of the overall general scheme. This plan would amount to the constitution of a League of Free Nations which, presumably, Germany might join if she accepted the principles and which in turn would be her guarantee of any hostile acts against her in the future. Thus Allied terms of peace were the conditions upon which Germany might enter the League. Her economic position after the war would, in consequence, depend upon her acceptance of its political conditions.

If such a statement could be taken as the basis of Allied policy towards Germany, then the task of propaganda would be much lightened since it was a positive programme which could be directed towards the moderate elements in Germany rather than a list of terms to be imposed upon a defeated enemy.

Finally, propaganda upon such constructive lines was unlikely to be of much use unless it was supported by public and authoritative statements at Allied governmental level, otherwise the

Germans would fear a trick. He thus urged most strongly the need for a policy statement*.

Shortly afterwards, a further letter dealt with the problem of the German colonies. Northcliffe expressed the view that it was premature to suggest a final settlement but that in broad terms they constituted a problem which either the Allies would be entitled to decide or which could be reserved for the general League of Nations at a later date.†

Both these letters arrived at the War Cabinet and were given official approval° but did not impel the authoritative statement for which Northcliffe had asked.

The theory of German responsibility for the war and the need to defeat her before the question of peace arose was thus axiomatic to Northcliffe and his colleagues, and inevitable therefore that they should react adversely to rumours and suggestions of a negotiated peace. Whilst the peace movement during the last weeks of 1917, as symbolised by the Landsdowne letter, had failed to ripen, it had reflected and interested much opinion in the country which had not yet given up hope of bringing the war to a speedy and less bloody end. The summer of 1918 brought further rumblings in this direction and the report to Steed that not only were some members of the War Cabinet in favour of the notion but that the Prime Minister himself was prepared to discuss it privately. Lansdowne was thought to have a second letter drafted and to rate his chances pretty high because of influential support at the highest level. All he was waiting for was "the occasion".+ The essence of the scheme was thought to be a bargain with Germany at Russia's expense and the most important member of the Cabinet behind it was Lord Milner. Steed's informant was Clifford Sharp× who wrote to say that he considered the War Cabinet as a whole was suffering from loss of nerve and its

* A full text of this letter is in *The Times History of the War*, Vol.21, p.342 *et seq.*

† See Steed, *op. cit.*, Vol.II, p.224 for an extract from this letter.

° Steed, *op cit.*, p.224.

\+ Steed, *op. cit.*, Vol.II, p.217.

× His letter is printed in *The Times History*, p.360.

leading members in particular suffering from cold feet. In contrast he had found that public opinion was "amazingly healthy".

Steed at once sent this letter to Northcliffe, Balfour and Hughes, the Prime Minister of Australia, all of whom could be relied upon to have "a sound" reaction. Balfour reported that the letter appalled him, Northcliffe was scandalised and an article of Steed's appeared in the *Daily Mail* of 18th June. Headed "Watch Lansdowne and others" it asserted that to make such a deal with Germany would be treachery.* Whils the matter was swallowed up in the Allied breakthrough which shortly followed, there can be no mistake about the policy desired by the propagandists or the direction in which their influence was asserted in the matter of war and peace.

III

Closely associated with propaganda directly to the nationalities within the empire was the question of that which should go to the Balkans generally, where the conflicting interests which had prevented the formation of a Balkan league behoved Great Britain to tread warily when advocating policies which might not be universally desired. Any wooing of Bulgaria, for example, in order to undermine enemy morale, ran the almost certain risk of offending Serbia, Rumania or Greece whilst propaganda towards the latter depended, not only on Allied policy towards Bulgaria, but also on that for Austria–Hungary. Thus on 25th May 1918, Northcliffe wrote to Balfour† urging the necessity for a definite policy for these areas in order that propaganda towards Bulgaria might begin. It was necessary, he considered, to avoid outright bribes to Bulgaria which would inevitably descend into competitive bargaining with the central powers and which would offend the Balkan allies. The memorandum suggested that the basic aim should be of a lasting territorial and political settlement on lines

* Steed, *op. cit.*, Vol.II, p.219 gives the text.
† Stuart, *op. cit.*, p.135.

of ethnography which could lead ultimately to a permanent league; such a policy contained the immediate difficulty that in order to be ethnographically whole, areas previously held by Serbia, Greece and Rumania would have to be ceded to Bulgaria and the only way in which their consent could properly be obtained would be to cede to them in turn those areas of Slav, Greek or Rumanian populations now in enemy hands. Whilst this necessitated the Allies adopting a policy of racial unity and independence, certain problems would arise in fulfilling it absolutely. In particular, economic and strategic injustice to Serbia and Greece might well result if Bulgarian ethnic claims in Macedonia were entirely fulfilled or to Bulgaria if Greece retained Salonika and Kavalla. Some form of international guarantee might be needed to secure these rights. Should Greece and Serbia refuse to countenance these concessions to Bulgaria perhaps an independent Macedonia could be created. In any case the necessary ethnographic delimitation should be done by a competent Allied commission. If such a policy could be agreed then Bulgaria could be told of it and informed that if she accepted, financial and economic support would be forthcoming from the Allies. If she rejected, ruin would surely follow. If Bulgaria refrained from further co-operation with the enemy then she could be told she would get the Enos–Midia line as a minimum; if she actively co-operated with the allies then she might be rewarded with an even better frontier, namely the Midia–Rodosto line. The inclusion of Silistua should also be made dependent on her behaviour.

On 6th June 1918 Balfour replied expressing his agreement with the general lines of policy there laid out but suggesting that the ethnographical issues should be played down until Allied policy in the area was more certain. He suggested propaganda should concentrate on the awfulness of the fate awaiting Bulgaria if she did not cease active enmity against the entente. In particular Bulgaria should be urged to expel Ferdinand, break off relations with Germany, establish democratic government and re-orientate Bulgarian policy towards a Balkan confederation under Allied aegis.

This reply was not, of course, entirely satisfactory for it confined propaganda to telling Bulgaria to "be good or else". A clear-cut policy was at this stage impossible for the Allies had not yet determined what their policy was to be in an area where the Italians were slipping away from the implementation of Serbian claims and the Serb and Greek suspicions of Allied policy once more aroused. That summer, Bulgaria had made secret overtures for peace but British policy was to refuse to respond to them until Bulgaria had given proof of her new policy. Even so, Serbia and Greece both had to be re-assured that Bulgaria was not about to benefit at their expense.* Once again, propaganda was prevented from its fullest development through the lack of a definite proposition to put before the Bulgars for their consideration.†

Propaganda had been entrusted to large-thinking men with definite ideas of their own both on war-policy and the role of the instrument which had been handed to them. They were thus bound to feel the need to enlarge the scope and importance of their work. One of their first felt requirements was of the need for greater unity among the Allies in their propaganda services. Steed perhaps, in particular, was conscious of the possibilities open to them to display to the world the allied view of the basic problems before mankind. Economic policies, international law, the new league of nations were all matters for serious and urgent study for which an "international Thinking General Staff" was badly needed. Whilst the creation of a permanent Inter-Allied body of true effectiveness was largely overtaken by the ending of the war, considerable strides were taken to co-ordinate and articulate allied policies through a series of Inter-Allied conferences.

The first major Inter-Allied meeting on propaganda assembled in London in February 1918 for far-reaching discussion of the nature of the war, the type of peace that should properly follow and the question of responsibility for the war since such topics

---

* Steed, *op. cit.*, p.229.

† The policy of "bribing Balkan bandits" defeated others than Grey.

could well form the basis for propaganda to the enemy. The recognition that development was dependent upon government policy and thus the need to press for such policy where it was lacking was almost inevitable and, as has been shown, the British element was not slow in implementing this belief during the ensuing months.

The successes which propaganda claimed for itself, the rapidly developing situation in the Balkans and the irritations felt through lack of a proper formulation of war aims lay behind a second allied conference called at Crewe House for 14th August 1918. It is clear that by now those who were concerned with propaganda had really got the bit between their teeth and were exhilarated at the potentialities their work contained. Discussion ranged over a wide plethora of issues. Once again it was urged that policy towards the enemy must be defined before propaganda could be fully effective. It was suggested that such policy should be for a "changed Germany"; that plans for a comprehensive world organisation should be worked out and for the greater co-ordination of Allied and American economic policy. Since the conference wished to undertake a further propaganda offensive against Austria–Hungary again it pleaded for the definition of policy towards the nationalities, and for an Allied declaration thereof. It declared itself in favour of a free Poland and the return of Alsace–Lorraine as a principle of international justice. As a matter of immediate urgency, the delegates found themselves yet again involved in the issues between the South Slavs and the Italians and the opportunity was taken to exert pressure on the latter to make a public declaration of acceptance of a free Yugo-Slav State.* In addition, the conference set about creating effective Inter-Allied machinery for better co-ordination of the work and was addressed by Northcliffe on the potentialities of propaganda not only as a war-winning but as a peace-making instrument. Here lay the seeds of the development of Northcliffe the peace maker which was to bring him into disfavour with Lloyd George.

* Such a declaration was issued on 26th Sept.

The British delegation to this conference had been an inter-departmental one with representatives from the Department of Propaganda, the Admiralty, the War Office, the Air Ministry, the Foreign Office and the Ministry of Information, and one result of the meeting was the creation of an inter-departmental committee with the mandate to formulate peace proposals acceptable to those departments and organisations at home which considered themselves entitled to make their opinions heard. This committee grew from a suggestion of the British General Staff* and represented the War Cabinet, the Admiralty, the War Office, the Foreign Office, the Treasury, the Air Ministry, the Colonial Office, the India Office, the Ministry of Information, the National War Aims Committee and the Press Bureau. A Crewe House sub-committee drafted their accepted peace programme. This document started with the belief that peace was dependent upon a clear understanding that Germany accepted certain principles as fundamental and upon the known willingness of the German people to co-operate in establishing the peace. The non-negotiable elements of peace included the restoration of Belgium, the freeing of French territory, the reconstruction of the invaded territories, compensation for civilian losses and injuries and the restoration of Alsace–Lorraine. The liability to replace the damage to merchant shipping through the use of unrestricted submarine warfare would have to be accepted by Germany, as also the intention to create an international tribunal for the trial of individuals accused of offences against the laws of war or humanity. Germany would have to lose her colonies because of her illegal aggression against Belgium. Other matters could fairly be subject to negotiation with the enemy, notably other claims for damage, the constitution and form of the League of Nations and the creation of a world of opportunity and security for the legitimate development of all.

Certain other particular matters were discussed. It was suggested that the northern frontiers of Italy should be readjusted along the lines of nationality wherever possible and that the

* Steed, *op. cit.*, p.242.

peoples of Austria–Hungary had the right to unite with their fellows beyond the frontiers of the empire. Russia would have to be evacuated by enemy forces and the appropriate agreements annulled. Poland should become independent, should include territories predominantly Polish, have access to the sea and be given an indemnity. As far as possible, Turkish rule over non-Turkish peoples should be removed and Rumania, Serbia and Montenegro restored and evacuated. The Associated Powers might well give their assistance in settling Balkan questions on an equitable basis.

It is clear from Steed's account* that the Prime Minister was not attracted to the proposal that he should bind himself to such a document before the Peace Conference had even begun. His argument that it usurped the functions of government and decided principles which properly belonged to the field of Allied responsibility was not unreasonable in a war-time Premier presented with a blue-print for the peace he was so shortly going to help to make. His annoyance no doubt combined with his unwillingness to tie his hands too closely in matters of policy at that stage of the war and his natural dislike of feeling that his hand was being forced. He nevertheless sanctioned its use for propaganda purposes provided Balfour approved its contents. With one amendment it proved acceptable to the Foreign Secretary and each department then adapted it to its own needs.

This document played its part in the breach between Northcliffe and Lloyd George which was now imminent but its purpose in this context is rather to show how the need for propaganda contained an impulse towards the determination of the peace. From the start it had not proved possible to separate war-time efforts of propaganda from the most fundamental problems concerning the nature of the struggle and thus the closing stages of the war saw an increasing preoccupation by the propagandists with the peace settlement and their desire to use the machine, which had been working so successfully in war, to put over the

---

* Steed, *op. cit.*, p.244 *et seq.*

country's views on peace. According to his latest biographers* Northcliffe was already hankering after regaining his independence as early as March 1918 by which time he had become increasingly critical of the government. On 19th April he resigned, but was persuaded by Lloyd George to stay on until someone else could be found as a replacement. Whilst Northcliffe agreed, his dissatisfaction continued. It seems clear that he wished to win for the machinery which had been created the official duty of keeping the British public informed of the deliberations of the Peace Conference, and of disseminating knowledge of the essential conditions of peace and of peace terms propaganda in collaboration with the Departments of State,† and this claim was in any case unacceptable to the Prime Minister. Thus the publication of "Northcliffe's peace terms" even though they were based upon a document officially approved and however "fair minded and moderately phrased" "could not fail to appear to the Prime Minister and others as a piece of blatant egoism and as an attempt to force his hand and dominate the British Peace Delegation from outside".°

Lord Riddell became responsible for publicity arrangements at Paris.

IV

Out of the development and expansion of the blockade and the deepening of the war was born the conception of a coherent economic policy in which the state would play a more constructive part than in pre-war days. At first, this was largely seen in terms of more effective economic pressure upon the central powers but, after two years of war, attention moved towards the possible form the post-war world might assume and the British place within it. Such speculation and planning was very often seen in terms of the continuance into the peace of the war-time alliance system in

* Pound and Harmsworth, *op. cit.*, p.627.
† *The Times History*, pp.385–6.
° *The Times History*, p.391.

which Germany would still be treated as an enemy. The modification of traditional trading patterns, the limitations on shipping space, financial and commercial restrictions and the pattern of joint Allied purchases of materials all meant that a controlled process of adjustment would be necessary when the war came to an end and one compelling problem was seen to be the post-war treatment to be accorded to enemy countries and whether their traders were to be allowed access to raw materials and markets on equal terms. Of similar concern was the question of whether to attempt consciously to develop imperial trade now that the Empire was becoming a more self-conscious community, of whether mutual support between the Allies should properly be expected or the encouragement and assistance which might be given by the state to British exporters when the war was over. During 1916, a Board of Trade committee began to study this last question* and its report indicated that large sections of British industry now favoured government support and sponsorship whilst the belief that Germany and Austria would be able to flood markets with supplies of cheap goods immediately the war came to an end seems to have been widespread. The desire to meet the needs of home industry and the interest in post-war co-operation with the allies for mutual benefit fused with the realisation that economic resources had to be fully utilised for the prosecution of the war to create the concept of an economic alliance, extending into the peace and implying little or no economic communication with the enemy. Considerable discussion along these lines is evident by the middle of the war and it gave rise to a certain pressure for more formidable governmental action.† The danger that this would arouse old party controversies on trade and tariffs was now felt less important than that the government should accept what were coming to be widely felt as its proper responsibilities. Whilst

* Report of a sub-committee of the Advisory Committee to the Board of Trade on Commercial Intelligence with respect to measures for securing the position, after the war, of certain branches of British industry. The findings are to be found in Cd. 8181 and the evidence of the firms approached in Cd. 8275.

† See e.g. Budget debate, 4-4-16. *Hansard,* Vol.81, Col.1049 onwards.

it is obvious that the government would not wish to pronounce upon a far-reaching economic policy for the country without very considerable reflection, it is clear that it was prepared, by the beginning of 1916, to envisage a much enlarged governmental role than had hitherto pertained. Official recognition was made of the impossibility of return to the *laissez-faire* ideal of pre-1914 and that, if only in self-defence, certain elements of British industry would in future validly be able to claim protection.*

The need for some special economic assistance after the war was felt particularly strongly in France in view of the physical damage she had suffered in comparison with Germany and it was thus her initiative which led to the decision in the spring of 1916 to hold an Inter-Allied economic conference and this focussed much debate on economic policy. It was announced on 21st March that the President of the Board of Trade was to be the chief British representative, accompanied by Mr Hughes, the Prime Minister of Australia and Mr Bonar Law as Secretary of State for the Colonies; the composition of the delegation giving point to the possibility of an imperial setting for trading policy when the war was over and certainly foreshadowing the removal of the reparations problem from the sphere of traditional diplomacy.

It most not be supposed, however, that the needs of the current situation were overlooked. It was to be "A conference for the education of the Allied Governments in the economic meaning of the war. ... an economic counterpart to the London Pact of September 1914" was now necessary wrote *The Times* Paris correspondent on the eve of its opening.†

The resolution° of the Allies from the Paris Conference must be seen within the framework of their determination to give a practical expression to their solidarity of views and interests.

---

* See e.g. Debate 23–3–16. *Hansard,* Vol.81, Col.503 onwards. Also 18–5–16 for A. Chamberlain's acceptance on behalf of the government of the impossibility of laissez-faire. *Hansard,* Vol.82, Col.1680.

† 14th June 1916.

° Cd. 8271.

They fall into three parts. The first and simplest dealt with the tightening up of Allied blockading policies and the provision of greater uniformity in Allied action based upon the principle of the complete prohibition of trading contacts. In particular it was intended that exports to neutrals should in future depend upon satisfactory guarantees concerning the destination of goods. This determination was of more consequence for those members of the alliance who had not been as vigorous as its two major members in blockading policies and for Britain herself the major necessity was an extension of the black list, but it perhaps symbolised government recognition of the fact that "in this struggle economic considerations are as vital as purely military or naval measures".* The second section referred to the transitory post-war period in which the rehabilitation of the devastated areas was to have a first priority. It was anticipated that during this time the allies would give each other mutual assistance in meeting needs for raw materials, that Germany would be excluded from any most-favoured-nation arrangements and might indeed continue to suffer even after the reconstruction period was over since the allies would be entitled to make permanent arrangements. Finally, enemy commerce and shipping would be subject to special regulations. For the permanent post-war world, the Allies were to decide what steps they would wish to take to render themselves independent of enemy countries in raw materials, to allow for the development of manufacturing industries deemed essential for their economic well being and to strengthen their financial, commercial and maritime organisations. In order to fulfill these objects permanent machinery for interallied assistance and collaboration was envisaged whilst state activities to assist industry, such as subsidy, duties and financial assistance for research and development was recognised to be necessary and acceptable. Over the whole rested the belief that the central powers were in the process of preparing for a conflict on the economic plane which would survive into the peace and indeed would then attain its full scope

* Lord Robert Cecil, *The Times,* 3rd Sept. 1917.

and intensity. Such action would place an intolerable yoke on other countries and "in face of so grave a peril the representatives of the Allied governments consider that it has become their duty, on grounds of necessary and legitimate defence, to adopt and realise from now onward all the measures requisite on the one hand to secure for themselves and for the whole of the markets of neutral countries full economic independence and respect for sound commercial practice, and on the other hand to facilitate the organisation on a permanent basis of their economic alliance".*

The implication of a document worded in such a way could well be thought to be some form of grand economic union when the war was over and, as such, was bound to arouse the suspicion of those who were outside its provision.† The idea of an economic boycott of Germany was not in fact fully acceptable to the allies themselves even at the time of signature and the Russians in particular at once made sweeping reservations. This was much to the relief of the British Foreign Minister and some of his officials to whom the policy appeared impracticable. "Personally, I have no great faith in the efficacy of the Paris resolutions (wrote Sir Victor Wellesley) if only for the simple reason that general agreement as to the manner in which effect should be given to them is impossible of attainment. The reservations which the Russian government make in the draft declaration are so wide as to enable any of the signatory powers to drive a coach and four through the resolutions. . . . To this Lord Grey added: I am in favour of all possible restrictions to German trade during the war; I do not believe in artificial restraints after the war."°

These private doubts were supported publicly. Simon was the most formidable opponent of the punitive philosophy in the Commons for he doubted firstly whether Germany was either willing for, or able to, pursue economic warfare in the unforseeable future and secondly whether British trading interests were really best served by an abandonment of a true multilateral solution to

* Preamble to the resolutions, Cd. 8271.
† e.g. America.
° Bell, *op. cit.*, p.557.

economic problems. He was supported by Philip Snowden who was also capable of rising above war-time feeling. Free trade, he thought, was still the basis of British strength whilst war-time alliances did not normally last long into the peace. He suggested that peaceful international relations were bound to be injured if based on hatred and enmity.

The dangers for British trade in cutting Germany off from international development were also stressed outside Parliament. The *Daily News,* whilst accepting the need for Allied collaboration and government encouragement for industry, did not welcome the negative and hostile side of the pronouncement*. The *Economist* also disapproved of the complete ostracism of Germany after the war.† Not only did it consider this impracticable but the paper considered it wrong that the peace should be based on passion, although it was all for a rational discussion of peace terms and the nature of the post-war world.°

The implementation of such principles could not be otherwise than a most far-reaching matter. As Mr Hughes himself recognised, it would affect and possibly fundamentally change the trading and economic relations of 600 million people. The consequence of the government's approval of the resolutions + was a considerable increase in political activity to discuss and elaborate them further. Already there was both a committee advising the Board of Trade on commercial and financial problems and a Cabinet Committee dealing generally with questions of reconstruction which included commercial and industrial policy + and in consequence of the Paris conference was added to them a number of specialist committees within the Board of Trade, whilst Lord Balfour of Burleigh's Reconstruction Committee was asked to

* 21st June 1916.

† 17th June 1916.

° Indeed the *Economist* considered that it was time to discuss the ending of the war and carried at the time a correspondence initiated by Lord Loreburn directed to this purpose.

\+ Prime Minister, 12–7–16. *Hansard,* Vol.84, Col.342.

× Statements in Commons, 13–4–16, Vol.81, Col.1982. 19–4–16. Vol.81, Col.2335.

report on post-war commercial policy including the resolutions of the Paris economic conference with the object of calling an imperial conference to discuss the whole matter.

Further evidence of the Board of Trade's serious intentions was given by its President on 20th March 1917 in his announcement to the Association of Chambers of Commerce that a British Trade Corporation was to be created and that his department intended to increase its activities in order to assist in the work of promoting British trade.

Such developments posed in a clear fashion the problem of the interest and concern of the Foreign Service in the country's trade. Whilst it is tenable to argue that before the war it had shown little enthusiasm in, or knowledge of, the problems of British traders, in part this was a reflection of the lack of any positive governmental policy for it to pursue. The war not only provided such political direction but brought the department into close working relations with business men from Britain and from overseas. This experience it found welcome for it is not to be supposed that the Foreign Service was utterly insulated from the thoughts and opinions current in the wider world or that it was unaffected by the desire to abandon that which was sterile in the old diplomacy for the pursuit of the true and non-aggressive interests of the country as a whole. The Foreign Office, we are told had found in its blockade work "a more satisfying field of activity and a more tangible touch with realities and personalities than had been afforded by the political moves and counter-moves of an older diplomacy".*

This is reflected in the report of an internal Foreign Office Committee† set up in 1916 to examine the appropriate form of government organisation to promote and assist British trade after the war. The sentiments of this Committee express a point of view concerning trade far removed from the lofty indifference which many had detected in the service in earlier years. Now it

* Percy, *Some Memories,* p.147.
† Cd.8715 contains this report.

was accepted that commercial matters were an integral and important part of general foreign policy and that the country was committed to "a national trade policy which will enter largely into the conduct of any foreign relations and may dominate them"*. Before the war, the essentially *laissez-faire* context in which British trade had operated had not been favourable to the development of state assistance to the business community. "Not only has this country omitted to create or use fully adequate channels of information, but other functions also of an efficient commercial intelligence organisation, such as the rendering of active diplomatic assistance in obtaining commercial or industrial concessions, or in obtaining orders for British supplies in connection with loans for foreign states, have been rarely exercised except to some degree of recent years."† If in the post-war world the fundamental approach to trade was to be different then a necessary corollary would be an improved statutory arrangement to provide coherent and adequate help.

A Foreign Office Committee could hardly be expected to recommend other than that the Foreign Office was the proper department to be charged with this responsibility since interstate relations must be "treated as a unit and conducted as a whole".° If trade was a part of foreign policy its agents must be part of the Foreign Service through the creation of a home "department of the Foreign Office on large lines worthy of its importance",+ and the development of the system of commercial attachés and of the consular service on more appropriate lines. Furthermore, the Foreign Service as a whole could be expected to have a different role in and attitude towards trade than heretofore. "In future the instructions issued to our diplomatists must place trade and finance in a different relation to general policy than was the case before the war, and their action in regard to such matters will therefore take on a new character. Trade and finance can no

* para. 16.
† para. 10.
° para. 3.
\+ para. 18.

longer be things apart, outside the sphere of their general diplomatic work. Trade and finance must become an essential subject of their study.* The way for this has been prepared and the attitude of the foreign service has already been radically altered by the work done, the experience gained, and the information collected during the war, and it is therefore a question of maintaining and extending tendencies already fairly well established."†

Whilst the Committee adumbrated the details of organisation, the Board of Trade was prepared to fight for its position. Out of a Cabinet tussle between Runciman and a "somewhat bewildered Grey"° emerged a brief minute of 3rd October 1916+ anticipating the replacement of commercial attachés by trade commissioners who, whilst part of the diplomatic staff, should receive their instructions from the Board of Trade. On the other hand the heads of missions might suspend such instructions when necessary for reasons of policy. This peculiar arrangement did not even constitute an armistice between the two departments and in the following January the new Foreign Minister and President of the Board of Trade set up a further committee "to enquire into the best form of organisation for promoting our foreign trade through representatives abroad, including the consular service and, in particular, to consider whether the agreement [i.e. 3rd Oct. 1916] requires any and what amendment or alteration".× This Committee consisted of Lord Faringdon and Mr Docker representing the Federation of British Industries, Mr Pennefather M.P. for the Associated Chambers of Commerce, and a representative from the Board of Trade and the Foreign Office respectively. Unfortunately the report of this committee reflected the perennial dilemma. Three were broadly for the implementation of the Foreign Ofice recommendations whilst the Chairman and the Board of Trade representative favoured the home department.

* The Committee was apparently willing for diplomats to be instructed by the London School of Economics.

† para. 17.

° Percy, *op. cit.*, p.147.

+ In Cd. 8715.

× Cd. 8715.

The minority accepted the need for an extended commercial attaché system, under whatever name, as part of the Diplomatic Service. Its personnel should be appointed by the Foreign Secretary but after consultation with the Board of Trade which should be "a reality".* Such attachés should not be bogged down with routine commercial work at the missions or with inspection of the consular service. At home, however, "it is essential, both to sound administration and to the convenience of the commercial community, that there should be in this country a single department charged with the compilation and distribution of commercial intelligence, from whatever source it is obtained. The manufacturing and trading interests of this country in Imperial and foreign markets overseas cannot be absolutely separated, and to compel the British manufacturer or trader to seek information and advice as regards overseas trade from two separate departments, which would inevitably tend to work upon different lines and by different methods, would lead to serious inconvenience and waste of effort. Similarly, we do not believe that in connection with commercial intelligence work a distinction can satisfactorily be drawn between domestic and foreign trade. The Board of Trade is the only Department of Government which is in a position to acquire the necessary knowledge of industrial requirements and industrial capabilities in the United Kingdom. . . . The Department primarily responsible for the trade interests of the country as a whole is the Board of Trade, which cannot divorce itself from interest in, and responsibility for, the promotion of British commercial interests in foreign markets. [If the Foreign Office were responsible] the Government might often receive conflicting advice from two Departments, each claiming to represent the commercial community. In the light of these considerations, it is our opinion that the proposals put forward by the Foreign Office Committee would be likely not only to cause inconvenience to the commercial community in this country, but also to lead to serious friction and embarrassment in departmental administration."†

* para. 5.
† paras. 13, 14, 16, 17.

Out of this battle emerged the inevitable compromise. In September 1917 plans were announced for the creation of a Department of Overseas Trade to be formed by the fusion of the Commercial Intelligence Department of the Board of Trade and the Foreign Trade Department of the Foreign Office together with such elements of the War Trade Intelligence and the War Trade Statistical Departments as were considered appropriate. This department was to be under the control of Sir Arthur Steel-Maitland as Parliamentary Secretary, in a dual role of responsibility to the President of the Board of Trade and to the Secretary of State for Foreign Affairs. The Controller-General* was appointed jointly, whilst an Advisory Committee of business men was to keep the department in touch with the needs of industry at home. The new department was intended essentially as a gleaner of commercial intelligence and thus intended to be in part the source of instructions for personnel overseas and be responsible for keeping them in touch with the commercial classes at home. It was also to train the Trade Commissioners and to provide a short spell of experience for entrants into the Diplomatic and Consular Services. Whilst the Board of Trade retained the responsibility for the appointment and control of Trade Commissioners with the empire, the Foreign Office similarly retained the commercial attachés, and the consular service. Instructions to them, or the Diplomatic Service proper, were to be channelled through the Foreign Office which retained its commercial and consular departments. It was intended that there would be a constant interchange of staff between the new department and its two parents and that recruitment could also come from the commercial attachés, consuls and men of business experience.†

It is clear that such an arrangement could solve nothing and that it is best viewed as a postponement of any fundamental decision whilst perpetuating the frustrations of the civil servants. Indeed one might well argue that on this level it had but made

* The first holder is best described as a Board of Trade man with strong Diplomatic Service associations.

† See *The Times*, 15th Sept. 1917.

matters worse by spreading them over three departments instead of two. The lack of a definite economic policy at governmental level giving the new department clear cut direction prevented its firm establishment in the official hierarchy and in consequence it fell increasingly into a backwater. Isolated from the Foreign Office it could neither receive the support of an older, more powerful department nor provide in its turn that effective contact with reality which the Foreign Office required. Whilst relevant information from the embassies could not be certain of reaching, and of being used by, the new department and its clients, neither was diplomacy improved by the greater association with commercial matters. "Never have diplomatists and consuls felt themselves more out of touch than at the present moment with the economic condition of the country whose interests they are supposed to be serving".* Long years afterwards, Tyrell too drew attention to the harmful psychological effect the creation of the Department of Overseas Trade had had upon the Foreign Office and which had deprived it of one of its chief functions.† The resignation of Sir Arthur Steel-Maitland in 1919 because he felt the Board of Trade was being unduly obstructive of his department's development merely pinpointed a problem which had never fully been considered.

* E. Percy, *The New Europe,* 15th May 1919.
† House of Lords, *Hansard,* Vol.126, Cols.970–1. 30th March 1943.

CHAPTER 7

ANGLO–AMERICAN RELATIONS

SOME of the wider influences necessitating re-consideration of the content and handling of foreign affairs have now been discussed, but it is also beneficial to see how the matter appeared from the viewpoint of the day to day handling of external relations. This chapter is therefore devoted to a discussion of some of the business that concerned America and Britain during war-time with particular reference to the year 1917; a time when the substance of diplomacy was changing rapidly and for which considerable information is available.

Anglo–American relations are not unique in that the atmosphere which surrounds their conduct is important for this is true of all negotiations in whatever context. It is simply that they take a special form in that, as in all human affairs, they have unique characteristics and to that extent are different from relations between any other pair of countries. A similarity of language and much cultural inheritance in common can easily lead to a widespread British feeling that Anglo–American relations are not "foreign" in the accepted sense and thus to the easy assumption that general "like-mindedness" must automatically exist. The danger in this attitude is that of taking too much for granted. The superficial likenesses can disguise differences in habits of thought or long-term objectives and the recognition of these differences in moments of crisis is liable to produce a sudden, unexpected and totally unpleasant shock. When relations are bad the other side seems peculiarly exasperating in just the same way that family quarrels can make one especially impatient.*

It has been a minority in this country who have taken a different view and who have warned against the dangers of being misled by the resemblances between the countries into the assumption that there are no causes of disagreement and that concord need not be worked for. Rather than assume that these ties imply a fundamental unity of outlook, they have preferred to see the necessity to use them to create harmony in order that the respective positions and needs of both countries may be properly appreciated and understood. In order to do this such persons have attached fundamental significance to the establishment of a general atmosphere of confidence and understanding that the underlying premise may in fact be correct. This school of thought has therefore attached the highest importance to the selection of the ambassador in Washington whose personal qualities can be used to help to create those enabling conditions in which differences may be solved. His peculiar contribution to this is considered to be to personify British sincerity and good intent and by his very nature to lull the ready American suspicion that the England of George III is still alive. Such a job is a long-term and undramatic one and its nature is not always recognised by those who prefer to take good Anglo–American relations for granted. At a time when more pressing problems face the British government it is tempting to push the question into the background and to assume that because Anglo–American relations ought to be harmonious that therefore they will be.

By the end of 1916, much of these relations had become enmeshed in a net of mutual exasperation and bad temper largely resulting from the neutrality of the one and the belligerency of the other. Whilst the worst dangers of this fundamental cleavage had been recognised and avoided by the men handling their country's business, after two years of war the friction between

* See, for example, Eden's account of the Suez problem, *Full Circle*, Book 3.

them was perhaps more readily visible than their common interests. This was the more ironic since, from the British side, the executants were men believing in the importance of working for Anglo–American harmony and the American ambassador in London a burning Anglophile. Grey had for long believed in the over-riding importance of taking positive steps to keep relations harmonious both in the immediate present and as a long-term investment for the future. Spring Rice, appointed to Washington in 1912, had many American contacts which, it was assumed, would facilitate his task,* whilst Walter Page steadily became more English than the English. Nevertheless, the problems created by the war sometimes appeared to be too much for them. During the years of American neutrality, the differences of view concerning the blockade and the nature of the war not only necessitated a practical modus vivendi but also raised the issue of Anglo–American relations in the fundamental sense of that degree of confidence, trust and fair dealing without which amicable human relations cannot exist at all. One of the most important contributions of those years was the tacit recognition that such problems, however important, were nevertheless but episodes in the permanent stream of relations which had, if possible, to be kept unpoisoned.

Whilst it is no part of this chapter to deal with the intricacies of the blockade, this provides a nice example of the way in which strained relations can disguise a situation which is in fact working to overall mutual advantage. The blockade is a weapon of war which in its very nature must cause divisions of opinion between belligerent and neutral and it has already been pointed out that traditional views were becoming superseded by the nature of modern war. Pressure of events necessitated that the British view and British action should work for an ever-widening interpretation of the blockade as part of an overall economic war strategy whilst the American view was under no such compulsion. Even though transatlantic thought developed after the American entry into the

---

* A. Willert, *Road to Safety,* p.51.

war, it never seems to have become quite so all-embracing as the British.* It was during the first two years of the war however that the divergencies of view were the most apparent due above all to the allied disruption of American trade with European neutrals. Here a working arrangement had been reached by the end of 1914 through the development of the navicert system by the British Embassy in co-operation with American shippers and under an unofficial blessing from the Department of State. It would, of course, be untrue to say the system was liked; at the most it was grudgingly accepted by American traders as the best they could get under the circumstances and which did at least enable them to continue that neutral trade which Britain was prepared to allow them with the minimum of delay, loss and inconvenience. That which remained however provided a bone of contention at the diplomatic level.

At first Great Britain felt partially tied by her signature, although non-ratification, of the Declaration of London and by the efforts she had made to obtain a restrictive interpretation of the blockade in that document. This reinforced the American position as the champion of neutral rights through which Walter Page was often enabled to make Grey thoroughly uncomfortable. Here the British Foreign Minister steered a difficult course. On the one hand lay Scylla in the guise of all neutral countries, of which America was the most important, with whom Great Britain would have to live and trade when the war was over and whose rights he personally had every inclination to accept. On the other the Charybdis of the fire-eaters at home who, in their eagerness to see a rapid extension of the blockade, were blind to all other considerations of policy.

In reality, the problem of trading relations contained both a mutual and a conflicting interest and the real need was to damp down the disagreements until such time as the mutual advantage could become apparent. The latter lay in the development of

* Percy, *Some Memories,* esp. pp.49–56, but A. Bell, *The Blockade of the Central Powers,* p.667 suggested the Foreign Office exaggerated the back-sliding of the Americans.

America as the reservoir of goods for the Allies, supplies which were to be demanded in ever-increasing quantities and variety whilst the former consisted of the hardships suffered by particular interests especially in the short-term until their trading patterns had been diverted. Such interests, especially when their sympathies also lay with the central powers, were vocal and to some observers, including the British Ambassador, the danger arose that these sectional groups might prove sufficiently powerful to force America to take action which in practice would damage both countries. If Congress were to place an embargo on supplies to all belligerents, or if America was to attempt to "break the blockade" then the development of trade between the two countries would be prevented to their mutual detriment. The problem therefore was to prevent the inevitable dislocations becoming so great that resort was had to draconian measures. It was such considerations that had underlain the delay in declaring cotton to be contraband despite strong pressure from members of the British government. It soon became clear that the overall American interest was not going to suffer for August 1914 was the last month in which she had an adverse balance of trade as purchases from Great Britain and France leapt up.* The problem indeed soon became one not of preventing distress in America but of how the allies were to pay for their requirements. As often happens, however, attention was directed not to the general but to the special interests and this meant a spotlight not on the benefits but on the dislocations. As a result, during the years of neutrality, Anglo–American relations had never been more delicate. Whilst the blockade was an Allied policy, its execution was largely in the hands of the British navy and it was thus on the one instrument that American odium largely fell. All these factors helped to account for the fact that, as Spring Rice reported on numerous occasions, American majority public opinion could be both generally pro-Ally and particularly anti-English.

In addition to the blockade a major difference between America

* *The Times History of the War,* Vol.21, p.88.

and Britain in the early years was in the view taken of the war. The inability of many Americans, often echoed by Wilson and House, to see any moral difference between the belligerents aroused resentment in many British minds, including that of the British Ambassador. It was only gradually, and particularly as Germany became more ruthless at sea, that the American attitude began to change, but her entry into the war was occasioned by the fact that she felt herself to have her own just quarrel with Germany. It was not that the Allies had been white-washed in her eyes and thereby freed from suspicion concerning the purity of their motives as was too easily assumed on this side of the Atlantic.

True to the minority view of the role of the British Ambassador, Spring Rice viewed his function as an exercise in public relations in the broadest possible sense. Firstly, he was convinced that Wilson would take no action of any sort until certain that public opinion was behind him and therefore a major task was to attempt to report to the British government the general tenor of belief. Secondly, Spring Rice was aware of the cross-currents of opinion in America and his despatches are full of warning against presuming too far on the friendly feelings of America for the Allied side and urging the necessity of concession wherever the British interest was not vital in order to placate her.* "The danger is that if 80% are in favour of the Allies, they are in favour of them as we are of church-going. The remaining 20% are in favour of Germany as we are of eating our dinners. There is indifference on one side and intense earnestness on the other."†

Thirdly arose the problem of putting across the British case about the nature of the war and it was in this respect that Spring Rice was to be most criticised particularly since the German Embassy was the centre of the most active propaganda for the central powers and indeed for acts of sabotage and espionage. The plea was heard that Britain should take far more positive

* e.g. 25th Aug. 1914. To Grey. *The Letters and Friendships of Sir Cecil Spring Rice,* edited by Stephen Gwynn, Vol.2, p.218; hereafter referred to as Spring Rice.

† To Grey, 21st Nov. 1915. Spring Rice, *op. cit.,* Vol.2, p.299.

steps to put forward her case and actively to influence American opinion in her favour. To this Spring Rice was deeply opposed both by temperament and conviction. He held strongly to the view that the facts were the best form of propaganda and that the more devotion Englishmen shewed to the cause by fighting for it rather than talking about it, and the more successful they were in their actions, the more likely Americans were to be impressed. "The only propaganda which really pays in proved facts."* Propaganda could only too easily suggest that an outsider was attempting to make up American minds or, even worse, preaching at the New World and it was thus likely to boomerang by arousing the hostility to England which lay so near the surface. The most that he would suggest therefore was to advocate the occasional visit of prominent and respected personalities to explain their point of view about the war. He came also to appreciate the need for a press bureau in Washington to issue factual information. But "A distinctive English propaganda would be a great mistake."† At this point a larger consideration entered into his calculations. Because of the undoubted divisions in American opinion and in particular the vocal German and Irish elements any attempt to force America's hand to take action for which she was not ready could only divide her more. This to Spring Rice was a serious consideration. America must not be antagonised because of her importance as a base for Allied supplies, because of the danger that she might be pushed beyond bearing into an attempt to "break the blockade" with the enormous danger of a clash at sea and finally because if America ever came to feel that she had a quarrel with Germany it was important that the nation should be united on the point. In any case, the blunders of German policy were largely doing the job of Allied propaganda.

This view point Spring Rice was constantly sending home° and

early 1916, p.320.

* *op. cit.,* Vol.2, p.321.

† *op. cit.,* Vol.2, p.278, Aug. 19, 1915.

° *op. cit,* Vol.2, e.g. Despatch, 25th Aug. 1914, p.218. Letter to Newton, 21st Oct., 1914, p.239. Letter to Chirol, 27th Nov., 1914, p.249, Despatch, 12th Feb., 1915, p.254. Despatch 19th Aug., 1915, p.278. Letter to Newton,

because the use of propaganda was relatively ill-developed, few positive steps were taken in America during the first half of the war and those few steps were empirical, *ad hoc* measures rather than part of a concerted policy. At home, the American section of Wellington House provided certain services such as that of sending lecturers of varying degrees of quality to the States; it also kept up a personal correspondence with individual Americans producing articles for the American press or helped American press correspondents in England to obtain news. The News Department of the Foreign Office, which was later to be merged into the Department of Information, was also available for newspaper men in London. This in no way, however, amounted to a propaganda machine and indeed was rather inefficient as a source of factual information. In part this was due to the lack of any clearly defined directive over the use of news but also because of the very rigid censorship exercised with excessive caution by the service departments. As a result it was difficult for foreign correspondents in London to get any news at all; people like Norman Angell who, unorthodox in view, might yet have helped to create a more realistic image of the Englishman, found it impossible or difficult to go to America; little news was published in the American press concerning the British war effort for there was nothing to publish and, so it was alleged, the Americans were rapidly gaining the impression that the war was being fought by the Canadians and the French.* By the middle of the war it had become recognised that this situation required a remedy and early in 1917 a member of Northcliffe's staff visited America, with the Prime Minister's approval, to report on what needed to be done to tighten up the situation. Burton recommended that more vigorous measures be taken to provide a source of reliable information, a policy report which met with the approval of John Buchan,† then Director of the News Department at the Foreign Office. As a result, a small British Bureau of Information was

* See Beaverbrook, *Men and Power,* p.268.
† R. Pound and G. Harmsworth, *Northcliffe,* p.551.

created and established in New York with the laudable intention of pulling the various strands together and which, by making the necessary factual material available, enabled both a better presentation of the British case to be given to the American public and the more obvious mis-statements of German propaganda to be proved false.

To Spring Rice the best service, in general terms, that he could render to his country's cause was in keeping quiet and in oiling the wheels of the blockade machinery but the man who does nothing is an easy target for criticism and to people at home, immersed in the urgencies and horrors of the war, this negative policy and the hesitations in America were frustrating. The Northcliffe press, in particular, had published criticisms of Spring Rice's inactivity in the spring of 1916 and even the Foreign Office felt their ambassador to be too cautious over the propaganda issue and over-alarmist concerning the possible effects on American opinion of the blockade policy.* "He is just a miscellaneous diplomatist" wrote H.G. Wells to Northcliffe, "Tokyo, Cairo, Petrograd, an all-covered-with-orders kind of person. We might as well have a messenger boy there." Wells thought Gilbert Murray would make a good ambassador for he would be able to talk to Wilson "like a brother".†

On this question there is always likely to be some difference of view but most serious commentators have agreed that in essentials Spring Rice was right and that any attempt to pursue a more positive policy, notably in the propaganda field, could only have reacted adversely on the Allies whilst America was fumbling towards a war decision. Once she had entered the war, however, the situation was changed for the problem was now one of harnessing the great might of America towards the winning of the war and for this task a new outlook was necessary. Spring Rice himself was conscious of this fact and felt that the man who

---

* Percy, *op. cit.*, p.51. See Spring Rice, *op. cit.*, Vol.2, p.317, indicating that elements in the Foreign Office, including Crowe, thought Spring Rice too fastidious.

† Pound and Harmsworth, *op. cit.*, p.531–2.

had suffered the strains and difficulties of representing a belligerent in the vast untidiness of American neutrality and the consequent obloquies that had been heaped upon him was not the best person to continue at Washington. He himself could recognise that his talents lay in the practice of traditional diplomacy rather than the mobilisation of the war efforts of two co-belligerents. The nature of the problem had changed with the technicalities of wartime needs which required the bustle, thrust and forcefulness of the market place for their solution; qualities which Spring Rice knew he had not got. He therefore offered to resign but was persuaded by Balfour to remain at his post to give the British government an opportunity of considering the new problem of representation more fully.*

Indifference and ignorance at home towards the problems met in keeping American opinion reasonably sweet were not the only difficulties faced by Spring Rice during these years. Much has been written of the difficulties of the Wilsonian system of government in which the President remained inacessible in brooding isolation whilst keeping the reins of government securely in his own hands. The difficulty of contact with him was increased by his liking for unofficial advisers in preference to normal established machinery. The capacity of an ambassador to do his job must obviously depend upon his ease of access to the fountain head of authority and this Spring Rice increasingly had not. He described his view of the American system of government to Mr Balfour on 22nd December 1916. "It is difficult to explain exactly the way in which business is conducted here. The President rarely sees anybody. He practically never sees Ambassadors, and when he does, exchanges no ideas with them. Mr Lansing is treated as a clerk who recetives orders which he has to obey at once and without question. His communications to the press have been several times contradicted from the White House. He practically never expresses an opinion to a foreign representative. He never discusses any serious step in consideration by his govern-

*** See Spring Rice, Vol.2, p.426. Percy, *op. cit.*, p.55.**

ment. The State Department is full of very pleasant gentlemen whose kindness and courtesy make it very easy to transact business. Mr Lansing himself is most sympathetic and agreeable. But the real business of foreign politics is transacted by the President alone. He has a pronounced taste for the employment of secret foreign agents, a long succession of whom have passed through the White House. He has also a succession of advisers, who one after the other are discarded. Sometimes he sends a message to a foreigner through one of these, but he rarely, if ever, appears to discuss matters face to face with any foreign representative, and with his own Cabinet he is supposed to have maintained the strictest reserve. It is actually doubted whether Mr Lansing knew of the President's intention to send his peace note. Both the President and Mr Lansing denied that there was any such intention, and Mr Lansing's denial in the most positive form was given the day after the despatch of the note, which was sent over his signature. You will see that under these circumstances it is rather difficult to do diplomatic business, or to obtain authentic information of what is going on in the mind of the administration except through communications through the press."* Of these unorthodox methods of doing business Spring Rice did not approve.

Whilst this situation created difficulties for all diplomatic representatives in Washington, Spring Rice in addition increasingly lost the confidence of the American Administration. The little incident in the early months of the war when his opinion was sought by House and Wilson in order to tone down an ill-tempered note from the State Department concerning the blockade† deteriorated into a situation in which House considered Spring Rice illfitted to be the British Ambassador at Washington. "Sir Edward Grey's mistake has been that he allowed Sir Cecil Spring Rice to remain here at the most critical time in the history of the two countries . . . Grey failed to see that conditions demanded radical changes and that the ordinary diplomatic corps was un-

† Hendrick, *op. cit.*, Part 1, p.378.
* Spring Rice, *op. cit.*, Vol.2, pp.366–7. Spring Rice to Balfour.

equal to the new situation brought about by the war."* Spring Rice, House had previously complained, was always seeing spooks.† For this unhappy state of affairs a number of reasons can be found. Spring Rice was in fact a sick man and it was no doubt his illness which made him forget at times the impartiality which it is proper for an ambassador to assume. He was cross and ill-tempered when he should not have been° and was betrayed into injudicious remarks which were bound to arouse hostility. A sally such as "If the President is the shepherd of his people, then McAdoo is his crook",+ whilst caustically witty, is not for an ambassador in office to make, at least where it may be retained and quoted against him and his country. Then again, Spring Rice felt deeply about the nature of the war and resented what seemed to him wilful American blindness to the issues involved. It is always irritating to have to deal with people who calmly assume they are on a higher moral plane and doubly so when one has a passionate conviction that one is in the right. Although he appreciated, none better, that Wilson was the prisoner of American opinion, the idea of neutrality in thought as well as in deed, revolted him. When the President likened the war to a drunken brawl in a public house it was natural that Spring Rice should take offence,× the more so when the American attitude appeared tinged with hypocrisy. He thus did not hesitate to point out to the Americans that "when the laws of God and man were violated, there came no protest from us, but that when our oil and copper shipments were interfered with, a most vigorous protest came."** The President, in his view, went too far in glorying in his neutrality whilst the American habit of writing notes in response to German sinkings of American ships

---

* House, *op. cit.,* Vol.2, p.399. 7–12–16.

† House, *op. cit.,* Vol.1, p.465. House to President 7–5–15. See also Spring Rice, *op. cit.,* Vol.2, p.214.

° As his biographer admits. Spring Rice, *op. cit.,* p.215.

\+ Willert, *Road to Safety,* p.53. Mr McAdoo was Secretary of the U.S. Treasury.

× Spring Rice, *op. cit.,* Vol.2, p.352.

** House, *op. cit.*. Vol.2, p.75, entry for Oct. 14th 1915.

struck him as contemptible. There was substance in Lansing's complaint that "what had annoyed him was not the Ambassador's point of view which he could understand, but the manner in which it was conveyed".* Thus both sides took up attitudes of moral righteousness which were bound to annoy each other and which, because they were sincerely felt, tended to become uncompromising.

When Spring Rice became Ambassador, one of his assets had been held to be his good relations with prominent Americans. Unfortunately his friends, such as Roosevelt and Cabot Lodge, were not only Republicans but moreover men anxious to see America taking a more active part in the war. His contacts thus tended to become a liability. Spring Rice was aware of these pitfalls and tried to see little of his friends but his known associations increased suspicion of him in official quarters. "the Administration has come to regard the British officials as Republican partisans." Wiseman reported home.† Even so, in retrospect House could write of him "What a ruthless and destructive force is war! Here was perhaps the ablest and best-trained member of the British diplomatic service. There was no one who possessed to a greater degree the affection and confidence of his chiefs, and no one was more deserving. With all his accomplishments he possessed a personal charm that made him a multitude of friends. But when war broke loose he had a serious illness. Under ordinary circumstances he would soon have righted himself, but with the stress of disasters coming day by day, he could not regain his normal health. ... He went as far and as hard as he could, but what he could not do he was willing should be done by others. He was one of the few I have known who did not hesitate to yield his prerogatives in order that his country's interests might not suffer."°

For such reasons Spring Rice became unacceptable to House and Wilson as a channel of communication and a mechanism of

* Willert, *op. cit.,* p.55.
† Quoted Willert, *op. cit.,* p.52.
° House, *op. cit.,* Vol.3, p.27–28.

interpretation and this at a time when it was essential for Great Britain to achieve the closest degree of intimacy in view of her growing dependence upon America and when the pressure of events was driving the two countries towards co-belligerency. This was all the more alarming since neither House nor Wilson considered the American Ambassador in London entirely reliable for his reports and advice were generally held to be coloured by his strong pro-Allied feelings. The decay of normal diplomatic relations between the two countries made it necessary for them to find alternative methods through which to transact their great business. The unfortunate result was to create an hiatus in representation at one of the most critical centres of the war for it was not until the appointment of Lord Reading in 1918 that the possibility of proper channels of communication between the two countries became a reality, albeit only for a short space of time. During the interregnum the immense task of creating machinery for the co-ordination of war efforts and the flow of American aid of all kinds in the most appropriate channels was left by the British government to a series of hasty and *ad hoc* improvisations whose relations with the British Embassy were left undefined. "Normal political communications", writes Percy "ceased between the two governments".* With the appointment as ambassador of a man of both personal stature and top political status British activities could at last be brought under some form of coherent control.

The question of British representation during the winter of 1916–17, was becoming the more urgent with the increasing likelihood that America would be forced into the war; with the fall of Grey and his replacement by a man whom House knew only slightly and with the realisation by the President that Anglo–American co-operation on a long-term basis would be essential if his scheme for a League to prevent war was to have any chance of working.

In 1915 a young Intelligence Officer, William Wiseman, had

* **Percy, *op. cit.*, p.55.**

been sent to America nominally as a member of the Purchasing Commission of the Ministry of Munitions though in actuality as a counter-espionage agent. There was much to be done to prevent delays and arson in the factories, docks and in the ships, to scotch the poisoning of animals, and food supplies, to expose enemy agents and their work. This activity was, of course, conducted separately from that of the British Embassy and it was this contact that the American Administration came increasingly to prefer so that towards the end of 1916 Wiseman began his career as liaison between the White House and the British government. By this time it was clear that some mode of communication other than traditional methods was necessary and because he was acceptable to House and Wilson, Wiseman was enabled to fill the gap which circumstances had created and he rapidly established himself on terms of great intimacy with the Americans. His relations were particularly close with House to whom Wilson had deputed the task of keeping in touch with European representatives.* So acceptable did he become that the Americans wished him to succeed Spring Rice as British Ambassador in 1918.† This ease of access to high places° and his consequent ability to interpret the two countries' view-points was all the more important since by the winter of 1916–17 Anglo–American relations had touched the depths of mutual misunderstanding. In the one country the unpopularity of the blockade had reached a peak whilst in the other annoyance with "peace without victory" was acute. "[It] brought us to the very depths of European disfavour,"+ reported Mr Page. In this situation, Spring Rice was able to do little except to recognise and acquiesce in his supersession since the close contact that Wiseman developed with the Administration was a necessary preliminary to doing business at all. The British government fell in with this arrangement during

---

* House, *op. cit.*, Vol.3, p.23.

† Willert, *op. cit.*, p.16.

° "He is the only person, English or American, who has access to Wilson and House at all times", Northcliffe to Churchill, 27th July, 1917. House, *op. cit.*, Vol.3, p.90.

\+ Hendrick, *op. cit.*, Part, 2, p.214.

Balfour's visit to the United States when Wilson, by specifically pressing for Wiseman to stay*, awakened the Foreign Secretary to his importance. From that time, a new direct link between Wiseman and Balfour was established which came to be increasingly used as a channel for personal communication between the two governments and by means of which Wiseman was enabled to express his own views on policy. With the American entry into the war, this channel if anything increased in importance by virtue of its speed and its ability to keep the war leaders in line with each others thought, thereby helping to overcome what many, including Wiseman, held to be one of the chief German assets, namely the width of the ocean between London and Washington. Both countries relied heavily on him and he made several trips to Europe both to explain the American view and to attempt to describe to the British government the essentials of the American scene. In December 1917 Wiseman was made the official liaison officer between the British War Cabinet and any representative it might wish to send out to America† and both Northcliffe and Reading, particularly the former, found they leant heavily on him for official contacts. The chain of communication thus increasingly became House – Wiseman – Balfour rather than Lansing – Spring Rice – Page – Balfour.

The declaration of war changed the stuff of Anglo–American relations. The blockade had now become a matter of adjustment rather than of policy° whilst both countries could agree that Germany, by her own actions, had put herself outside the pale of civilised society. But whilst no longer putting the belligerents on the same moral plane, American opinion continued to believe that its cause was not fully that of the Allies whose involvement

* Willert, *op. cit.,* p.80–1.

† Willert, *op. cit.,* p.81.

° When Mr Balfour raised the question of an extension of the black list by America to neutrals, Mr Polk (of the State Department) replied "Mr Balfour, it took Great Britain three years to reach a point where it was prepared to violate all the laws of blockade. You will find that it will take us only two months to become as great criminals as you are". Hendrick *op. cit.* Part 2, p.265. If over-optimistic, this symbolises the change in atmosphere that war brought.

in the sordid intrigues of European politics was an example it did not wish to follow. Neither did the new situation imply that the old suspicions of Great Britain had been miraculously swept away. The immediate problems were of a practical rather than a policy nature but even so their solution had to be sought, from the British side, with due regad to American susceptibilities. It was necessary to avoid any appearance of pulling the wool over the eyes of the innocent giant or the suspicion that requests for aid from America were but cunning tricks to push the burden of the war onto the gullible newcomer. Any suggestion that the Allies knew best was almost bound to be resented. This theme was to recur with monotonous frequency as the slow business of hammering out effective forms of technical co-operation pursued its weary way. Once again, therefore, the creation and maintenance of an atmosphere of confidence can be delimited as an essential part of the business of conducting relationships. At the same time the practical tasks involved had to be tackled, and with speed, for the allied position was rapidly becoming desperate.

To most observers in the early months of 1917, including President Wilson, it appeared that America's main contribution would not be in the field but as an arsenal from which supplies of all kinds could be drawn to sustain the fighting forces* and it was to this task that minds were immediately turned. In order that America should fulfill this function it was necessary that the allies should explain in what directions American productive capacity should be developed that it might be most immediately useful and that experiences, often bitter, that they had undergone in organising themselves for total war should be placed in the hands of the New World still unprepared, both physically and mentally, for the demands of the war. Even though war had been drawing closer, Wilson's desire to walk the tightrope of neutrality had prevented him from taking steps necessary to make American participation immediately effective with hostilities whilst the Allies

* It was the failure of the spring offensives and later the Russian collapse that brought a change of view in America and an appreciation of the urgency of help. House *op. cit.*. pp.5–7.

were in reality at their last gasp and practical aid had become an urgent necessity.

It was only gradually that the true facts of the desperate situation of the Allies were realised across the Atlantic and in the meantime it was important for them not to create the impression of jockeying America into a position that she did not wish to occupy as in their anxieties they might so easily do. William Wiseman produced for the British government a memorandum on the situation as it appeared from the American side which was approved by Wilson and House before it was despatched. This pointed out that American sentiment was against a formal treaty for the people felt themselves to be arbitrators rather than allies. Their desire to crush militarism and to make future wars impossible was sincere; their war aim was therefore an idealistic one to serve the cause of democracy rather than to protect themselves against any felt danger. It was necessary for the Allies to pronounce that their aims were in general accord with this sentiment. He commented on the general mistrust of Great Britain and the historical sympathy for France which would make Anglo–American co-operation more difficult. Although, therefore, Great Britain had the most urgent need to obtain supplies from the United States she must go carefully and make no attempt to wield any pressure. Her only hope was in a long term process of education of Congress and the American public to create confidence and to produce an awareness of the size of the problems involved. Finally the American administration was too far from the war and possessed too little information to be able to judge the merits of the demands which would be made upon it.*

This difference in atmosphere between America, snug behind her ocean and unaware of the need for speed, and the realisation in the war capitals that the life of the Allies hung by a thread accounted for many of the difficulties which lay ahead.

Whilst there remained immense problems to be solved, the American entry into the war had an enormously heartening effect

* House, *op. cit.*, Vol.3, pp.32–4.

on the Allied populations of Europe to whom the war had become an ever-increasing and never-ending burden. The opinion of America in England changed overnight. Gone were the sneers at notes and neutrality, gone was the resentment of America's moral superiority, the Lords and the Commons expressed their thankfulness, the press their commendation, the President's speech to Congress was lauded and all for once could agree on the significance and wonder of the event.

The desire to convey this change of view point and to begin to grapple with the problems involved underlay the sending of the Balfour mission as the first big attempt to make war-time co-operation a reality and to dispel the clouds of mistrust that had settled over the relations between the two countries. Already the War Cabinet, in the days when an American declaration of war appeared imminent, had discussed the problems that would arise and had come to the preliminary conclusion that a special mission was the right way of dealing with them. The matter was referred to the Imperial War Cabinet which approved the proposal. The American Ambassador, too, welcomed the idea. He had long held the view that a personal meeting between leading statesmen would lead to the clearing up of many misunderstandings on both sides* and was strongly in favour of the proposal that a British mission should be sent to America and that Mr Balfour should head it. When a British approach was made to him it was thus natural that he should give it his full approval. Reinforcement of the plan had also come from across the Atlantic for Wiseman had reported an 8th February that the President would favour an allied commission.† No time was lost. On 4th April the Cabinet decided that a mission should be sent, that it should be headed by someone of high status and should include representatives of the Admiralty, War Office, Munitions, Food and Shipping Ministries and the Bank of England. The next day it was determined that Balfour should head the mission and that it should include

* Hendrick, *op. cit.*, Part 2, p.248.
† Willert, *op. cit.*, p.70.

Labour representatives. This mission had two functions. On the technical side lay all the problems involved in developing American strength for the common war effort. Certain matters were here singled out as requiring the highest priority in view of the needs of the war as seen from the British side.* In broader terms, however, its significance lay in its capacity to create a better understanding between the two countries and to dispel the deep-rooted mistrust extant in America about Great Britain and her war aims so that co-operation between them would ultimately prove to be fruitful. In its most important aspect it was a goodwill mission to establish confidence and understanding so that the various technical problems which were to be handled by the appropriate experts on a permanent basis might function with the maximum efficiency. Balfour was selected as the head because his personal qualities appeared to be those that were required. The enormous significance of the American entry into the war made it essential to send an important member of the government; Balfour had a known history of friendly feelings and actions towards America and was of a personal stature to make his name an acceptable one. On 5th April, Page notified his government of the wish to send Mr Balfour on a mission to America. "Mr Balfour is chosen for this mission not only because he is Secretary of State for Foreign Affairs, but because he is personally the most distinguished member of the government,"† Colonel House supported the concept of a British mission and the choice of its head and President Wilson agreed. "I do not see" wrote House to

* These were (i) The need to develop American shipbuilding capacity and the possibilities of diverting existing American shipping to carrying for the war effort.

(ii) The need to despatch some American troops quickly for morale purposes on both sides of the Atlantic who could if necessary complete their training in Europe, in which the western allies would be prepared to help.

(iii) The advantages which would follow if America were to adopt British type guns.

(iv) The necessity for an increased steel production and the short-sightedness, in the British experience, of recruiting skilled workers for the armed forces.

(v) To assess the importance of the Irish question in Anglo–American relations.

† Hendrick, *op. cit.,* Part 2, p.252.

Wilson on 5th April "how you can well refuse this request, . . . Balfour is the most liberal member of the present British Cabinet and it would be of great service to the relations of the two countries to have him here and to talk to him in person."* Wilson decided to welcome the mission although with some misgivings "Of course there is nothing for it but to reply . . . that we shall be glad to receive such a commission and to see Mr Balfour at the head of it.

"The plan has its manifest dangers. I do not think that all of the country will understand or relish. A great many will look upon the mission as an attempt to in some degree take charge of us as an assistant to Great Britain, particularly if the Secretary of State for Foreign Affairs heads the commission."† To help to counteract this possible appearance of America as a milch cow he asked for it to be announced as a diplomatic and not a military affair.

Spring Rice, in clear terms, pointed out the pitfalls which the mission needed to avoid. He described first of all the division between the Democratic and Republican parties whose members were on bad terms with one another. The Republican party contained the leaders of finance, the leaders of society and the more vocal protagonists of American participation in the war. "The persons with whom [the mission] would naturally come in contact, and with whom they would be naturally inclined to associate, are precisely those with whom the President is on bad terms. Any intimacy with these persons would be regarded with suspicion." He pointed out that America had entered the war reluctantly and not because of any desire to help the allies but because she felt she must fight Germany. Furthermore the mission would be likely to lead to a belief that Great Britain had inveigled America into the war and was now sending a representative to offer unasked-for advice. There was a great fear in the States, he asserted, of America being dominated by Great Britain and any appearance

* House, *op. cit.*, Vol.3, p.36.
† Baker, *op. cit.*, Vol.7. p.3.

of British control must be avoided. Finally, the Irish question might prove to be an insuperable stumbling block to the establishment of good relations.*

Balfour stayed a month in the United States and there is no doubt that in the delicate task of creating confidence he succeeded remarkably well. "I hope that the English people realise how successful Mr Balfour's visit to America really was. There is no man they could have sent who could have done it better. He and the President got along marvellously well" wrote Colonel House.† It was not only with the President that Balfour succeeded but in the wider field of public relations as well. "You probably know what a wonderful success the British Mission has been, but I do not think you can realise what a deep impression they have made on all of us. Mr Balfour really won the affection of us all".° Spring Rice, too, commented on the personal influence of Arthur Balfour whose visit was in the "nature of a new light and a new atmosphere".+

The chief value of the mission, from the British side, lay in the fact that it had taken the first step to bridge the chasm of resentment and suspicion which lay between the two countries and which, if allowed to persist, would have inhibited the development of the closest possible practical co-operation between them. The latter was something that other men could do but the former was essentially a personal achievement. This did not mean, of course, that no potential cause of disagreement remained or that the mission had successfully created a pattern of administration to deal with day to day problems of finance, shipping and the like. This form of organisation was not Mr Balfour's forte and remained for other hands to arrange. Furthermore, the delicate problem of war aims still lay between them. House himself had felt that this was a sleeping dog best left to lie for fear it might prejudice the immediate object of whole-hearted practical co-

* Spring Rice, *op. cit.*, Vol.2, p.393. Despatch April 13, 1917.
† Hendrick, *op. cit.*, Part 2, p.263.
° Mr Polk to Mr Page, Hendrick, *op. cit.*, Part 2, p.263.
\+ Spring Rice, *op. cit.*, Vol.2, p.400.

operation* but Wilson was not be entirely dissuaded from a general discussion with the Foreign Secretary in which the main outlines of the secret treaties were communicated to the President. No bargaining or accord was, however, attempted for Wilson had no wish to make an issue out of these matters at that time. His main concern was to explore the likemindedness towards the whole problem of a lasting peace rather than to haggle over bargaining details.† He was, however, of the opinion that the two countries represented differing view points "England and France *have not the same views with regard to peace that we have* by any means. When the war is over we can force them to our way of thinking, because by that time they will, amongst other things, be financially in our hands; but we cannot force them now."○

Whilst in America, Balfour suggested to the British government that it would be desirable to appoint a permanent head for the technical missions. For this both he and House favoured Grey+ but although he was approached the offer was rejected on the grounds of ill-health.× At this point Balfour asked for a decision on the appointment to be postponed until be returned home.

The problem was a difficult one whose solution depended upon the way it was viewed. The need for further co-ordination of the technical missions provided a suitable moment to consider the whole question of British representation in the United States, particularly necessary in view of its unsatisfactory character. Within this whole context, the work of the missions could be seen as one problem only and viewed from this angle the appointment of Grey had much to recommend it in view of his concern with Anglo-American relations and the degree of respect afforded to him in America. He would not appear to be an obvious choice to deal with affairs of a purely business character. In the event, this overall reappraisal was omitted and it is difficult not to sense

* House, *op. cit.,* Vol.3, p.39.
† Baker, *op. cit.,* p.44, footnote. House, *op. cit.,* Vol.3, p.52.
○ Wilson to House, 21st July 1917. Baker, *op. cit.,* Vol.7, p.43. footnote.
\+ House, *op. cit.* Vol.3, p.55.
× George, *op. cit.,* Vol.III, p.1688.

a missed opportunity through the consideration of the immediate problems in isolation from the whole.

To Lloyd George, however, the main consideration appeared that of co-ordinating and fusing the competing interests and claims of the missions themselves for which a business man appeared a more suitable choice than a diplomatist. "Although the person selected would no doubt have a great deal to do with Americans, his primary duty would be to control our own operations, . . . and the priority of the various claims."* Political motives also played a part in the selection of Lord Northcliffe as the appropriate choice. Although Northcliffe had approved the change of government in 1916 because he was anti-Asquith this did not imply, as many thought at the time, that he was pro-Lloyd George and in the developing struggle between polticians and generals he was strongly on the side of the military. Then again Northcliffe was a vehement opponent of Churchill whom Lloyd George was increasingly anxious to bring back into the government. The Prime Minister therefore had strong reasons for finding it advantageous to send Northcliffe to the States if he could persuade his colleagues to agree. It is a measure of his personal position at the time that he found this possible in view of the distrust in which Northcliffe was held by the politicians. Curzon, Cecil, Austen Chamberlain and Walter Long had indeed made it a condition of their taking office that he should be given no post. Whilst certainly is impossible, it seems likely that a major motive of Lloyd George's was in fact to get Northcliffe out of the way for he had previously offered him the Washington Embassy although this had been refused.†

Lloyd George prepared the ground with care. He obtained first of all Bonar Law's agreement to the proposal and followed this up by a discussion with the Heads of the Departments concerned with purchases in America and found them prepared to accept

* George, *op. cit.*, Vol.III, p.1688.

† Pound and Harmsworth, *op. cit.*, p.528. See also *Diary of Lord Bertie of Thame,* entry for 11th July 1917 "Lloyd George wanted to substitute Lord Northcliffe for Spring Rice but that was stopped". Vol.2, p.136.

Northcliffe as head of the British War Mission. On the 25th May the matter was discussed at the War Cabinet and the advantages of a business man displayed. The Cabinet agreed that Northcliffe should be appointed, subject to the views of Balfour and Spring Rice. It appears clear that both these gentlemen expressed their strong disapproval of which the Cabinet was not told.* Balfour, indeed, wrote what appeared to House to be "a very earnest argument against sending any such representative",† and pointed out that the President's permission should first be obtained. In any case he had already asked for a decision on the appointment to be deferred until he reached home. Shortly afterwards, when severe criticism of the appointment was being expressed, Bonar Law publicy admitted that Balfour had not been consulted.° The appointment was however confirmed by the Cabinet on 30th May.+

Northcliffe himself seems to have accepted the job with certain misgivings. He viewed himself pre-eminently as a journalist rather than a business man and feared that his many enemies would make his task more difficult. He cannot, too, have been unaware that his relationship with Spring Rice would be delicate, if not impossible. "It was decided by the War Cabinet," he wrote "after consultation with Americans in London,× that I was to be marked down for the difficult and delicate task, from which, in my judgement, it is impossible for anyone to emerge with credit; that does not matter. Anything I have achieved at home has been won by my press. In the U.S. I am to be without my source of influence. My coming will be resented by the Embassy, by the Missions, by the Consulate, and eventually by the Americans themselves."** His alarm increased during his voyage to the States as he perused the documents the government had given him and the full awfulness of the situation dawned upon him. "Nothing but my intimate

---

* Beaverbrook, *op. cit.*, p.65.

† Baker, *op. cit.*, Vol.7, p.95–6. House to Wilson. 31st May.

° 4–7–17. Hansard, Vol.95, Cols. 1105–6.

\+ George, *op. cit.*, Vol.III, p.1689.

× Page approved the project. See House of Lords, *Hansard*, Vol.25, Col.532.

** Pound and Harmsworth, *op. cit.*, p.529.

knowledge and instinct of the grave national danger would have led me on this lonely and dangerous venture. Even *I* had not a full understanding till I read the gloomy documents dumped on me for the voyage. My task is a terrific one and most delicate. I am sent forth literally to *beg* for assistance of all kinds and in colossal quantities and from a people whom certain of our public men and journals have attacked up till the last few weeks. Most fortunately, I have never allowed any criticism to appear in my Press . . . I have always felt, as you know, that when this war *did* come we should eventually have to ask for their assistance. On the scale on which I am being sent forth to plead, it looks as though the British nation will be in pawn to the United States, and, though I do not fear for the future, it is obvious that people don't realise the coming linking up of nations . . .

"The brazen impudence of some of these Government begging suggestions fairly staggers me. They are written by people who obviously have never been in America and who seem to think that we are conferring a favour in allowing the Americans to join the alliance. I shall do my utmost. I will slave 18 hours a day. But I should like a whirlwind visit of the Prime Minister, not merely to the East but to the money and munitions centres of the great West. We are begging from a people who want munitions for their own army, who have been humbugged by the censorship, so that their notion of the war is quite different from ours, their sympathies pro-French and in many states vigorously anti-English, with German propagandists working against my Mission night and day."*

Having decided to go, Northcliffe acted with despatch and set sail for America with all speed and secrecy. Whilst it may have been considered prudent to by-pass the inevitable criticism of his appointment with a *fait accompli,* one consequence of haste was that he left England singularly ill-prepared through the absence of prior discussion with anyone really knowledgeable about his assignment. The limits of his briefing appear to have been one

* Quoted Pound and Harmsworth, *op. cit.,* p.536.

lunch-time meeting with the Prime Minister and Hankey.* Not only was he launched off into the blue to do the best he could by himself but equally there had been no preparation on the ground for him in Washington. Having decided on the mission, the Prime Minister took "no steps whatever to see that the various authorities in America were informed" wrote Geoffrey Dawson.† One can imagine only too easily what this meant. No one knowing what he would be doing, whom he ought to meet, where he ought to go, or what degree of importance the British government attached to his mission. In particular no prior attempt had been made to reach a *modus vivendi* with the British Embassy. The degree of success which the mission had was despite its opportunist birth.

The object of Lord Northcliffe's mission as laid down by the War Cabinet was to supervise and co-ordinate the work of the various departmental missions and to prevent any conflict of interest between them with consequent loss of effort. He was expected to maintain friendly relations both with the Allied organisations in America for the same purpose and with the United States authorities. In carrying out his duties, Northcliffe was given the right to communicate directly with the Prime Minister and the Heads of Departments and full authority over the missions in America.° He was expected to keep the British Ambassador in Washington informed of his actions and reciprocally, because he had no diplomatic status, the Embassy was expected to give him all diplomatic support. It was thus unclear with whom it was anticipated the Americans would deal over particular issues whilst the precise relationship between Northcliffe and Spring Rice was peculiarly ill-defined. Such circumstances necessitate a working

* Lloyd George states it was intended by the Cabinet that he should have interviews with the Heads of Departments before he left. *op. cit.,* Vol.III, p.1689.

† Quoted Pound and Harmsworth, *op. cit.,* p.544.

° See text of the telegram sent to Heads of missions quoted by Bonar Law in the Commons, 13th June 1917. Hansard, Vol.94, Col.956 and George, *op. cit.,* Vol.III, pp.1689–91 details the instructions to the mission given to Northcliffe by the War Cabinet.

arrangement being hammered out on the spot and the personal relations between the two men were bound to be a critical factor in determining what this relationship was to be. This was a situation in which prior consultation could have provided an opportunity for the exercise of that tact and understanding which it obviously demanded; not only on personal grounds but in order that the effectiveness of British representation in America might be maximised. Two people who could work less harmoniously together it would have been difficult to find. All the more reason for trying to smooth their path. If the canalisation of the goodwill of both countries was peculiarly dependent on the atmosphere in Washington, it seems the more unfortunate that no attention was paid to the consequences of this arranged marriage.

As Northcliffe had foreseen, his appointment raised considerable criticism at home. To the long-standing animosity to the tenor of his press was added the objection that the perpetrator of popular journalism was not a suitable person to represent the country in America. It was impossible to prevent the impression that he was to some extent to succeed Mr Balfour and to supersede the British Ambassador* although both these implications were officially denied. On 7th June, however, *The Times* carried an announcement "British Missions in America. Lord Northcliffe's Task. Successor to Mr Balfour. The War Cabinet have invited Lord Northcliffe to go to America to co-ordinate the work of the several British Missions that are already established there, and to continue the task so successfully initiated in that respect by Mr Balfour. Lord Northcliffe has accepted this invitation, and has already sailed for the United States". This caused considerable indignation whilst the whole episode additionally provided an opportunity for the expression of hostility to Lloyd George, his penchant for amateurs and his alleged subordination to the press. These discontents were partially expressed in Parliament on 7th June, 11th June, 13th June and 4th July. Bonar

* See House of Lords, 20–6–17, *Hansard,* Vol.25, Col.522; House of Commons, 13–6–17, *Hansard,* Vol.94, Col.956; 4–7–17, *Hansard,* Vol.95, Col.1105.

Law's replies on these occasions together form the official view of Northcliffe's appointment as a technical and co-ordinating function which would carry on the work begun by Mr Balfour "in this respect" but which was not diplomatic and which would not supersede the British Ambassador.* A fuller discussion took place in the House of Lords on 20th June† to which Curzon replied in emphatic terms. He stated that there was no analogy with Mr Balfour's appointment, or his powers, functions and duties and that there was no encroachment on the diplomatic function. For whatever reason, Curzon rather played the mission down, limiting it in his view to the need for co-ordination of the work of the missions which arose essentially out of their competition for freight. A problem with which Lord Northcliffe was "supremely well qualified" to deal. But the general feeling of unease concerning the appointment was not stilled. His task appeared woolly, his precise standing vague, his personal qualifications and experience not obviously those befitting a man to fill high public office. Under such circumstances suspicion that the government's real motives were other than had been admitted was only to be expected.° David Davies faithfully reported the hostility. "If Northcliffe is to go to U. S. A. as head of the British Mission you will be making a damn bad appointment and you will raise a devil of a storm in the Liberal Party, which is just what you want to avoid just now. Northcliffe is one of the biggest intriguers and most unscrupulous people in this country. It is a gratuitous insult to the Americans to send him there – he will do more harm in a week than Balfour has done good in a month. He is not a business man — in the sense that you want for this job. If you are sending him there to be rid of him, you are making a huge mistake. The restless devil will be back here in less than two months, having in the meantime played hell all round and injured your reputation. Here it will be said that you are

* *Hansard,* Vol.94, Cols. 324, 606–7, 956; Vol.95, Col.1105.

† House of Lords, *Hansard,* Vol.25, Col.522 *et seq.*

° See e.g. *Daily Chronicle,* 21st June 1917; *Daily News,* 21st June 1917, *Morning Post,* 30th June 1917.

afraid of the Harmsworth Press. Rothermere at the War Office; Cecil [Harmsworth] in the Garden City; Northcliffe in New York! . . . We shall soon have a Government of the Harmsworths, through the Harmsworths, and for the Harmsworth Press!"*

It was not only in this country that people found the appointment strange. Sections of the American press considered it odd that the British government had found it proper to send to America a man from whose press bitter attacks on the British Embassy had emanated or that it could suppose that Americans could ever accept Northcliffe stepping into Balfour's shoes. Once again, it was assumed that he was in fact to have the status to do this and he was widely reported as the "successor to Mr Balfour".† At least one editor wrote directly to Balfour to express his disgust° but after the first shock of surprise was over the tenor of the American press settled down to be generally friendly to the newcomer.

Neither was the appointment particularly welcome to the Administration. The President was not convinced that any further appointment was necessary or that, if it were, Lord Northcliffe was the proper person to fill it. On 31st May, Wiseman delivered to House a memorandum from the British government setting out its reasons for wishing to send a non-diplomatic head to co-ordinate the British work in America and suggesting that Lord Northcliffe was the man for the job. House and Wilson agreed that Balfour was right to consider it best not to send anyone at that juncture. Wilson wrote to Colonel House "Action mentioned in your letter of yesterday would be most unwise and still more unwise the choice of the person named."+ "I don't believe in Lord Northcliffe any more than I do in Mr Hearst" he wrote on 3rd June.× Colonel House agreed with him. "I am sorry Northcliffe is coming. I thought Balfour's cable had headed him off...

* Quoted F. Owen, *Tempestuous Journey*, p. 381.
† Pound and Harmsworth, *op. cit.*, p.530.
° Beaverbrook, *op cit.*, p.73.
+ Baker, *op. cit.*, Vol.7, p.96.
× Baker *op. cit.*, pp.99–100.

It is to be remembered that Northcliffe comes apparently with your approval and of course expects to be cordially received. I am afraid his visit may stir up the anti-British feeling here that at present is lying dormant."* On 6th June, Lansing expressed to Page the Administration's doubts† but it was, of course, too late for Northcliffe had already sailed. Page attempted to reassure his government. Northcliffe, he cabled on 7th June, was on a purely commercial errand with no diplomatic standing; his duties had no reference to what Mr Balfour had done and he would have no official relations with the American government different from the British commercial interests then in the United States.° But this view was not altogether accepted there, any more than it had been at home. "The British government" wrote House on June 12th "have given him the widest possible powers and it would therefore seem necessary to give him proper consideration."+ Since in any case they were largely faced with a *fait accompli*, after some hesitation, they decided to make the best of it.×

The other storm centre was the British Embassy. No established institution likes to see its work taken over by a new broom but this had already begun to happen in the sphere of Anglo–American relations in the same way that at home the Foreign Office found its exclusive concern with foreign affairs being shared with others and largely for the same reasons. Specialist problems were now involved where the need for specialist knowledge could be justified and accepted as an unfortunate but temporary necessity. As the problems gained in volume and importance they began to form the main stuff of Anglo–American relations thus inevitably leaving the Embassy high and dry and concerned with peripheral matters. Simultaneously, other developments seemed to swallow up its remaining functions. Firstly,

* Baker *op. cit.*, p.102 footnote. House to President.
† Baker *op. cit.*, p.102.
° Baker, *op. cit.*, p.104.
+ Baker *op. cit.*, p.108.
× Baker *op. cit.*, p.108. See also Pound and Harmsworth, *op. cit.*, p.532 quoting House diary for 9th June 1917.

Wiseman was rising in importance as the general channel of communication between the two governments and Spring Rice had been prepared to acquiesce in this arrangement for his country's good. Secondly had come the Balfour mission which was partly a reflection on the work of the Ambassador. Its very success in establishing a better atmosphere pointed the extent to which this had been lacking previously. The Northcliffe appointment was not only the latest but also the biggest blow. Whilst Balfour was part of the family, Northcliffe was "the incarnation of all that he [Spring Rice] disliked in the twentieth century".* The popular journalist with his appeal to mass emotions and the consequent crudities of expression could not have been more distasteful to the cultivated intellect which Eton, Oxford and the urbanities of diplomatic circles had united to produce. Sadly, Spring Rice had been a personal sufferer from the weapon of the Northcliffe press and was consequently filled with bitterness against him. Both before and during the war, *The Times* had attacked the Ambassador's competence and indeed patriotism. His somewhat subtle and admittedly negative view on the scope of British propaganda was poles apart from that of Northcliffe who was increasingly concerned to see its extended use as a war weapon generally and who felt his knowledge of the United States gave him a special competence to judge what should be done. These criticisms had been bitterly resented by Spring Rice. Nor did the manner of his coming help. It was obvious, we are told,† that consulting Spring Rice in the first place was only a matter of form; his objections to the project had been ignored whilst Northcliffe's hasty departure left no time for friends or superiors to attempt to soften his feelings or, indeed, for Spring Rice himself to consider how best to deal with the situation. Here was a man whom Spring Rice considered his bitter enemy, landing unexpectedly upon him, requiring close diplomatic support, whose terms of reference were insufficiently defined and whose

* Willert, *op. cit.*, p.97.
† Willert, *op. cit.*, p.96.

mission was being reported as to "replace the ambassador".* His anger was still at fever heat when Northcliffe landed.

Northcliffe knew before he arrived that there would be difficulties and was inclined to believe that the Ambassador interfered with the Mission's work. "if as I . . . believe," he recorded "he is a man of small parts, inclined to make mischief, I shall come back after duly acquainting the War Cabinet and the Foreign Office with the circumstances."† He was not, however, prepared for the shock of landing in New York to find that no one from the Embassy was there to meet him. "Northcliffe was not received by any of the staff of the British Embassy and he was angry beyond words."° Kind peace makers tried to make excuses but Northcliffe in his anger protested to the Prime Minister and threatened to return.+ Spring Rice tried to make amends by sending Northcliffe a letter of welcome and explaining that since his instructions had been to keep the mission a strict secret he had not felt any official representative could properly be sent to the ship. (A somewhat thin excuse since it had been swarming with newspaper reporters.) The two men, however, had to meet and a stormy interview took place which both protagonists recorded home. At the end of a most bitter conversation, as Northcliffe was preparing to leave the house Spring Rice "rushed after me, put out his hand, and said: 'We have to work together whatever we may feel about each other'. I accepted his hand".× Northcliffe nevertheless recorded his opininon to Lloyd George "Sir Cecil Spring Rice is either overwrought by the strain of war, or is not quite right in his head".** This personal antagonism continued throughout Northcliffe's stay in the United States with consequent detriment to the work he had gone there to do. Although outwardly there was civility in practice "There is no co-

* Even J. Davies, *op. cit.*, p.130. records the matter as '"The wireless has brought surprising news. The Prime Minister has sent Lord Northcliffe to take the place of Sir Cecil Spring Rice as ambassador to the United States."'

† Pound and Harmsworth, *op. cit.*, p.533.

° House. Recorded June 12th. See Baker, *op. cit.*, Vol.7, p.108.

\+ Pound and Harmsworth, *op. cit.*, p.538.

× Northcliffe to Lloyd George, *op. cit.*, Vol.III, p.1695.

** Pound and Harmsworth, *op. cit.*, p.541.

operation whatsoever".* Although Northcliffe seems to have tried to be friendly "You need have no fear" he told the Prime Minister "that I will have friction with the Ambassador, if it can be helped"† he found it difficult to be tactful. It must have been a blow to Spring Rice to hear from Northcliffe himself that Lloyd George had offered him the British Embassy. On enquiry to the Foreign Office the Ambassador was informed that Balfour knew nothing of it and doubted if it was true but since Lloyd George had the habit of taking decisions without his colleagues it could hardly be disproved.° Small comfort for Spring Rice in that.

Within this somewhat complicated net-work of personalities, reservations and unofficial methods of doing business, Northcliffe had much practical work to do. By this time a wonderful miscellany of people had gathered in the States, all busy with their own concerns to the detriment, very often, of each others. There were experts on finance, on purchasing, on arms and munitions, experts on transport, on docks, on sugar, on wheat, on oil and timber, in addition to three service missions. He estimated he had a staff of ten thousand people strung out over the United States and Canada between them spending two million pounds a day. All these missions were essentially independent of each other and acted under direct instructions from their Ministries at home. Thus the Ministry of Munitions was represented, the War Office dealt with its own needs of recruiting and horse-purchase and also with special purchases of munitions and railway equipment for Russia for which the British government was financially responsible. The Admiralty, and later the Ministry of Shipping, was concerned with the internal transport of goods to the ports and then across the ocean; the Ministry of Shipping dealt with the purchase of steamers and the placing of building orders; a special wheat company purchased grain for the Allies and had offices up and down the continent; the Treasury had a

* Willert to *The Times,* July 1917 quoted by Pound and Harmsworth, *op. cit.,* p.542.

† Pound and Harmsworth, *op. cit.,* p.542.

° *op. cit.,* p.546. But see *supra* p.286.

special representative concerned with the supervision of all British financial interests in the United States. At the same time the British government made huge purchases through J. P. Morgan & Co., who acted as its financial agent. It was essentially Northcliffe's job to pull the whole of this work together, to cut out competitive bidding, to prevent duplication of demands, to centralise all decisions of major importance and to create special departments to deal with particular purchases. Nor did his work end there for more specialists kept arriving from Britain. It became the job of the War Mission to look after them, to see they knew the appropriate rules and regulations affecting their work and that they made the right contacts. As American war production got into its stride requests began to be received about British war organisation which again were channeled through the War Mission which provided the answers, sought them from home or brought over yet more experts to answer them.

Northcliffe soon found however that this was not the end of it for he was in competition too with other allied missions in America for the same purpose and Inter-Allied machinery to co-ordinate requests had not yet been evolved. Finally, as America's own war effort increased, the American government also entered the field as a purchaser of goods. It was impossible therefore for him to limit himself simply to co-ordinating British activities or to suppose that his contacts with the administration would be minimal. Thus he found himself up against the difficulties of official Washington and the ambivalent American attitude to Great Britain. Writing home to Lloyd George to describe the problems of his work he pictured a "mysterious force" in Washington making for endless discussion and delay. He commented on the anti-British views emanating from American Universities. The Administration, as he thought, tried to do its best but 'does not know how to' and he found that everything, even the smallest detail, had to go to the President, surrounded except for one or two by people not of the greatest calibre.* It was also impossible

* Pound and Harmsworth, *op. cit.*, p.545.

in practice to limit his dealings to matters arising out of his mission. The American reaction to British requests for aid was partly determined by her picture of the British war effort or by the suspicion that help was wanted which would give Britain an advantage over America in the post-war world. Thus Northcliffe's work was in fact inter-twined with other policy issues such as propaganda, or indeed, war aims and because he saw that this was so he was soon to be writing home on matters which were not strictly in his brief. When all personal considerations are left on one side, it is difficult to see that this could have developed otherwise. The neglect of prior consideration of the question of overall British representation in the United States resulted in an arrangement which was essentially unworkable for it rested upon a false division of labour. Since war problems were increasingly the real stuff of Anglo-American relations, it was the British War Mission rather than the Embassy which was in a controlling position and Spring Rice's decline increased the likelihood of its rise to power. As Percy was to write to Balfour, there was in effect no Ambassador at Washington. Spring Rice lacked the power to organise, to control, to direct or stimulate his staff. "We cannot go on like this. There will be a mess. Northcliffe will become ambassador."*

Northcliffe himself soon came to realise what in fact was involved in his presence in America. His method of dealing with it was to shelve the fundamental problem and do the best he could under the circumstances. "I propose to leave the whole question to Reading to go into the whole matter and to advise you."† But that he found the situation inherently irksome is clear "It is a curious experience to have only partial authority when one has been accustomed to absolute authority".°

Meanwhile, his bad relationship with Spring Rice partly accounted for his decision to settle in New York rather than Washington so that personal contacts could be kept to a minimum and

* Pound and Harmsworth, *op. cit.*, p.543.
† Willert, *op. cit.*, p.107.
° Pound and Harmsworth, *op. cit.*, p.549.

it seems likely that this decision made his task more difficult. As American production got into its stride, Northcliffe's contacts with the government were bound to increase and, as he soon found himself, this meant Wilson and House. In addition the absence of any synchronisation of Allied demands upon America meant a certain element of competition between them and British observers felt that this continued refusal to settle in the capital left the French and the Italians with too clear a field. In theory, New York, as the heart of the business world, might seem the ideal spot for a business mission but, as has been seen, this was a false description of it. It could not be separated from politics. Washington was becoming the centre of increasingly critical decisions and from this centre Northcliffe had severed himself.

Neither was Northcliffe really a business man in quite the sense which the mission required. His power was founded on his newspapers and although he had here an uncanny flair for knowing what was to the public taste this is rather a different ability from taking decisions about ships, food, timber or transport and establishing a smoothly running business to deal with them. It is true that even here Northcliffe's contacts proved invaluable in that he was enabled to settle various difficult problems because of them* but these were incidental advantages arising from his appointment rather than a justification for it. It was the press that Northcliffe knew and loved and sympathetic, though watchful, observers began to question whether he was really the right man for the job. The trouble, thought Wiseman, was that Northcliffe was ill-fitted to organise the enormous business of the British war mission† and his latest biographers concur in that opinion.°

It was indeed true that the press and publicity were in Northcliffe's blood. Although of retiring habits, he exerted himself to

* Thus on one occasion his ability to handle Henry Ford eased tractor production in Detroit; on another his contacts with Standard Oil solved a crisis for the British Navy.

† Pound and Harmsworth, *op. cit.,* p.577.

° Pound and Harmsworth, *op. cit.,* p.590.

give parties to counteract the aloofness he associated with the British Embassy; he wrote articles; he gave interviews; he travelled the country and made speeches in an endeavour to bring home the meaning of the war and the importance of the British war effort. To some extent this had the effect that Spring Rice had always feared of arousing American resentment of an outsider claiming to know their business best. "The newspapers announce that when Lord Northcliffe has put some of the President's punch and pep into the British government and removed the dead wood, he will return here again. There is some anxiety lest he should perform a similar function for the U. S. Government, which prefers to do its own forestry, but I don't believe Northcliffe's return would be as fatal as some people say."* Both Willert and Wiseman tried to persuade him publicity was better left alone and might well prejudice his major task. It was natural that American officials would exercise more than usual reticence when speaking to someone who might use the material in public indiscretions. Wiseman reported "Northcliffe cannot keep his hands off propaganda, and is even now engaged in writing a series of articles for American magazines which criticise the President and have given some offence in that quarter. He is convinced that he is doing it in the best interests of the country, and simply cannot see that no British official ought to write articles of any kind, still less of a controversial nature. Apart from these two things, he is getting on very well with everybody, and undoubtedly spares no effort to further our cause in the way which seems best to him."†

It would not be fair to suggest, however, that the effect was wholly bad for his publicity did bring home to the Americans what the demands of belligerency were likely to be and his remarks were the more acceptable in that they came not from the stuffed shirt official but the self-made success story of known friendship to the United States. "Moreover, if Northcliffe's un-

* Spring Rice to Balfour, 23rd Nov., 1917. Spring Rice, *op. cit.*, Vol.2. pp.404–5.

† Willert, *op. cit.*, p.110.

bridled publicity shocked Washington, it did much to make the country understand the meaning and demands of belligerency and without annoying it, for to the American public Northcliffe was not a high official behaving improperly, but a great and friendly English newspaper proprietor talking sense."* Nevertheless he had "trodden on just a sufficient number of sensitive toes . . . to make it highly undesirable for him to return"† to America in November. "Northcliffe's recent utterances" wrote Spring Rice "have not given unqualified satisfaction here."°

Because he saw an intimate connection between British propaganda and the success of the War Mission, Northcliffe deluged London with requests for more constructive application in this filed and in particular with the need to publicise the British military effort about which nothing had appeared in the American press and which, in consequence, had been largely unappreciated. How could the American public or Congress be expected to go on lending money if they were never told what it was for or if they remained unaware of the extent to which Great Britain was subsidising her allies? "The majority of people with whom one comes into contact . . . have no notion of the immense sacrifices we have made and are making. I do not know who was responsible for the suppression of this information, [i. e. about the war effort and casualities] in the early days of the War, but whoever he was he has rendered our position here, as beggars on behalf of the British nation, most difficult."+ He suggested that prominent personalities, he instanced General Smuts, should be sent across the Atlantic to put the British case or that more active use could be made of the Press Bureau if the Foreign Office gave it more backing.× On 15th August Northcliffe was writing home to complain that there was no proper military mission in America and that nothing seemed to be known about the

* Willert, *op. cit.*, p.111.
† Percy, *op. cit.*, p.57.
° Spring-Rice, *op. cit.*, Vol.2, p.405, 30th Nov. 1917.
\+ Northcliffe to Lloyd George, 17th July 1917 on the financial situation. George, *op. cit.*, Vol.III, p.1699.
× Pound and Harmsworth, *op. cit.*, p.583.

work of the British navy. Could a high-ranking officer be sent?* The pressure was kept up throughout August and September and gradually London began to thaw. As time went by the mutual interchange of ideas and contacts which the war had often interrupted began once more to flow. Active steps were taken to send both people and information across to America. Neither was a standard pattern adopted. Personalities ranged from the Archbishop of York to Harry Lauder, from members of the Labour Party to representatives of the Y.M.C.A.; there were authors, war correspondents, travellers and sailors. At American request, serving men made a short visit to help launch the Liberty loan; films, photographs, war exhibitions, and speakers for local meetings were organised. All these activities were channelled through the Information Bureau which undoubtedly received a stimulus from the presence and energy of Northcliffe. It thus began to play a far more active role in the field of Anglo–American relations than Spring Rice could ever have envisaged as proper. Whilst he may generally have been over-sensitive about the problem, the successes of the Bureau do not necessarily prove him to have been wrong, only that with the American entry into the war a more forthright presentation of the British war effort had now become acceptable to the recipients.

The financial capacity of England to continue the war was rapidly waning. The large loans she had made to her European allies and her immense purchases of food and raw materials in America had been made possible by financial reserves which by the time of the American entry into the war were near exhaustion point. In order that she could continue to acquire material from America large scale credits or loans were rapidly becoming necessary. This point was at once appreciated by Page who, on

* House, *op cit.*, Vol.3, p.95. Sir Henry Wilson was asked but wouldn't go. Wilson's diary entry is revealing. "I asked who I would be under, and he [Lord Derby] said he thought Northcliffe. I flatly refused to go. We then went over to see Bonar and he tried to persuade me to go; but I said that I could not see any good in it and that I would not serve under Northcliffe, which rather irritated Bonar because he said Northcliffe represented the British Government, to which I naturally replied by asking whether we had not got an Ambassador". See Callwell, *Field–Marshal Sir Henry Wilson*, Vol.II, p.11.

5th March had already informed the President, "Great Britain and France must have a credit in the United States which will be large enough to prevent the collapse of world trade and the whole financial structure of Europe. If the United States declare-war against Germany, the greatest help we could give Great Britain and its Allies would be such a credit".* It is interesting to see that he put forward his view not only as a means of helping the Allies win the war but also as in the best interests of American trade. In the States, however, the problem appeared differently and British negotiators found themselves up against two major difficulties. The one was the general unawareness which was to be found at all levels of opinion of the scale of war-time finance. There was reluctance to believe that the demands being made were really necessary: consequent suspicion that the purchases being made in America would, by re-equipping European industry at American expense, ultimately work to the detriment of the American trader. The need thus existed, first to convince the Administration of the realities of the situation and then for the government to convince Congress in like manner. That this was never done completely came to the surface in the later war-debt controversy. The second main difficulty was that America had never done any large-scale lending abroad; it was thus an unfamiliar field to her in which the appropriate institutions did not exist. On both counts, therefore, a favourable climate of opinion had to be created before American financial resources could be properly mobilised. In consequence, financial matters were not a separate, technical issue with no political implications any more than supply problems had been. Once again the ability to persuade the United States government of the need for credit impinged upon the publicity given to the British case and the acceptance by the American public of the British war effort. It also depended upon reassuring America that money was required for immediate war purposes and thus upon detailed explanations of its use. Such matters were wider than a mere brief to co-ordinate

* Hendrick, *op. cit.*, Part. 2, p.270.

the work of the British war missions and once again Northcliffe found that the pressure of necessity was driving him outside his immediate terms of reference. At the same time these financial questions could not really be handled by the Embassy which was not equipped to deal with specialised financial transactions at this level and which, if it had attempted to deal with them, would have interfered thereby with the work of the Mission. In any case, the United States government did not wish to handle financial questions through normal diplomatic channels. "It is [Mr McAdoo] who distributes proceeds in the forms of loans to the Allies. He naturally wishes to keep financial administration in his hands. But financial administration covers practically all the more important matters in discussion between our Governments. He does not wish these negotiations to be carried on through the State Department. It would be impolitic to take a different point of view. At the request of the Secretary of State I went to see the President to communicate to him the statement of the financial position sent to me by Mr Balfour. The President said that financial matters were in the hands of Mr McAdoo, and that I was to apply to him in all matters of this nature. This express command of the President . . . entitled me to apply direct to Mr McAdoo. I accordingly called upon him and discussed the whole situation. I pointed out to him that Sir Hardman Lever is a financial secretary of the Treasury, and that Lord Northcliffe is charged by H.M.G. with the supreme control of their financial matters in this country. It would therefore be advantageous for all matters of finance to be considered direct in consultation with these two gentlemen. Mr McAdoo is unfortunately resentful of what he believes to be a regrettable misunderstanding arising out of some conversations with Sir Hardman Lever. He also seemed to think that Lord Northcliffe's experience had lain chiefly in the sphere of journalism and not of finance. He evidently would prefer the presence here of a high independent official of the British Government."*

* Spring Rice to Balfour, 13th July, 1917, Spring Rice, *op. cit.*, Vol.2, p.402–3.

Whilst the essential financial problem was, of course, that of making money available to Great Britain in order that she could continue to make her necessary purchases, the spring and summer of 1917 saw two particular difficulties which further complicated the situation. The first was the Morgan overdraft which held the promise of considerable ill-feeling on both sides. Until April 1917 Britain had financed her buying through J. P. Morgan & Co. but with the American entry into the war it was desired to transform the matter into an inter-governmental transaction in which purchases would be made through the United States government and payments made through the United States Treasury. It was not until August 1917 that satisfactory purchasing boards were established to deal with the first side of this problem and in the interim only hand to mouth arrangements existed. Meanwhile at the time of the transfer of the British account from Morgans a large overdraft was outstanding upon which a payment of 400 million dollars was due on July 1st and the problem of repayment of this overdraft was to be a constantly recurring problem not finally settled until June 1919. Considerable security had been lodged with Morgans which, in April 1917, the United States government was unwilling to see flooded onto the market partly because it was itself anxious to raise a war loan. Whilst the Balfour mission had established the principle that the Treasury would lend Britain money out of this war loan, confusion arose as to whether past commitments were also to be covered. Mr Balfour and his party thought that this point had been agreed; Mr McAdoo was firmly of the opinion that it had not. When therefore, at the end of June, Messers Morgan, acting on British instructions, applied to the Treasury for payment the request was refused on the grounds that it had not been promised and that Congress would never sanction such a payment. This item bedevilled financial transactions for many months.

The second problem was the need for speed. It was largely unappreciated in America at first that Great Britain had no more money left and therefore leisurely arrangements to underwrite her were of no use. The need was immediate, pressing and large-scale and all British voices joined in pressing this fact home. On 29th June, Northcliffe saw Colonel House and explained the British requirements very concretely "35 million dollars on Monday; 100 million on Thursday 185 million a month for two months beginning ten days from next Thursday."* The appeals continued with ever increasing frequency. On 1st July Spring Rice, on Balfour's instructions, appealed for urgent financial aid "there is danger that the ability of His Majesty's Government to effect payments in America from today onwards will be in jeopardy".† Back came Northcliffe to the attack. He paid a further visit to House to produce statistics of British expenditure and to press the need for regular financial aid. "It is after having supported an expenditure of this magnitude for three years, that the United Kingdom ventures to appeal . . . for sympathetic consideration in financial discussion, . . . our resources available for payments in America are exhausted. Unless the United States Government can meet in full our expenses in America, including exchange, the whole financial fabric of the alliance will collapse. This conclusion will be a matter not of months but of days."° On 20th July, Page cabled information from the Chancellor of the Exchequer to the effect that British reserves in America were exhausted. The same day Balfour cabled direct to Colonel House asking him to see that the need for immediate cash received the personal attention of the government and stressing the urgency of the situation.+

Although immediate cover was provided, the situation remained full of uncertainties. McAdoo held to the view that it was impossible for him to judge the situation rationally, or to get the necessary authorisation from Congress unless he was given more information about British needs and unless there was greater co-ordination of Allied demands on America so that relative priorities could be established. He pointed out that the United

* Baker, *op. cit.*, Vol.7, p.134 footnote.
† Baker, *op. cit.*, Vol.7, p.139.
° House, *op. cit.*, Vol.3, pp.109–10.
\+ Baker, *op. cit.*, Vol.7, pp.176–7.

States had no positive undertaking to meet needs, that she must reserve her freedom of decision and that she had no commitment to meet the Morgan overdraft.* "America's cooperation" he wrote "cannot mean that America can assume the entire burden of financing the war".†

It had become obvious that more long-term arrangements must be made in which British needs were presented as a whole, some Inter-Allied co-ordination achieved and a British representative capable of pulling together the politico-financial problems involved, appointed. Northcliffe was aware that he had not the status for this, and that he was not really the man for the job. On 12th July, Wiseman reported to Northcliffe and House that the President was pressing for more allied information about their financial needs and general policies. He thought that, as far as the British were concerned, there was no one who could speak with sufficient financial authority to discuss both financial and political problems. It appeared that the President was in favour of the establishment of a council in Paris to determine what was needed from America and the relative degree of urgency underlying the requests.° Northcliffe duly reported home on 17th July "It does not require any imagination to foresee great difficulty in obtaining money from the United States in the future. When we come to the actual point of contact with members of the Government and others . . . all that we have done seems, even if they know it, to be ignored by them . . .

"Mr McAdoo and subsequently Colonel House plainly told us that they insist on knowing whether or not the supplies for which we are asking are of strict military necessity . . . what authority have [we] for saying so? . . . There is a general suspicion that much the huge Russian locomotive and general railway order is in the nature of a 'job' to put the Russian railways in order after the war.

---

* Baker, *op. cit.*, Vol.7, p.153, entry for July 9th.

† *op. cit.*, p.158. McAdoo to Balfour, entry for July 12th.

° Baker, *op. cit.*, Vol.7, p.171.

"... Tardieu,* as a Frenchman, is in a far better position to obtain money than are the English, but he sees the coming danger.

"The Americans are not accustomed to our huge financial operations and it will be a very long time before they are."

The letter continues by urging that "the British Government sets up a co-ordinating War Council, which shall state why each article of supply the Allies require is needed. If that Council be not set up, we shall one day be face to face with one of those abrupt actions on the part of the United States with which by this time we are, I presume, becoming accustomed".†

Spring Rice in a letter of the same month echoed the general difficulties as explained by Northcliffe. It would be very difficult, he thought, to get a new loan through Congress, impossible unless the Administration had the fullest information on where the money had gone in the past and was to go in the future. He reported on an American request for a high level British representative and added his opinion that it must be someone positively acceptable to the President. Despite Northcliffe's progress "The fact remains that the President did not ask for his appointment, and being known here not as a statesman but as a very influential proprietor of newspapers his opinion would not carry very great weight in itself ... This is written to show you that the question of the direct representation of the British Government here is not entirely solved by sending Lord Northcliffe. The only way it could be solved is by taking the President's wishes which it will be extremely difficult to do".°

Thus by July it was clear that finance had become the most important single question in Anglo–American relations and for its proper handling yet further rearrangements would need to be made. Meanwhile Northcliffe seems to have found the irritations of his job increasingly irksome. At the end of the month Spring Rice was reporting that Northcliffe seemed rather tired of busi-

* French High Commissioner in Washington.

† George, *op. cit.*, Vol.III, pp.1699–1701.

° George, *op. cit.*, Vol.III, p.1715. Despatch of 5th **July.**

ness.* It appears he was beginning to hanker after his press and the influence it gave him. His limited authority, his relation with the Ambassador, his involvement in problems which were not his specialist concern must all have grated on him. Neither was he accustomed to working as part of a team and he found it difficult to accept the delays which the British government inflicted on him. He addressed himself thus to the Prime Minister "I have always in my mind the possibilities of friction between the American and British Governments. That is not in my department, but in that of the Ambassador's. I can do much, however, to keep this Government in good humour, but when the Government asks me, for example, for the personnel and power of the Air Board at home, in order to assist them in their discussions here, and no reply is sent to my pressing cable, my position then confirms what they already believed – that they only see us when we come to ask for something"†.

The trouble was wrote Lloyd George that "He was naturally impatient of even inevitable delays. Not accustomed to being thwarted or to have his decision questioned or delayed, in his experience an order rung down the telephone had to be executed forthwith and he expected a report on the same telephone at latest in an hour's time. He had thus acquired a telephone mentality. He was now in a world where the autocrat had to submit to being an all-round subordinate. He was subject to approval of the Home Government – to acceptance or acquiescence by the American Government; to protracted conversations and negotiations – palavering instead of commanding.

"In politics and diplomacy long intricate persuasion is an essential prelude to action. Lord Northcliffe had not even the experience of a provincial Mayor to guide him in the activities which depend more on co-operation than on dictation. For a man of his dictatorial temperament and experience he did well. He was not always ready to make allowances for conditions

* Pound and Harmsworth, *op. cit.*, p.563. Spring Rice to Drummond.
† Pound and Harmsworth, *op. cit.*, pp.557–8.

which neither he nor the British Government had power to control".*

It seems probable that for such reasons Lord Northcliffe began to consider a return to England and as the summer drew on it looked as though he might "prepare an exit".† In November he sailed for home although it was not until he was in England that he finally decided not to return preferring to remain in London as Chairman of the London end of the War Mission and to take up the direction of propaganda to enemy countries.

It is, of course, impossible to say whether anyone else would have done the job better or worse than Northcliffe. He had been sent to pull together the varied strands of British activities in the States before they got out of hand. This he had done. He had found himself involved in matters outside his narrow brief and he had reported on them to his government in the same terms as its other advisers in America. He had carried out his work without fulfilling the worst fears that he would seriously offend the Americans. Northcliffe cared for good Anglo-American relations and was prepared to work for their betterment however much he may have differed from the Ambassador on how to set about the job. And this fundamental good will came through "Northcliffe" says Seymour "brought interminable energy and complete disregard of the impossible, gilded with never-failing good temper".° His ire was directed, not towards the Americans but, as has been seen, towards the British who did not realise the penury of the country and expected the Americans to jump to it to fulfil British requirements. This was an attitude he deplored and had no intention of adopting being more sensitive to the delicacy of the situation than some of his fellow countrymen. Thus the danger that Northcliffe would prove personally unacceptable to the Administration did not develop. As early as the 14th June Spring Rice reported to the Foreign Office that the State Department

* George, *op. cit.,* Vol.III, pp.1701–2.
† Percy to Balfour, Pound and Harmsworth, *op. cit.,* p.547.
° House, *op. cit.,* Vol.3, p.90.

seemed quite reconciled to Northcliffe's arrival* and his later reports were more glowing. "I hear he made an extremely favourable impression"† and his influence steadily increased. On 19th June, House reported that Northcliffe was charmed with Wilson and very anxious to work in harmony with all° and on 5th July, Spring Rice wrote in similar vein. "Lord Northcliffe is making an excellent impression and is seeing a great number of prominent persons here. He must be collecting a great deal of valuable information. There is no objection to him on the part of any official and the President has given him a very favourable reception . . . He is on very good terms with M. Tardieu, who is an old friend, and this is a very important matter at the present moment." + Nor were these only first impressions. Colonel House's opinion of him increased as the weeks went by "Northcliffe is doing good work and is getting along well with everyone".× The mission had important side benefits. The time was now ripe for a more constructive presentation of the British case than had hitherto obtained and Northcliffe's pressure on the government to increase the amount of information made available performed a valuable function. His speeches, whilst a drawback in official circles, made a positive and favourable impact on general opinion. He discovered, too, a common interest in propaganda as a war weapon with Colonel House and it has been suggested that the long discussions they had together on the matter contributed towards the way Northcliffe handled the propaganda machine he was shortly to set up.**

The balance of advantage would thus appear to have been in his favour. Lord Hardinge was the only one to see no good in the Northcliffe mission "He was a complete failure and returned to England in a few weeks' time. The Americans felt that they were as good business men as Northcliffe, and better hustlers

* Pound and Harmsworth, *op. cit.*, p.539.
† On Wilson. Spring Rice to Balfour, George, *op. cit.*, Vol.III, p.1695.
° Baker, *op. cit.*, Vol.7, p.116.
+ George, *op. cit.*, Vol.III. p.1715.
× House, *op. cit.*, Vol.3, p.91, 11th Aug. 1917.
** Pound and Harmsworth, *op. cit.*, p.584.

than he, and they realised that he had none of the charm or distinction that had endeared Balfour to them".* Today this reads simply like ill-tempered professional spite and even Spring Rice, the most affected, had found it possible to be more generous. Whilst he may not have been ideally suited for the job and it is possible to argue that a business man would have been more at home with the internal problems of the Mission the despatch of anyone would equally have been an encroachmen on the traditional authority of the Diplomatic Service, and thus likely to be resented. It was not Northcliffe's personality but the nature of the work itself which led him into fields where other skills were needed. Nowhere was this more true than in the field of finance and once again there is a *prima facie* case for arguing that the diplomatic corps was not the obvious source for the appropriate talent. Personal politics apart, the circumstances of the time would appear to have created a strong compulsion towards the decline of Foreign Office responsibility for Anglo–American relations.

By July it was recognised in Washington circles that more competent financial representation was required since money had now become the key problem. The Americans were quite clear about what was necessary. House held the view that Britain needed to send a man of political experience supported by the appropriate military, naval and technical staff to explain economic and war strategy, to translate these policies into specific demands for money and supplies so that the United States government would know what was going on, why things cost so much and the nature of the desired achievement.† He thus early came to the conclusion that a new representative who could do this was necessary.° The President agreed and Wiseman reported his desire for someone with "sufficient financial authority to discuss the whole situation, both financial and political".+ Mr McAdoo also found the set-up confusing. The British Ambassador,

* Hardinge, *op. cit.*, p.213–4.
† House, *op. cit.*, Vol.3, p.102.
° E.g. House to Wilson. 11th July 1917. House, *op. cit.*, Vol.3, p.108.
+ Wiseman to Foreign Office, 7th August. George, *op. cit.*, Vol.III, p.1718.

Sir Hardman Lever, Lord Northcliffe were all in constant contact with him over financial matters. With whom was he supposed to deal? "Am I to understand that Lord Northcliffe has been designated financial agent of the British Government, and that he will conduct all negotiations? I am really confused by the number of people who undertake to speak for the British Government."* As has been seen, from July these requests from the American government were going back to London with general support. A decision, however, seemed very slow in coming. At first there was a suggestion that Bonar Law should go and this proposal was welcomed by the Americans,† but in default of this possibility they expressed themselves as happy to have Lord Reading. House, Wilson, McAdoo, Northcliffe, Wiseman and Spring Rice all united in believing his would be a successful apointment. The British government, however, hesitated and Northcliffe asked his brother to encourage the Prime Minister to act swiftly. He received the reply that Lloyd George was afraid to confirm the appointment for fear of resurrecting the Marconi scandals.° Finally Wiseman journeyed to London, partly at any rate to persuade the British government to take action in this matter. On 12th August he wrote to Northcliffe "I have now discussed the American situation with the King, the Prime Minister, Bonar Law, Balfour, Milner, Carson, constantly keeping in touch with Geoffrey Dawson whose advice has been invaluable. My conclusions are as follows: The Government realises every day more clearly the importance of the United States and are coming to the view that she must be treated as our most important ally. There is, however, need for this to be kept constantly before the Cabinet owing to the great distance of America and to the fact that members of the Government have little personal knowledge of Washington affairs."+

But another reason also lay behind the British government's

---

* McAdoo to Page, 12th July 1917. Reading, *Rufus Isaacs, 1st Marquess of Reading,* Vol.2, p.58.

† Northcliffe to Lloyd George. George, *op. cit.,* Vol.III, p.1719.

° Pound and Harmsworth, *op. cit.,* p.570.

\+ Quoted, Willert, *op. cit.,* p.118.

dilatoriness for once again it raised the problem of overall representation in the United States. On August 25th Cecil wrote to House "I am afraid lest it should complicate still further our representation in United States, unless in fact it was part of some general rearrangement. ... What powers should Lord Reading have, and how should they be made to fit in with the position of the Ambassador and of Northcliffe if he remained?"* The following day House replied advising that "Lord Reading" or someone like him, who has both a financial and political outlook "be sent to the United States" and given "entire authority over financial questions, Northcliffe to retain charge of all commercial affairs". What was needed he thought was someone who could dominate and compose the situation and who would have the entire confidence of the President.†

On the 28th August the War Cabinet approved Reading's appointment on a special mission to the United States. "Though primarily concerned with finance, he would be authorised to deal with any subject which he considered desirable for the proper discharge of his mission."° Thus once again true discussion of British representation had been shelved; indeed in order to disguise the problem the full importance of his mission and his credentials were not made public. It was thus assumed in Washington, reported Wiseman, that he was but a Treasury representative and indeed mainly concerned with the Morgan overdraft.+ In consequence, for a little while, British relations were handled by three organisations whose business was inevitably interlocked and whose relations were to some extent coloured by personal factors. The shipbuilding programme was being handled by the Embassy but Northcliffe too had been concerned in it. War Mission business was Northcliffe's preserve but this had involved him in other matters also; Reading was concerned with what remained and especially money matters which came into every-

* House, *op. cit.,* Vol.3, pp.123–4.
† Baker, *op. cit.,* Vol.7, pp.235–6.
° George, *op. cit.,* Vol.III, p.1720.
\+ Willert, *op. cit.,* p.121.

thing. Relations between Spring Rice and Northcliffe were bad and although the Ambassador welcomed Reading's appointment as a financial expert, Willert is of the opinion that he resented him as an "outsider" and that Reading in turn found Spring Rice "unhelpful". Neither did the newcomer trust Northcliffe very much.* Perhaps, therefore, it was as well that Northcliffe's sojourn in America ended at the point where he had been able to recognise the need for alternative representation. "He does not seem to mind about his own position"† recorded Wiseman but there was no real reason why he should.

An indication of the true importance attached by the British government to the new appointment is found in the fact that Lord Reading was the bearer of a confidential letter from the Prime Minister to the President which set out Lloyd George's views on the general war situation and the comparative failure of the Allies during the previous year. For this he thought the two main reasons were the Russian collapse and the Allied failure to obtain unity in their military operations, a point which was increasingly occupying his attention and for which he was anxious to obtain the President's support.° Reading also presented a British memorandum on the blockade policy of which neither the Foreign Office, nor the Ministry of Blockade, nor the British Embassy was cognizant and which indeed cut across the lines of approach which the British Embassy was then currently pursuing in Washington.+

The Reading mission resulted in an immediate improvement in the situation in that a further loan was passed by Congress and "House told me . . . that the financial situation would eventually be eased by the coming of Reading and his experts".× What remained was the unsolved problem of the co-ordination of Allied demands upon America which Reading was soon to realise as an imperative necessity. This now became a major problem of

* Willert, *op. cit.*, p.121.
† Willert, *op. cit.*, p.120.
° George, *op. cit.*, Vol.IV, pp.2348–2357.
\+ Percy, *op. cit.*, pp.56–7.
× Northcliffe to Lloyd George, 21st Sept. George, *op. cit.*, Vol.III, p.1724.

Anglo–American relations. In retrospect, the idea of a common cause demanding a common effort and harmonised action within which the respective roles of each nation might be rationally determined appears elementary. At this time, however, the notion of pooling resources in an organic whole was an unnatural one which could not be artificially imposed but which had to be allowed to grow under the forcing house of necessity. Even so, it was impeded by the realisation that the subordination of the national interest to supra-national decision taking was only temporary and limited to the one object which made up the common cause, namely the winning of the war. It was clear that when peace came the cracks in the alliance might gape alarmingly. For such reasons, the necessary machinery could only be created gradually and in consequence those who were convinced of its necessity suffered acute frustration.

An early suggestion that some form of Allied coordination was necessary had come when Balfour had discussed the difficulties resulting from the separate ordering of goods. The mission announced that a joint Allied buying commission could shortly be expected so that the Allies would pay standard prices for their purchases, extortion would be prevented and supplies would be distributed "scientifically and economically".* In the ensuing months, American pressure was exerted towards this object so that she might both be given guidance on relative priorities and would be enabled to explain better to the American public what the goods, and the money to pay for them, were wanted for. After a while came too the need to correlate the growing demands of the U.S. government with those of the Allies in order to prevent them falling over each other's feet in clamouring for the same suppliers, or even more importantly, determining what those demands should be.

A first stage in the process was reached by August 1917. In July, McAdoo had suggested that an Inter-Allied council on war

---

* *The Times History of the War*. Vol.21. British Missions in the United States, p.77.

purchases and finance be created for the Allies and a comparable American purchasing commission to handle affairs for the American government. On 26th July a joint Allied reply expressed hesitation about lodging so much power in a commission over which home governments would have insufficient control, and expressing the need for further discussion of the project, but by August a system of handling requests in the States had been evolved. A joint Allied body was created in Washington through which all demands were passed direct to an American commission composed of Mr Bernard Baruch, Judge Lovett and Mr R.S. Brookings. These gentlemen then became responsible for seeing that allied requirements were met cheaply and promptly subject to first priority being given to the U.S. government and the shipping board. This arrangement, though a help, did not go to the root of the problem for it was simply an administrative technique for dealing with independently determined Allied demands; it did not synthesise them at a policy level as McAdoo and others had had in mind. The delay in facing up to this problem caused growing concern to those in America whose despatches home were increasingly devoted to it. In October, Reading wrote at length upon the matter. Considerable criticism of the handling of the war existed in America, he reported home, but for rather different reasons. Firstly were those who charged that the Administration was ill-organised for war and not sufficiently enthusiastic about waging it and secondly were those who agreed that America's real interest in the war was limited and who were thus suspicious of Allied policies and the danger of America being humbugged. Both these pressures worked on the Administration in the same direction, he thought, namely to emphasise the part America was playing in the war to the detriment of the Allies' contribution and for it to run the supply programme mainly with American needs in mind. Thus a vast American programme had been drawn up with no regard to the existing programmes of the Allies or to the date at which they might become effective as compared with Allied plans. He foresaw that in the ensuing three months particular pressures would work to the detriment of Britain and indeed to the Allied cause as a whole. The first of these was that U.S. Treasury officials, who were nervous and depressed, would hesitate to commit themselves. Thus, although in the end the money would come, the process would never be clear cut but full of anxious delays. Secondly, American demands would always come first, any shortages of funds would thus fall on the Allies. Thirdly, in the future, the essential shortages would not be monetary but real and it was obvious whose interests were likely to suffer when priorities were determined. "The growing lack of co-ordination between the programme of the Administration here and the programme of the Allies is probably, on every ground, the biggest question in front of us."* Thus Reading posed the problem. Would American help be more efficient if applied to existing Allied plans and armies than if it were built up as an independent war effort? If so, then this implied both a greater definity in Allied plans so that America knew what she was aiming at and the need for greater American participation in their shaping. Supply and financial problems could not be isolated from war strategy or, indeed, from politics and Reading suggested that a U.S. mission be sent to Europe to thrash the matter out.

Northcliffe wrote in similar vein. He pointed out the need for centralised control and the need to re-consider military plans in view of the Western deadlock as well as the mounting confusion on war aims because of the entry of so many powers into the war. Wiseman, too, urged that House should be asked to Europe in order to provide the impetus to bring all efforts under some form of unified control. He also pressed his view on House. "I believe that the greatest asset Germany has today is the 3,000 miles that separate London from Washington; and the most urgent problem we have to solve is how our two governments can effect the close co-operation which is undoubtedly necessary if the war is to be quickly and successfully ended".†

The Prime Minister was ready to comply. Not only was he concerned with economic co-ordination but he hoped that Ameri-

* House, *op. cit.*, Vol.3, pp.186–7.
† Willert, *op. cit.*, p.126.

can backing would be available for his plans for greater military unity and for a second front. The matter was thus soon arranged. On 16th October the Allied Ambassadors in Washington were told of America's willingness to send a delegate to the Inter-Ally Council of War Purchases and Finance in a consultative capacity for by now the Administration was extremely concerned with the critical nature of all the practical problems of the war. Finance, supply, shipping and the blockade, all presented grave and urgent difficulties for which more constructive methods were required,* for McAdoo's letter of 18th July had not yet resulted in any effective co-ordination. Later that month House sailed for London.† "Nobody" he wrote "except those on the inside can know of the wasted effort there has been."° He arrived fully committed to the view that there must, at the very least, be much fuller co-operation between the allies to determine the needs which they expected America to fulfil. "Here in Washington," wrote *The Times* correspondent, "the officials have struggled for six months to find out just what the Allies want."+ Before proceeding to Paris, House had preliminary discussions in London. In so far as these related to his desire for a public declaration of liberal peace aims, he was unsuccessful. Through Wiseman he sounded both the Prime Minister and Foreign Secretary but neither felt the moment opportune and both feared the ill effect on public morale of any suggestion of a compromise peace. It was submitted that allied war aims were sufficiently well stated already.× With regard to greater material co-ordination, however, he was preaching to the converted and, at Paris, Allied agreement was at last reached. Joint allied councils covering the fields of purchase, finance, shipping, food and blockade were created whereby, *inter alia*, allied needs might be correlated, discussed with American representatives and orders be ultimately submitted to the United States

* House, *op. cit.,* Vol.3, p.193 and Baker, *op cit.,* Vol.7, p.309.

† House's arrival was announced in *The Times* on 9th Nov. The next column but one is headed "Coup d'etat in Petrograd. Lenin deposes Kerensky."

° Willert, *op. cit.,* p.132.

+ *The Times,* 6th November 1917.

× Willert, p.134.

Government on a priority basis. Obviously these arrangements contained the promise of a very much more orderly system which would also satisfy the American demand for information on the need for borrowed money. Naturally the machine was not perfect and it was always possible for those nearer the war to get impatient with delays. "We have so often had large promises in the past which have invariably been falsified in result that I am sincerely apprehensive that this last undertaking [i.e. sending troops to France] may not be carried out in actual practice. Everything depends upon your going beyond the ordinary province of an Ambassador and exercising personal supervision over the carrying out of pledges. . . . Immediately a hitch does occur we rely upon you to bring pressure to bear to secure its immediate removal."* In broad terms, however, the practical problems involved in waging total war in an alliance had impelled their solution and this was one which lay outside the normal scope of diplomatic machinery and for which other types of persons seemed to be better suited.

The letter from Lloyd George anticipates a further development in the problem of British representation in the United States. Although it was not generally known, Reading had been asked to survey the whole question and to submit a report,† a matter self-evidently necessary and only rendered more important by the friction between Embassy and Mission. Spring Rice accepted the fact that keeping affairs in watertight compartments would not work and that some form of centralised control was necessary.° Northcliffe and Reading talked about the need to bring all political, diplomatic and financial affairs together under one head as they journeyed back to England that November.+ The problem simply remained to decide who would be best fitted to do this. It could not be Spring Rice, by now described by House as an "excitable invalid"× General agreement appeared to exist that

* Lloyd George to Reading, March 1918, quoted Willert, *op. cit.*, pp.141–2.
† Willert, *op. cit.*, p.120.
° Spring Rice to Chirol. 26–1–18. Spring Rice, *op. cit.*, Vol.2, p.426.
\+ Pound and Harmsworth, *op. cit.*, p.590.
× Pound and Harmsworth, *op. cit.*, p.577.

the person appointed would need to be able to deal with the changed content of Anglo–American relations; to possess the confidence of the American government and be intimately connected with the inner workings of British politics. Such a one was not to be found within the ranks of the career Diplomatic Service for due to the nature, scale and speed of the problems as well as for their solution a semi-political appointment was necessary. Lord Reading himself seemed a fairly obvious choice and his appointment was announced on 8th January 1918. He was designated as High Commissioner and special Ambassador with full authority over the members of all British missions whose work was brought completely under his direction and control. In addition, as the recognised channel between the American and British governments he was called upon to deal with many other problems as the fortunes of war brought them to the surface.

Mr McAdoo received the appointment enthusiastically, but the President was more lukewarm.* There seems to have been some slight American prejudice against him because of his German–Jewish wife† and his connection with the pre-war Marconi case.° This may have made the President a little reserved. Essentially, however, Reading was concerned with immediate, practical war-time problems and in the event he did not stay long in America. It appears that from the start he had never intended to do so.+ These problems were essentially different from the normal content of diplomatic business; they were also ones which in their nature required urgent executive decision. As Balfour was later to write "The difficulties were great; they were without precedent; they were quite outside ordinary diplomatic routine; they involved most complicated questions of finance, shipping, food-supply, troop-transportation and armaments. Though they profoundly affected the fortunes of all the Allies, they had to be dealt with in the main between Great Britain and America, and you provided

* Pound and Harmsworth, *op. cit.*, p.590. McAdoo had specially asked for his 'skilled advice'.

† Pound and Harmsworth, *op. cit.*, p.590.

° Willert *op. cit.*, p.120.

\+ Reading, *op. cit.*, Vol.2, p.74.

the most important personal link between the two great Associated Powers".* The first problem with which Reading was faced was the urgent need to get more food to Europe; this in turn gave place to that of getting more American troops immediately to the fighting lines and, constantly recurring, was the emptiness of the British purse. In each case the problem can be divided into two stages; the first that of convincing the Administration of its urgency and size and the second that of participation in the means of its solution. In both stages Reading was helped enormously by the fund of American goodwill and eagerness to participate with maximum effect in the common purpose, and in negotiation his job was simplified by the essential willingness to reach agreement which existed on both sides. This is not to imply however that personal factors had become negligible, for Reading brought great advantages for these tasks He had already been in America on financial missions during 1915 and 1917 and was thus not only knowledgeable about one of the specialist problems with which he was called upon to deal but was already *persona grata* with many of the United States officials with whom he was now brought once again into contact. His legal training and gifts of advocacy provided an analysis of technical problems, and a decisiveness in urging a plan for their solution. The fact that Reading was a man of high political status who was fully *au fait* with the current situation at home and who was acceptable to both House and Wilson was of great importance in achieving a cordial atmosphere of good will in which matters could be discussed. In July 1918, Willert wrote home that Reading was a great success. His handling of American officials had been a vital factor in settling the food situation; to him belonged much of the credit for American troop movements and for the conclusion of the Russian issue. He had made for himself a commanding position in Washington "and in a few months has effectively rescued the Embassy from the slough into which it had fallen".† The enhanced status of the

* Reading, *op. cit.*, Vol.2, p.146. Balfour to Reading.
† Willert, *op. cit.*, p.139. Willert to *The Times,* July 1918.

Embassy doubtless contributed to his acceptance by the diplomatic staff who had viewed his appointment with the reserve and apprehension natural to those who watch the supersession of a colleague by an outsider who, in addition, becomes their chief.* Nothing, however, succeeds like success and Reading had helped to restore the Embassy to the centre of affairs, even to the extent of relying less upon the Wiseman link than Northcliffe had done,† though the ability to do this depended in part upon the willingness of Wilson to see it superseded. In any case there were precedents for the appointment of a non-career diplomat at Washington and a strong case could be made out for Reading in view of the problems with which Anglo–American relations were currently concerned and the need for contact with a multiplicity of government departments and officials rather than simply the State Department. Certainly his handling of affairs commended itself to the British government and in July 1918 Balfour expressed the hope that he would find it possible to continue as Ambassador.°

That month, however, Reading asked for permission to return to England to discuss the complications of the Russian situation. According to Willert he was, even then, in two minds whether to return because of the barriers which existed between the President and the foreign representatives and his suspicion that he could accomplish no more than any other Ambassador might.+ How far this influenced his actions it is impossible to say but the fact of the matter is that once he reached England in August he was at once swept into the hurly-burly of activities at home. As a result he did not return to America until February 1919 and then only to clear up. Once again an interregnum in diplomatic representation had occurred. Anglo–American relations had been allowed to go by default through lack of awareness of the need to take positive and continuous action to maintain their cordiality.

---

* The apprehension was not entirely one-sided being felt by Reading too, Reading, *op. cit.*, Vol.2, pp.71 and 75.

† Willert, *op. cit.*, p.138. The author states Reading agreed to use Wiseman on Embassy matters but not War Mission affairs.

° Reading, *op. cit.*, Vol.2, p.135.

\+ Willert, *op. cit.*, p.139.

The day to day work of any organisation must inevitably suffer if it is left without an effective head but this is not perhaps the most important criticism to be made. The damage was done not so much in a less-effective war effort as in the more nebulous sphere of atmosphere and good will to whose importance reference was drawn at the beginning of this chapter. It was a little hard for the Americans to understand why the British government should assume their Ambassador was of more use first in London and then in Paris rather than in Washington. This is perhaps one of the dangers of using the politician rather than the career diplomat as Ambassador; to the former the job is only one of many responsibilities to be viewed as of an essentially temporary nature in the larger scheme of things. But in those critical months of 1918 this viewpoint denigrated the importance of Anglo-American relations to the point of absurdity. By implication, at the very least, it appeared that Britain attached little importance to America once she had got what she wanted for immediate war purposes. The American pressure for Reading's return to Washington increased,* whilst *The Times* came out publicly in defence of the American interest "Lord Reading left Washington as long ago as last July, for a flying visit home, and he has been detained until this week by a series of unexpected duties in London and Paris. Doubtless these duties have been of great importance to the affairs of the Allies. But his failure to return to the United States has not prevented serious heart-searchings among our friends across the Atlantic. There is abundant evidence of dissatisfaction there that during the last six critical months the Embassy should have been left without a head. The evidence accumulates by every American mail until it is obvious that, however much modern means of swift intercourse may have impaired the independence and hence the prestige of Ambassadors, Americans are convinced that their local conditions require, as one of the key stones of really satisfactory Anglo–American relations, a first-class British representative in Washington".†

* Reading, *op. cit.,* Vol.2, p.144.

† *The Times,* Feb. 14th 1919.

CHAPTER 8

THE DEMAND FOR A DEMOCRATIC FOREIGN POLICY

I

The closing stages of the war were notable for a wide-spread demand for greater democracy in international affairs as part of the new world which was to arise from the ashes of the old. In the larger sense this aspiration implied the creation of a new moral order based upon 'the reign of law, the consent of the governed and sustained by the organised opinion of mankind'; in the narrower, a closer and more detailed control over the practices of diplomacy. Whilst the main stream of new hope came from across the Atlantic, an important tributary flowed from Great Britain whose Radical tradition developed and expounded what had been begun before the war into a coherent theory of international relations. War, it was believed, was eradicable from human society provided the people in fact sanctioned the main lines and vital decisions of foreign policy.* Now that whole continents were involved in war with consequent devastation and loss for millions of ordinary people, it was essential that diplomacy should be controlled by them and operated in their interests. Provided the democratisation of Europe was general, foreign policies could for the first time express the true interests of the nations rather than the wishes of small governing classes who equated their own desires with those of the people. Within this broader context therefore we must place the desire for the adoption by Great

---

* See, for example, *Foreign Affairs,* July 1919.

Britain of foreign policy objectives which were wholesome and good; the creation of a system in which democratic control over the conduct of foreign affairs would be assured and the reform of the Foreign Service as the executive arm of the state. This desire for improvement arose directly out of the faults of the past and the necessity to avoid them for the future, for it is clear that critics had found much to deprecate in the traditional ways whilst the experiences of the years preceding 1914 had led to the conclusion that the whole system, and its trappings in the form of traditional techniques, must be washed away for ever. Viewed from this angle the old diplomacy had not only been the servant of a system which contained, and even in its extreme form approved of, war but was now held to be in part responsible for it.

There is something ironic about the fact that the air was thick with enthusiasms for a more realistic and representative diplomacy at a time when the traditional checks on executive action were at a minimum. Both Cabinet and Commons had abdicated their responsibilities whilst the existence of a free Press was questionable. It was a curiosity that did not go unnoticed that the negotiation of a democratic peace, and the handling of the tremendously complex aftermath of the war, was left in the hands of those whose political position was virtually one of dictatorship.* The opposition to Lloyd George's methods of government, however, took further time to mature into an irresistible force, in the meanwhile enthusiasm fixed upon the creation of a new international order and a reformed and pacific foreign policy executed by an agency appropriate to, and sensitive of, the needs of a new world.

It is customary, when writing upon problems of diplomacy, to insist upon the separation of policy and technique in order to avoid the confusion of two elements which are in fact distinct. Professional writers suggest this is a common public error.† This may be so, but it is not a charge which can fairly be levied against

* See e.g. L. Maxse, *Fortnightly Review,* 1st May 1922.

† E.g. H. Nicolson, *The Evolution of Diplomatic Method,* p.86.

the articulate critics of diplomacy at the end of the first world war when Ponsonby, Morel and their supporters in Parliamentary debates took pains to deny that they were naive enough to suppose that day to day control over negotiation was either possible or desirable.* They did however see a connection between the objects of foreign policy, the control thereof, the types of persons who became diplomats and the influences which were brought to bear upon the process of policy-making. The gravamen of their charge was that "diplomacy" in its largest sense was a class business which needed reform both at the level of policy and execution. "The possession of the Eton manner or the correct ritual of a Christ Church address is a far straighter road to diplomatic success than the surest grasp of Balkan intrigue."† As aggressive national policies, secret diplomacy and a caste-ridden foreign service had gone together before 1914, so internationalism, democratic diplomacy and a reformed foreign service were linked for the post-war millenium. However much we may wish to separate them today, "open convenants openly arrived at" expressed shortly the totality of the new international world in which both aspects were intertwined. Indeed the new role of diplomacy was a matter widely accepted, even, apparently, by the British government for it "is no longer a question as between Court and Court, but it operates as between people and people."° For this reason the reformers thought it to be of particular importance that the composition of the delegation to the Peace Conference should be such as to represent, understand and be responsive to, the new feelings and aspirations abroad in the world. Persons with first-hand knowledge of the problems involved, delegates from labour, Parliament and the workers would represent the whole people in a way that traditional diplomacy could not. "We fear, however, that the

* See e.g. Ponsonby, *Democracy and Diplomacy,* p.25. Numerous articles in Foreign Affairs; *Hansard* 19–3–18, Vol.104, Cols.852–3 "Control over foreign affairs does not mean interference with the conduct of actual negotiations."

† Diplomaticus. The Reform of Diplomacy. *The New Europe,* Vol.IV, No.47, 6th Sept. 1917.

° Cecil, 31–7–18, *Hansard,* Vol.109. Col.569.

Government as a whole, and the "War" Cabinet in particular, are treating far too lightly the whole matter of preparing for the Inter-Allied Conference, which will be much more important than the final Peace Conference. Various names of prospective British delegates are being mentioned, together with those of the chief technical advisers to be sent from the Foreign Office. The latter are frankly disquieting. They include the names of several diplomatists and officials whose past record has been marred by some obvious failures, and whose ignorance of the subjects upon which they will presumably be the chief advisers of the delegates can be fully appreciated only by those who have had dealings with them. It is indispensable that men of sound first-hand knowledge should be employed to advise the Government in regard to the many critical questions that await treatment and settlement. There are none too many such men in the British Empire, and there are next to none in the diplomatic service. Diplomatists and departmental officials rarely, if ever, acquire first-hand knowledge. They live in a world of "papers", "minutes" and general second-hand unrealities. Fortunately, the Dominions are likely to be well represented. India also may find good spokesmen. The Navy will doubtless make its voice heard; but what provision is being made for the proper representation of Parliament, of Labour, and of the nation-wide classes that have supplied men and women for the Army, for munitions and for the land, and are therefore directly interested in securing a thoroughly sound and lasting peace? Diplomatists are not capable of making the kind of peace the nation wants. They have no sense of the things about which the people of this country are really thinking. Nor do they know that, despite the restrictions that have prevented the nation as a whole from understanding many of the features of the war and the requirements of a just peace, public comprehension of the general problem awaiting solution is far in advance of the degree of comprehension yet exhibited by the official world."* The war,

---

* How to Make Peace. *The New Europe,* Vol.IX, No.111, 28th Nov. 1918. See also A. F. Whyte in *The New Europe,* Vol.V, No. 65, 10th Jan. 1918.

after all, had had a revolutionary character and men's minds were turning to the possibility of rebuilding the world on new, democratic principles. "Under the stress of these three mighty factors [i.e. the overthrow of Czardom, the entry of the U.S.A., the enormity of war-time sacrifice] the conflict in the war between the principle of right and the principle of power was decided in favour of the principle of right."* Since "The diplomacy with which the Allies were equipped at the beginning of the war drew their inspiration very much more from the balance of power than from the principle of right" the conclusion followed that "Great Britain positively invites a repetition of disaster if she leaves the negotiation of peace in the hands which have so grievously failed her in the test of war."† As long as the Foreign Services of the nations were drawn from "the old, discredited school" the fear remained that, if the country had won the war, the Old Gang was now about to lose the peace.

The end of the war was in any case a convenient moment to consider afresh the responsibilities of the Foreign Service. The growth of governmental interest in community life necessitated a general reconsideration of the tasks of the civil service, and perhaps the Foreign Service, least of all the departments, could expect to remain immune in view of the vast changes which were taking place both in the world and in Britain's position within it. The war had shown that British overseas concerns were no longer solely political but at the very least contained economic and informational problems, whilst the peace opened up a vast new area of work in the setting up of the League of Nations. To consider the organisation of the Foreign Service was thus a practical necessity as well as a moral imperative.

One must not give the impression that these ideas were held only by men hostile to traditional diplomatic circles. On the contrary, a wide measure of agreement on the need for reform existed.

---

* Bankrupt Diplomacy. An article reprinted by *The New Europe*, Vol.IX, No. 111, 28th Nov. 1918.

† Diplomaticus, "The Reform of Diplomacy", *The New Europe*, Vol.IV, No. 47, 6th Sept. 1917.

It was a moment when a consensus of opinion was fumbling towards a vision of the national interest truly expressive of the aspirations of all and which could be served by a machine of first-class efficiency. Thus much concrete and sensible suggestion came from persons who had their own experiences and knowledge to contribute whilst the Foreign Service itself was not resistant to change or unaffected by these vitalising winds stimulating the vision of a new international order. On the contrary, it too was anxious to play its part in building world society on a saner basis and to spring-clean itself that it might be better fitted so to do and in the process to provide more satisfying opportunities for the men who worked within its walls. "Nowhere were these hopes more vividly cherished than in the Foreign Office itself,"* for the constructive desires expressed from within, or from persons very close to the working problems of the Foreign Service, amounted to the hope that the opportunity would be grasped to destroy, once and for all, the association, whether real or assumed, with the élite and the image of the Diplomatic Service as a home for the incompetent fop in favour of the creation of a machine truly representative of the country which could get to grips with the stuff of reality rather than be kept "playing politics" in an unhealthy pre-war way. One can therefore detect a certain coalescence of view as the war came to an end between reformers from without and reformers from within in which both parties could recognise that, far from being irreconcilable opponents, they were partners in a co-operative enterprise.† Most thinking people were probably ready to admit that the phrase "secret diplomacy", although used wildly on occasion, did imply something undesirable which had been practised in the pre-war system and to recognise that its condemnation was not just a foolish notion of the irresponsibles. "Secret Diplomacy is undeniably in some disrepute today, not only among Pacifist 'cranks', . . . but with the generality of sound and sensible people, as being incompatible

* Percy, *The New Europe,* Vol.XI, No.133, 1st May 1919.
† G. Young, *The New Europe,* Vol.VII, No.86, 6th June 1918.

with the spirit of the age in which we live."* Mr Seton-Watson, in a review of Lord Loreburn's book *How the War Came,* made the same point. "Lord Loreburn is perfectly right in drawing the conclusion that the old secret diplomacy has utterly failed and ought to be ended once and for all [and we must abandon] the intolerable atmosphere of secrecy in which a few mediocre and by no means well-informed statesmen played with the lives of millions during the Great War."† It is, of course, possible to distinguish different emphases in the desires for reform in that those from outside dealt more with first principles whilst the "professionals" emphasised the improvement of technical efficiency. Each was necessary and neither incompatible with the other. It remains to be considered what these wishes were and to what extent they were fulfilled.

It is noticeable how often the comment of the day fastens on the loss of confidence felt by the country in the handling of foreign affairs as the divorce between press, Parliament and people on the one hand and government and Foreign Service on the other grew noticeably wider.° It was this above all that reformers were anxious to remedy as the key problem of democracy in relation to foreign policy in order to create that intimacy of contact and daily understanding without which true appreciation of differing points of view can never be expected. It was this very lack of confidence in "the system" which Balfour failed to appreciate in his scathing attack on the proposal to set up a Foreign Affairs Committee of

---

* L. Maxse, Some Studies in Secret Diplomacy, *The National Review,* July 1918.

It is common to point to Lloyd George's diplomacy as an awful example of what happens when the old, tried ways are abandoned for new-fangled notions and in consequence a certain denigration of open diplomacy and a swing back in favour of old diplomacy occurred. This seems unfair since Lloyd George's system of diplomacy bore little relation to the demands at present under discussion. His methods were characterised by their use of non-specialist personnel and advisers, *ad hoc* arrangements and, indeed, their secrecy. Hence Bertie's comment, as early as Jan. 1918 "With regard to secret diplomacy, there is more of it now by those who decry it than when it was not accursed." *op. cit.*, Vol.2, p.244.

† R. Seton–Watson, *The New Europe,* Vol.XIII, No. 161, 13th Nov. 1919

° See e.g. *Hansard,* Vol.97, Col.1652; Vol.109, Col.552; Vol.116, Col. 490–1. Also G. Young, *Diplomacy Old and New.*

the House of Commons,* a proposal which attracted considerable support. Impractical and unworkable it may have been but its purpose was anything but trivial and the short shrift given to it by the government was an indication of how little the true needs of the situation were understood.

The argument in favour of a greater association of the people with foreign affairs rested ultimately on the belief that it was only through such a connection that a moral element would be injected into foreign policy and thus the creation of an informed public opinion was a necessary condition if the world was to be saved from destroying itself in the future. It was remarked that in the days of Gladstone when the public had been more closely linked with events abroad foreign policy had also had some connection with humanitarian problems and moral questions, whilst in the years before the war, as the public became less concerned, so foreign policy became increasingly a-moral. "the immorality of the diplomatic mind lies in its making concessions not on principle but under pressure."† Whilst it could thus be argued that it was both necessary and right that the public should truly be the arbiter of foreign policy, the advocates of the people were also determined that such control should be exercised responsibly. Their concern was thus a twofold one embracing the proper consultation of the people and the offer by the public of an informed and intelligent opinion on the issues placed before it. Perhaps naively, they believed that this was a reasonable objective largely dependent upon the provision by the government of the day of adequate information concerning public events; the proper control of the Commons over the Executive and the democratisation of the Foreign Service. If the people understood, then the people would be peaceful; it was their ignorance which caused both their bellicosity and their emotional responses to international affairs. If, therefore, the ignorance were to be removed, the aggressiveness which was its symptom would also be destroyed to be replaced

* 19–3–18, *Hansard,* Vol.104, Col.867, *et seq.*
† George Young, *op. cit.,* p.18.

by a pacific influence based on the intelligent participation of peoples and the publicity, discussion and debate which was necessary to ensure it.* The basic object, therefore, was to replace the existing divisions between the Foreign Office and the country at large with a situation in which both were working together in the same direction. National policy should not be a duel of opposing impulses but a co-ordination of national forces and governmental function. "Confidential communication, whether with foreign representatives or representatives of the people, is not what is attacked as "secret diplomacy". "Secret diplomacy" stands condemned because it is not secret when success needs that it should be, and is secret when success needs that it should not be; and also because it is out-of-date diplomacy. The diplomacy of today works with public forces and facts. These forces may be pacific and progressive or they may not; but if they are not, it does not follow, therefore, that democracy does not make for peace in external relations. For when democracies are not pacific in their foreign relation to each other, it is because in this relation there is no democracy – that is no co-ordination of forces with functions. The more democracy there is in that relation, the more pacific will it be and the more progressive the diplomacy on both sides."† In order to achieve this fusion of interest, citizens had an obligation of concern but the government was responsible for their education. Here the traditions of the nineteenth century were once more invoked to explain that it had once been customary to include foreign affairs in party speeches, electioneering campaigns, public meetings and the like. This had declined with the doctrine of continuity but if the Foreign Minister were to consider it his duty to make periodic statements, especially when Parliament was not sitting, the public would be better able to participate. Furthermore, so it was argued, a better informed public would ultimately work to the benefit of the government for it would be capable of appreciating the reasons for policy and thus be less likely to

---

* See, for example, A. Ponsonby, *Parliament and Foreign Policy,* published by the Union of Democratic Control.

† G. Young, *The New Europe,* Vol.VII, No.86, 6th June 1918.

indulge in the volatile emotionalism over poorly understood issues which made it so difficult for governments to pursue a rational line. Far from being a drag on the government, an educated public opinion would be enabled to support and succour statesmen as they carried out their policies.* Thus whether the question of foreign policy was looked at from the outside in terms of democratic theory and the urge for instruction that the people be no longer deceived or from the more professional viewpoint of the despatch of government business the conclusion was the same. Somehow a way had to be found to minimise the gap between the governors and governed.

It is a tribute to British parliamentary democracy that it was assumed the necessary mechanism for achieving this could be found fairly easily within it. All that was really necessary was to make the Commons an effective institution for the control of foreign affairs thus curbing the traditional freedom of the executive to which reference was made at the beginning of this work and which, it was now clear, could be exploited. The revelation of the French relationship had given a shock to the fabric of parliamentary government from which many people never recovered. Confidence in the operation of the system, already weakened, was finally destroyed for them by the shattering experiences of the war whose very onset might in part be attributed to these dislocations. If sometimes the criticisms of the period seem far-fetched, they may yet be understood if this essential fact is borne in mind. What was looked for was not revolution but the tightening up of arrangements whose faults were those of omission rather than commission and where the laxity of public and Parliament was, in the last analysis, to blame for the sins of the past.† Whilst "there is no custom or understanding that Parliament shall be consulted beforehand in any class of foreign affairs . . . Obviously no prudent Ministry would venture on any new departure in foreign policy without being, in one way or another, assured

* L. Maxse, *National Review,* July 1918. Some Studies in Secret Diplomacy.

† Ponsonby. 19–3–18, *Hansard,* Vol,104, Col.848. G. Young. *Diplomacy Old and New,* p.15.

of its ground. Certainly it may be said, and I think with too much truth, that attention to these matters in the House of Commons has been neither so continuous nor so competent as it ought to have been. That has nothing to do with the system. Ignorance and indifference in the House merely reflect the same state of mind in the constituencies. There has always been a group of well-informed members . . . but they have never been numerous or made much impression on the public."

The result of the lack of general intelligence and comprehension in the House "has led to much time being wasted on petty curiosity and carping censure of details with small profitable results."* It had been no one's full responsibility to ensure that the government kept up to the high standard which had once been expected of it and thus out of drift, indifference, ignorance and mistaken judgements had developed a situation which was unacceptable to the British tradition. "Properly, Parliament or the press should criticise, the Cabinet should control, the Foreign Secretary conduct, and the Ambassador counsel. But the way our system really works now is that a Foreign Office clerk counsels, controls and conducts, the Foreign Secretary criticises, and nothing else counts at all".† Some, it is true, detected a more sinister element in that traditional arrangements enabled the development of a governing group whose interests were pursued with cynical disregard of the well-being of the nation in favour of that of class and whose policies were executed under the cover of hypocritical lip-service to the cause of democracy. For these critics, the vital problem was to deal with the existence of 'a camarilla'; namely the ruling oligarchy of the country whose stranglehold on foreign policy was only too effective. E.D. Morel defined this most completely. To him it consisted of a small group composed normally of the few dominating personalities in the Cabinet, and including the Secretaries of State for Foreign Affairs and War, the First Lord of the Admiralty; the chief members of the Parliamentary Opposition;

* F. Pollock, *The New Europe,* Vol.VII, No.83, 16th May 1918.
† Young, *op. cit.,* p.49.

the service heads of the Army and Navy, the members of the Committee of Imperial Defence; two or three powerful ambassadors and the top permanent officials of the Foreign Office. Such a group might at times include the court. Round this hard core revolved certain other individuals from the world of high finance, banking, industry, society and journalism to form the real rulers of the country. Furthermore, "our ruling oligarchy is the most subtle in the world" and because it saw the rise of the common people with fear and distaste was taking the necessary steps to retain power whilst pretending to work for the emancipation of the people. The withdrawal of foreign affairs from party debate through the agreement of the two front benches was one way of excluding the mass of the people from participation, whilst the encouragement to a vulgar and soulless journalism, and the lack of money spent on education reinforced this exclusion by turning public attention elsewhere, encouraging its emotionalism and making it unable to participate.* Thus one of the objects of the Union of Democratic Control was to convince the workers that their vital interests were threatened at every point by a system under which the relations of one nation with another, and therefore the issues of Peace and War, were conducted by a small and narrow oligarchy, out of touch with democratic sentiment and opposed to democratic progress.†

Echoes of this approach can be found elsewhere. "But neither in constitutional theory nor in actual practice is there anything to prevent ministers reverting at any moment to the old basis. Public opinion is fitful in its action, and the League of Nations as yet remains a paper covenant. And meanwhile the Crown's prerogative has in foreign affairs, as in so much else, become little better than a convenient legal fiction behind which two, or at most a tiny group of ministers, are free to take immensely important decisions almost unobserved and without any sustained or authorised attempt at control upon their actions. One of the first duties of Parliament is to assert itself in the field of foreign

* E. D. Morel, *Foreign Affairs,* Vol.III, No. 3, February 1922.
† *Foreign Affairs,* Vol.1, No.2.

relations and to insist upon the formation of a properly constituted Foreign Affairs Committee, analagous to those which work so successfully in the French Chamber and in the American Senate."*

The immediate problem was seen as the need to reassert the supremacy of Parliament. It was not difficult to state the case for believing that during the war the Commons had abdicated from its traditional position of control over the executive for the best of patriotic reasons.† It had been easly for the government to represent inquiry as injury to the war effort and the abasement of Parliament had continued under Lloyd George. The growth of bureaucracy during the war had made it more difficult for the Commons to find out what was happening. "For some time it has been apparent that the control of Parliament is being undermined, that the Executive and the permanent officials have assumed the power which, if not checked, threatens to become a menace to our Parliamentary life."° Thus a key point of reform was the demand for an annual discussion of foreign affairs in which the Foreign Secretary should make a far-reaching survey of events and policies. Such a survey could well take place on the Foreign Office vote and would provide the opportunity for a general discussion and summing up of British foreign policy. A full dress occasion such as this would help a great deal to educate the ordinary member in international problems and to keep the links between Parliament and executive alive. Never again, it was argued, must the country fall into the position where foreign affairs were the least discussed of the country's business or where so few back benchers were really knowledgeable about external affairs. Never again must the country become the victim of the doctrine of continuity and the elevation of foreign policy above party politics. Constant discussion in Parliament was one method of overcoming the disadvantages which such principles, enunciated with the best of intentions or not, could now be seen to have.

* R. Seton Watson, *The New Europe*, Vol.XIII, No.161, 13th Nov.1919.

† E.g., C. Trevelyan, The House of Commons in War Time, *The U.D.C.* Vol.3, No.5, March 1918.

° Henry, 4–4–17, *Hansard*, Vol.92, Col.1363.

Secondly, men insisted that, for the future, no treaty should be valid until ratified by Parliament. It will be remembered that Dicey's view had been that this was unnecessary for the sake of legality but essential for that of democracy. When, therefore, Grey denied* that it was necessary to submit treaties to Parliament for its sanction, although he believed it proper to do so for treaties of an unusual character, he was in good company. No longer however could the country rely upon the good faith of the executive. Its experiences of what the government, or certain sections of it, could hide led to the conclusion that all that was secret was bad and to find the remedy in the insistence upon the openness of all engagements. "Was ever a fact of our political life brought home more tragically than the fact that the House of Commons has no control over the treaty-making powers of the Executive? ... What is the use of talking of democratic control, or even Ministerial control, when a great nation like this can be practically bound for years to war and the representatives of the people have no knowledge of the facts."† Thus the express consent of Parliament to all agreements, alliances or commitments was demanded for the future with the periodic review of all obligations to see if they were still in accord with the country's needs and interests. Perhaps it is unnecessary to add that the same view was applied to the declaration of war which should not be possible without the consent of Parliament. "it should be regarded as a definite rule that no treaty which would involve important consequences, certainly no treaty involving peace or war, should ever be made by the Executive of the day behind the back of Parliament. Any such treaty should be definitely laid before Parliament and an opportunity given to it to express its views. It appears to me that these large and grave matters are too vast to allow them to be dealt with in any country that claimed to be self-governing without an opportunity being given to the representatives of the people as a whole to express their views."°

* 29–6–14, *Hansard,* Vol.64, Col.127.
† O'Connor, 4–4–17, *Hansard,* Vol.92, Col.1376.
° Samuel, 4–4–17. *Hansard,* Vol.92, Col.1374.

In addition to the closer association of Parliament as a whole with the business of foreign affairs the idea of a Foreign Affairs committee gained considerable currency.* This was thought of as a body of representatives of the main parties, perhaps containing as many as thirty or forty members, which would be concerned to exercise a more continuing contact and control than the Commons itself could effect. Mr Hyndman, it is true, had a rather different version in that he argued for an independent, non-party committee not necessarily drawn entirely from Parliament;† whilst George Young° added the necessity for a secretariat to ensure a high quality of knowledge and expertise. The New Europe, asking for a new foreign policy, made point 14 the "Formation of a Foreign Affairs Committee in the House of Commons, and definite establishment of the principle that no treaty or international agreement is valid without the sanction of Parliament and the publication of its full text."+ Perhaps the most important function of such a committee was to be a recognised channel for information in that it could expect to receive documents, be informed by the Foreign Secretary and, if necessary, interview officials. One of the difficulties before Parliament in contributing effectively to the conduct of foreign affairs was the ignorance of most members who, when all was said and done, had to rely upon the press for their main information. A great deal of unnecessary secrecy surrounded foreign affairs and such a committe would help to keep it to a minimum, particularly if all agreements were put to, and considered by, it before they were finally sanctioned. Such a system would surely be beneficial to the government as well for if the committee knew what was really going on and the reasons for it, the Foreign Secretary, instead of working

* It was supported by Mr Hyndman, Mr Young, Mr Ponsonby, the U.D.C. and the New Europe group. See too the Debate on 19th March 1918, *Hansard,* Vol.104.

† H. M. Hyndman, British Policy and the Rights of the People, *The New Europe,* Vol.I, No.11, 28th Dec., 1916.

° *op. cit.,* p.61.

+ *After Three Years;* the Need of a Foreign Policy, Vol.XIII, No.157, 16th Oct.1919.

in lonely isolation in which he was driven into an unhealthy dependence on his permanent officials, could draw support and encouragement from his fellow-parliamentarians. The committee would act as a watch dog over the application of broad and acceptable principles, it was not intended that it should try to control every act of the executive, or that it should "pry into all the detailed secrets" of the Foreign Office; neither was it intended that it should be associated with execution in any way, or even be advisory for the government of the day but that it should be a deliberative body keeping foreign affairs under constant review. "It has been the practice of the present Foreign Secretary to refuse his approval to such projects as a Foreign Affairs Committee, on the ground that the Minister cannot share his executive responsibility with a deliberative body like the House of Commons; and he is wont to expatiate upon the absurdity of attempting to conduct delicate negotiations under the prying eye of parliamentarians. Parliament asks for no such illegitimate privilege. We do not seek to pry into each act and protocol of Foreign Office transactions while they are in the making; but we do demand, and a rapidly-awakening public opinion in the country supports the demand, that the Foreign Office and Parliament shall find a new *modus operandi* by which the voice of legitimate enquiry may be heard."* Through the interaction of committee on the executive and vice versa, mutual confidence between them could at last be properly established. In such a way it was hoped that the gap between Parliament and foreign affairs might be closed and the faults which both sides had shown in the past be reduced to a minimum. Did not the Permanent Commission in France perform such a function and perform it well?† Public opinion there was well informed and diplomacy kept constantly alive to a sense of its own responsibilities. Finally, such a committee might well form the nucleus of Parliamentary contact with other representative assemblies and thus help to keep foreign

* A. F. Whyte, *The New Europe,* Vol.VII, No. 86, 6th June 1918.

† Whyte, *op. cit.* See also Sir Charles Henry's support of the French system of Commissions. 4–4–17, *Hansard,* Vol.92, Col.1363 *et seq.*

policies on the side of the people. "It is commonly said that the people of Europe, henceforth warned against the evils of secret diplomacy, will never again relinquish the control of foreign affairs in peace or in war entirely to their governments. This would appear to mean that the national will is to be extended to cover a wider area, and that foreign affairs must undergo the control and revision of democratic parliaments. In a word, these parliaments will have to be consulted before the ratification of treaties. And if this ratification cannot take place by means of public debate it will either have to be done by secret session or by the action of a parliamentary commission. And, indeed, if the Government desire to consult Parliament on such a matter, it would almost certainly, as a first step, take the older and more experienced members of the Chamber into its confidence. It is true that the Chamber would, in all probability, entrust the task to its most distinguished men, who, however, would not necessarily be those most closely in touch with public opinion or most alive to the needs of the coming generation. A meeting of the elder statesmen, so to speak, is not a fit body with which to rejuvenate the world. It therefore would seem that, at such a moment, a commission truly representative of all parties in the Chamber could render the highest service to the nation."*

From the government side however the idea received short shrift. The notion of a commission or of a Foreign Affairs Committee was firmly rejected on the grounds that not everything could be made public in the national interest. Whilst broad intentions could be made public, the processes must remain secret. Mr Balfour still believed some secret treaties were a necessary evil if only because the other party to the agreement found secrecy essential. There was nothing secret, he thought, about the main lines of British foreign policy but the daily adjustment of policies and interests could not possibly be done publicly without embittering negotiations and making a settlement more difficult. Since it would be undesirable for the committee to deal with

* Étienne Fournol, *The New Europe,* Vol.VIII, No. 94, 1st Aug. 1918.

current business and quite impracticable for it to keep *au courant* with what was going on, it would not in fact be able to act as a check. He suggested that the proposition arose from the "familiar platitude" concerning the opposition of democracy and secret diplomacy, claimed that he too was in the House as an elected representative, and poured scorn on the "fantastic picture" of foreign ministers spinning their evil diplomatic webs in some occult and mysterious obscurity.*

II

The need to overhaul the Foreign Service in order to create an instrument more in keeping with the demands of the time was a matter which commanded widespread agreement. Whilst this was in part a question of creating a department drawn from the whole nation and thus expressing its true interests, it was also seen to be a problem of internal reform that the department become more efficient and through which the stranglehold of the camarilla on the conduct of foreign affairs be finally destroyed. The implementation of the recommendations of the MacDonnell Commission, which had been shelved during the war, were an obvious ingredient of reform. Cecil's speech of 31st July 1918† was warmly in favour of changes upon these lines and the announcement of 21st May 1919° of the government's specific intentions went some way towards meeting the criticisms of the pre-war arrangements. At long last, the property qualification for the Diplomatic Service was to be abolished, with its corollary of proper pay for the attaché from the start of his career. The examination for the Foreign Service was to be amalgamated with that

* See Balfour, 17–8–17, Hansard, Vol.97, Cols.1667–72; 19–3–18, Vol.104, Col.867 *et seq.*

A Foreign Affairs group in the House of Commons was in fact formed independently in March 1918 but, unsurprisingly in view of this cold reception, accomplished nothing much.

† *Hansard,* Vol.109, Col.564 *et seq.*

° *Hansard,* Vol.116, Col.524 *et seq.*

for Class 1 entrance into the Home Civil Service and, although special qualifications in languages were still to be required, the applicant was no longer to be barred from consideration for a post in one of the Home Departments. Finally, the Selection Board procedure was to be changed, for the interview was now to occur after the examination and was to be as similar as possible to that operated by other departments.*

Thus some of the more obviously undesirable features of the old system vanished. No longer was it necessary to have private means, or to obtain prior nomination or for intending candidates to forego their chances of the Home Civil Service. The proper payment of the Diplomatic Service also enabled the two branches of the Foreign Service to be amalgamated and thus made it possible for exchanges between home and abroad to take place more frequently.† The reforms, as far as they went, met with approval. "The essence of Lord Robert Cecil's speech lay in its closing words. Throwing overboard the Victorian conception of diplomacy as a close corporation which none but the *élite* may hope to enter, and adopting a wide and liberal interpretation of the duties of the Diplomatic Service, he may be said to have brought the Foreign Office abreast of the thought and the needs of the time."° Nevertheless, some doubts remained, for fear that these intentions of the government only gave the smallest possible concessions. The reforms amounted, after all, to little more than the necessary minimum required to bring the Foreign Service into line with the Civil Service as a whole; a change which, whilst essential, could hardly be considered very startling. The improvement of pay and in the status of junior diplomats was only a beginning "If reform were to stop there, if the power of vested

* The Board was to consist of the Chief of the Civil Service Commissioners, 2 representatives from the Foreign Office and 4 others. As at 21st May 1919 these were 2 M.P.'s and 2 members of the War Office, see Sir Arthur Steel-Maitland, Hansard, Vol.116, Col.524 *et seq.*

† The frequency of the charge of lack of interchange of posts is interesting in view of the transfers noted for the pre-war period.

° A New Charter for the Diplomatic Service, *The New Europe,* Vol.VIII, No.95, 8th Aug. 1918.

interests in the Foreign Office – and where is it greater? – prevails against other and even more necessary reforms, the door will have been opened in vain to new talent."* The Selection Board procedure of the past had not eradicated the appearance of the closed shop and for this reason it had been urged that any interview deemed necessary should not be peculiar to the Foreign Service but that recruitment should both be, and be seen to be, part of the general pattern for the Civil Service as a whole. "But, granting all this, special limitations, the limitation of nomination and approval by a special selection board, I have come to the conclusion that really does more harm than good. They do harm by leaving the impression upon the public outside that the Service is still a close borough, restricted to a particular class, and on that account they shake the confidence of the country in the Service. I do not believe that they are really necessary."† Nevertheless. the Board procedure was not entirely assimilated with that for other Departments.

Neither did it escape notice that other suggestions designed to improve the efficiency of the service did not appear to meet with a ready response. As this became appreciated, the reformers began to fear that the old trick of dealing with the worst abuses of a situation and thus by-passing the need for more fundamental rearrangements had once again served its allotted purpose. Although the government's promises of reform had been given a welcome by, *inter alia,* "a considerable majority within the Diplomatic Service itself",° a suspicion remained that not everyone was ready for effective spring-cleaning. "Indeed, the pathetic attempt ... to discount in advance what Lord Robert himself was about to say, showed how little the old guard realises the urgent need and, indeed, the inevitability of reform. The proposals outlined and the hopes expressed by Lord Robert Cecil in his speech may yet meet with that kind of quiet, yet effective oppo-

* *The New Europe,* Vol.VIII, No.101. 19th Sept. 1918.
† Hoare. 21–5–18, *Hansard,* Vol.116, Col.493 *et seq.*
° *The New Europe,* Vol.VIII, No.95, 8th Aug. 1918.

sition of which the bureaucrat is a past master."* Thus "One of the lesser losses due to our success in the war has been that of Foreign Office reform. That somewhat decrepit but still debonair devil, Old Diplomacy, was very sick after the diplomatic disasters of the first years of war and seriously thought of seeing about sainthood. He got out of their dusty pigeon holes all the prescriptions of Royal Commissions for converting his soul by curing his system, and all the preachments of the radical prophets that said he could only be saved if he were born again. . . . And now, though he has gained the whole world, he has lost that soul again."† The true demands for reform within the Foreign Service had not, in fact, been met and this is the general tenor of the articles written by Lord Eustace Percy during the spring of 1919° "But there is a psychological moment for reform which, once missed, does not recur"+ but alas, this appeared already to have passed the government by.

Cecil had in fact admitted on behalf of the government the necessity for the adoption of two further points of principle but did not announce any particulars of how they might be carried out. The first was the possibility of some form of "post-graduate" training through which men might be encouraged to know more about the countries to which they were accredited,× whilst the second was the need for a greater systematisation of promotion. He was, however, somewhat guarded over the method whereby this suggestion should be implemented but the question touched deeply what some saw as the very heart of the problem. "There are many diplomats who regard this proposal as the root of all reform, . . . It is probably the most radical [reform] and therefore the hardest to reconcile with the existing system. Sincerely applied it would so revolutionise the present condition of affairs as to entail the entire disappearance of the old *régime* . . . We are in-

* *op. cit.*

† G. Young, *The New Europe,* Vol.XIV, No.182, 8th April 1920.

° *The New Europe,* Vol.XI, A Series of 5 in this volume.

\+ *op. cit.*

× Note the connection with Crowe's aim to get more systematised knowledge about foreign countries; see Chapter 2.

clined to believe, therefore, that it will not be won without a fight, and that the reformers within will need all the support that they can get from public opinion without."* In the past, appointments, transfers, promotions and movements from one post to another had been effected by the private secretary† and it was through this lever that what Morel called the camarilla and the New Europe "the old *régime*"° in the Foreign Office retained its supremacy. It was feared that a system existed in which the officials were unhealthily dependent upon patronage and favour which stemmed ultimately from the little group at the top. This demanded "elegant incompetence" from the Diplomatic Service by which it was kept in thrall through the discouragement of independence and initiative. The private secretary could make or mar man's career and, it was charged, very often had. Promotion depended on the favour of the camarilla to whom alone the quality of a diplomat's work was known. Some of the worst disasters of British diplomacy in recent years had been due to the promotion of persons the service knew to be no good and who ought to have been quietly disposed of. This fate was reserved for those who had tried to get improvements.+ It was wrong, thought *The New Europe,* that these matters should depend upon the word of a single official in the Foreign Office because then influence and personal relations could count for far too much. The appointment of a diplomat, especially a younger man, to a foreign post "depends largely upon his personal relations with a single offical in the Foreign Office, and is, therefore, with the best will in the world, a matter of influence, if not of caprice."× A proper com-

* *The New Europe,* Vol.VIII, No.101, 19th Sept.1918.

† Cd. 7749. See Tyrell's evidence to the MacDonnell Commission; especially Questions 40938–41002, Question 43464. Also Question 39339.

° 19th Sept. 1918.

+ The two cases often quoted are those of Arthur Ponsonby who had been prominent in the 1904 reform movement and the dispersal of the members of the Washington embassy who had been "bold enough to submit a petition of rights." See e.g. G. Young, *op. cit.,* pp.22, 27–9. See also Ponsonby's evidence in Cd. 7749. Q. 39,396. "And it was not resented by your superiors? Well, it was not received with any favour."

× *The New Europe,* Vol.VIII, No.101, 19th Sept. 1918.

mittee to control postings in the Diplomatic Service and an effective Promotion Board were both necessary in order that staff questions could be conducted on rational lines. "It has been the practice hitherto for these appointments to the lower ranks to be largely in the hands of the private secretary to the Secretary of State, who is an extremely important person. ... That is a most undesirable state of affairs. Attachés and secretaries in the Diplomatic Service have to go to the private secretary and ask him to go from one post to another to effect an exchange in the Foreign Office for some special appointment, subject, of course, always to the sanction of the Secretary of State. ... This private secretary has complete power over these appointments and changes. I do not think it is all a good system. I think there ought to be a Board of Appointments."* Furthermore "I believe that if merit is to be kept to the fore, and if the best people are to rise to the top, you must have in the Foreign Office at home, committees or boards dealing with promotion."† In addition, a method of retiring people before they had completed their full service was necessary that the dead wood be discarded before it reached the top where it might do serious harm. "Lord Robert Cecil was more guarded on the subject of promotion, but we gather that he takes a friendly attitude towards the drastic measures suggested by Mr Whyte and Mr Ponsonby. At the same time we feel we must lay some insistence on this matter. The Diplomatic Service is like a great tree full of ancient and decaying boughs which long ago should have been cut away in order to give the tree itself new life, and unless some provision is made at once for reasonably rapid promotion and, therefore, for the retirement of the older diplomats who have no future, the other reforms can hardly have their full effect. But once the Service as a whole has been purged, there is no doubt that the manifold talent which it contains will quickly show itself, and thus provide

* Ponsonby, 31–7–18, *Hansard,* Vol.109, Col.559.

† Hoare, 21–5–18, *Hansard,* Vol.116, Col.499. The bare announcement that there was to be a committee on promotions and the interchange of staff did not satisfy the critics that the system would in practice be reformed.

the Foreign Office and the public with an immediate justification of these reforms."*

It will be noted that the demands for a more efficient service with an operative career structure relate particularly to the Diplomatic Service and were aimed, in many people's minds, to restore its balance with the Foreign Office through bringing it up to the level of competence reached by the home-based department through its pre-war reorganisation. The relationship between the two departments had led, so it was argued, to the Foreign Office achieving an over-riding position in which diplomacy was largely dependent upon it.

Whilst the development of telegraphy had done something to militate against the initiative of the diplomat it was feared that tradition was the far more important influence. The growth in power of the Foreign Office had led to the assumption that the diplomat was only a mouthpiece,† subordinate to some junior clerk at home whose experiences were limited, who had rarely been abroad, had never been faced with the effects of a decision which to him was entirely "academic" and who had not had to deal with the difficulties of residence in other civilisations. The clerk at home often had no grip of realities, he led a comfortable and secure life where he had no need to think out the facts and in which tradition meant that the right accent was more important than knowledge when advancement was under consideration. Under such circumstances, the diplomat did not feel inclined to exercise initiative; he assumed he was there simply to report conversations almost without comment and that he was not free to interpret his instructions within reasonable limits. If one added to this the fact that until middle age he was confined to routine work, it followed that when he at last obtained the possibility of responsibility he no longer knew how to exercise it.° "The present system tends, on the whole, to repress talent. It

* *The New Europe,* Vol.VIII, No. 95, 8th Aug. 1918.

† See Diplomaticus, *op. cit.*

° See Ponsonby, 31-7-18, *Hansard,* Vol.109, Col.558; men "have been prevented from developing their natural capacities".

would be hard to conceive of any service in which less stimulus is offered to energy or skill. At the age of twenty-four or twenty-five, the *attaché's* seniority is fixed by his position in the entrance examination, and he retains this relative position until he reaches the rank of Senior Counsellor, usually at the age of forty-five or fifty. No effort of any kind can alter his rank in the slightest degree. Promotion in the true sense of the word does not exist... It is rare, during the first ten years of his career, for a diplomatist to have any opportunity of showing either capacity or initiative... One result of this complete absorption in the details of routine is a growing incapacity to judge great issues... Initiative, always hindered by any hierarchical system, is rendered entirely impossible, and the qualities of judgement, decision, and wide comprehension, which are most necessary to the senior diplomat, are precisely those which our modern diplomatic training kills."* If, therefore, the Service was in truth ineffective as the eyes and ears of the government or even in negotiation, the conditions under which it laboured were very often at fault. "the enterprising and intelligent young man goes – either to better himself or to the bad, but he goes."†

The release of the diplomat from the deadening routine that made up the major portion of his day in order that he might be able to show his abilities properly for the first time was a demand echoed by the younger members of the Service.

> "A leaf from an attaché's Diary.
>
> 31 Dec. 19–. This is the moment of good resolutions. I shall employ it in drawing up a list for the Secret. of State, who is my particular bête noire among those strange fauna called the powers-that-be in Whitehall. Tonight sees the close of my seventh year in his service, and I think he ought to know what we poor devils of attachés think of him and of

---

* Diplomaticus, *op. cit.*

† George Young, Foreign Office Reform, *The New Europe,* Vol.XIV, No.182, 8th April 1920.

that little world – what a close corporation it is – over which he rules. So here goes! Resolved:

1. To adopt the principle of the living wage among those servants of His Majesty who are called diplomatists, and thus to give up using sweated labour.
2. To persuade the Diplomatic Secretary that the practice of squeezing square pegs into round holes in good neither for the peg nor the hole.
3. To correct the impression that independent means connotes intelligence.
4. To remember Napoleon's remark about the Field-Marshal's baton and *la carrière ouverte aux talents.*
5. To give the "man on the spot" more opportunities of distinguishing himself – or of hanging himself.

"But alas, I find – as many a good man has found before me – that the practice of copying reports on stupid commercial subjects tends to atrophy my native wit; and my resolutions for the S. S. do not quite live up to my hopes. A square talk with him – which I may hope to have when I am on the doddering side of sixty, but not before – would give him some of those home truths which are the common coin when diplomatists talk shop; though most of the crowd I'm with here have long ago given up the airing of grievances and simply have a good time when they can get it. I shall reach that point soon; but I haven't reached it yet, else I shouldn't bother to keep this diary. God preserve our sense of humour, à tout prix, must be the prayer of all like me who are caught in the wheels of this system and can't get out. Let me see; I spent goodness knows how long in learning one of the most difficult languages in Europe, with the result that I was sent to the opposite end of the continent where I only use the knowledge in capping stories with the naval attaché at the club. That is the excellent operation of the square peg principle. And that reminds me, Jack and I agreed over a bottle of P. J. at the Carlton last year that we'd swop diaries at the end of a given time. When

I wrote reminding him of it, the beggar sent me the following on a half sheet of paper:

'Any old hour – Get up.

Three more hours – Pretend to be a typist.

One or more hours – Lunch.

Three more hours – Type again and pretend to be an expert paper file.

One more hour – Seal one bag.

One more hour – Unseal and disembowel one bag.

One minute – Realise that I'm engaged in the practice of diplomacy.

Next minute – Forget it, and go out to dine.

Last hour – Go to bed.

'Note. – Multiply by 365; deduct x for Sundays and leave, neither being obtained; result my diary for one year.'

"Jack's a humorist; but he's not far wrong."*

Here also, the government promised reform, for Cecil† had accepted that the attaché would be released from the more elementary clerical and routine work so that the "wasteful use of raw material" should truly be a thing of the past.

Running through the traditional criticisms of the Diplomatic Service has always been the thread of its social exclusiveness. The charge that it was isolated from the real stuff of life and unable to make contacts with a broad range of people or to experience a wide variety of movements and ideas presented a many-sided problem for reform. At home this question was seen to be closely linked with that of the need to widen the channels of recruitment but abroad it was feared that the conditions of life so often militated against full experience for the diplomat. The social tradition condemned him to a narrow official circle but the difficulty he experienced in developing wider contacts was enhanced by factors which lay more directly under the control of the service itself. Thus the release of the young diplomat from an over-

* *The New Europe,* Vol.VII, No. 87, 13th June 1918.

† 31-7-18, *Hansard,* Vol.109, Cols.565-8.

preoccupation with routine work and the relief of his 'linguistic poverty' could both help him to develop those links with the life of the country to which he was accredited made necessary as the nature of foreign affairs itself developed.* Superficially the latter point might be questioned since fluency for the diplomat was expected in French and German and he was also entitled to be examined in Spanish or Italian. Allowances were given for competence in certain oriental languages where these were the vernacular. But it one considers Europe alone then diplomats had no certain means of communication with people in Norway, Sweden, Denmark, Holland, Portugal, Hungary or in the Balkans generally unless Turkish was spoken. Thus it could be argued that they were effectively confined to circles where the most obvious European languages were spoken. Perhaps, too, the suggestion that diplomats were too often sent where their linguistic knowledge was useless was not as frivolous as might at first sight appear particularly in those cases where it implied a specialist interest in the problems of another country. The first candidate to take Russian in his entrance examination never went to Russia; the diplomat who was an international authority on Turkey could not get reappointed to Constantinople; the Foreign Office clerk who was an expert on Spanish commerce was brought home to edit blue books. All three left the service in middle life.† In less serious vein, but more felicitous language, Spring Rice had made the same point a few years earlier. "I am delighted to hear that you and other experts have not been consulted on any subject in which you were particularly well informed. This gives one the assurance that in this time of change and evolution the Foreign Office maintains untroubled a due regard to its noblest traditions."°

---

* Diplomaticus, *op. cit.*

† G. Young, *op. cit., The New Europe,* Vol.V, No.53, 18th Oct. 1917.

° Spring Rice to Maurice de Bunsen, late Ambassador at Vienna; undated but about Spring 1916. Spring Rice, *op. cit.,* Vol.2, p.318.

But some think there are dangers in too much knowledge for diplomats, e.g. H. Nicolson, *Foreign Affairs* (New York), Oct. 1961, Diplomacy Then and Now.

What is curious to a later reader is the lack of apprehension felt concerning the effect of these reforms which were, after all, designed to result in a more efficient and, potentially, more powerful service through giving, not to half of it, but to all the ability to recruit the most able and to provide them with an attractive, worthwhile professional life. In view of the charges made against the Foreign Office in the pre-war period and the dislike of its rise to power, it seems curiously optimistic to assume that a larger and more effective service would be less likely to violate the democratic conventions than before. Thus these internal reforms must be seen as part of a wider pattern for it was the greater effectiveness of Parliament that was to deal with the control of the Foreign Service as a whole and to prevent government department aga n pursuing an independent life of its own. "whereas, theoretically, the Foreign Office is merely a connecting link between the people's representatives in Parliament and the Empire's representatives abroad, practically it has made itself the sole organ, not only for the conduct of foreign affairs, but for the control of foreign policy."* The over-dependence of the Foreign Secretary upon his officials was widely credited. "the natural inclination of the political chief is to repose more and more confidence in his subordinates, . . . whom he cannot discharge. If these permanent officials are attacked and their influence denounced, this is claimed to be unfair."† "Working in this rarefied atmosphere, the Secretary of State, oppressed by the amount of business he has to transact, becomes more and more drawn away from any sort of outside influence and begins to rely exclusively on expert advice."°

It was intended that the Foreign Affairs Committee would counteract this through destroying the isolation of the Foreign Secretary at a political level. "It will be urged that there should

* G. Young, A Defence of Diplomatists, *The New Europe,* Vol.V, No. 53, 18th Oct. 1917.

† H. Hyndman, British Policy and the Rights of the People, *The New Europe,* Vol.I, No.11, 28th Dec. 1916.

° A. Ponsonby, *Democracy and Diplomacy,* p.47.

not be a Committee on the Foreign Office. I believe that in regard to the Foreign Office there must be a certain amount of secrecy, but I think there is great danger on the other side of allowing a certain number of high officials and one or two men to make great and tragic decisions. For my part, I would be willing to set up beside the Foreign Secretary a body of sane business men, carefully selected by this House, who would bring to the discussion of proposals affecting foreign affairs the joint intelligence of the House."* Furthermore, the Foreign Secretary was dependent, not on the top men of the service *per se*, but on a personal clique, centred on the private secretaries. "Thus, while Parliament has delegated foreign affairs to the Cabinet, and the Cabinet to the Foreign Secretary, the Foreign Secretary depends not on the departmental heads, still less on the diplomatic chiefs, but on a personal entourage or clique that I shall, for convenience, call the "camarilla". This camarilla is centred in, but not confined to the private secretaries – the principal private secretary being, not as elsewhere a junior, . . . but a personage – a K.C.B. at least – whose term of power is limited only by the frailty of mortal man and is based on two or three main points: first, the complete command of all access to the Foreign Secretary, . . . second, complete control of the appointments . . . as of the promotion, transfer and reward . . . and thirdly, the outside support of certain cliques that are almost all-powerful in the official world."† Internal reorganisation was designed to curb this freedom but the possibility remained that, if a power vacuum were to be created, the reformed, more able and united service might fill it with the minimum of fuss; for the tendency of the Foreign Secretary to rely upon his professional advisers was surely in some sense a natural one, in that the growing complexity, volume and specialisation of international affairs made some such enhancement inevitable.

* O'Connor, 4-4-17, *Hansard,* Vol.92, Col.1380.
† G. Young, *op. cit.*

III

By the time hostilities ceased, the position of the Foreign Service was hardly one of strength in Whitehall and in view of the changed world circumstances in which it now found itself it was unlikely that it would ever fully recover its position. The reasons for this were far deeper than the personal idiosyncrasies of Lloyd George and made it necessary for executive action to be shared with other departments in an unaccustomed way. The enormous growth of gevernmental concern with economic and financial international relations, the development of specialist international organisations such as the I.L.O., the rise of the Dominions to a position where their right to be consulted over foreign policies was admitted, all helped to prevent a return to the relative simplicity of pre-war days. It was no longer a workable assumption that the Foreign Service was the pre-eminent source of advice or the most suitable machinery for execution now that the content of foreign policy was changing. Thus a transitional period of considerable difficulty was inevitable in which the lines of communication were upset and the seat of responsiblity not fully clear. Under such circumstances it is not surprising that the members of the Foreign Service felt uncertain and insecure, and that their reactions ranged from the waspish and bad-tempered to a genuine desire to seize for the service the real opportunities now opening up before the country's foreign policy in a constructive attempt to adapt a very traditional institution to the modern world.

A question which the development of external relations was now posing in an acute form was that of appropriate departmental responsibility and thus the proponents of the view that the country be represented overseas by one department only, for otherwise separate policies would surely follow, endeavoured to make their voices heard. Much of this argument centred round the old question of trading responsibility and the necessity, or otherwise, of allowing the service to handle commercial matters as an essential part of the totality of the national interest. In this connection, some thought the time had surely come for the abolition of the artificial distinctions not only between the Foreign Office and Diplomatic Service but also with the Consular Services. Such watertight departments and lack of flexibility had long ago outlived any usefulness they might once have possessed and the substitution of one single, graded department was long overdue.* "You cannot run your Foreign Service as a train with first, second and third class coaches without communicating corridors or third class admission to the dining car. Such an arrangement of classes has worked in the Whitehall Civil Service, where it corresponds to what is still the structure of West End society, and it may continue to work there for such time as the middle class continues to enjoy this rather artificial and archaic atmosphere. But it has not worked well in the open air of life abroad, even within the cloisters of the *Corps diplomatique,* where caste conventions are still religiously respected. It will not work at all in the new Europe emerging from the revelations and revolutions of the war. If we try and maintain these obsolete classifications, we shall never get proper representation abroad of our political and commercial interests or enter into real touch with foreign ethnic and economic movements."† Hope was indeed to be found in Cecil's belief° that the time had come to extend the functions of diplomacy and especially to questions of commerce; indeed he felt they were inseparable matters and commerce now required some consideration of the political as well as the economic conditions of a country; but the arrangements that were made to deal with commercial policy, which have already been described, can hardly be said to have fulfilled the promise of these remarks.

One of the most hopeful activities for the service had been its involvement in economic affairs and its recognition during the

---

* The Consular Service was to be disappointed of such lofty elevation at this time.

† G. Young, Foreign Office Reform, *The New Europe,* Vol.XIV, No.182, 8th April 1920.

° Commons, 31–7–18, *Hansard,* Vol.109, Col.568 *et seq.*

war of its role in the totality of purposeful activity. During the war, we are told,* the Foreign Office developed both in spirit and in organisation and as its work departed increasingly from traditional activity, so its members acquired a new and healthier self-confidence and a sounder view of the nature of the country's interest and their part in fulfilling it. When one considers the network of relationships that developed as a result of trade and commercial relations with both neutrals and allies it is clear that in so far as the Foreign Service was responsible, and it largely was, it had indeed moved into the world of reality. Thus the creation of the Department of Overseas Trade symbolised a very real threat to the new significance which the service had found, since it removed the field of economic relations from the sphere of the Foreign Office proper. Whilst the relationship of the two departments and of them to the Board of Trade was anything but clear, even more fundamental was the fear that if the Foreign Office were to be shorn of its direct interest in commercial and trading questions, except in a post-office function, it would in practice be relegated to a political backwater where the real stuff of international affairs would pass it by. "The indefinable residue to be called politics"† did not appear a satisfactory prize, or even an adequate one, provided the Foreign Service were satisfactorily reformed.

A certain bitterness is evident amongst the senior members concerning the staffing of the Peace Conference. Hardinge claims that "Unfortunately Mr Lloyd George, whose knowledge of many of the problems involved was non-existent, insisted on employing a staff or his own unofficial creation who had no knowledge of French and none of diplomacy, and the Foreign Office organisation was consequently stillborn."° "although the Staff from the Foreign Office was only eighteen in all, the War Office,

* Percy, Foreign Office Reform, *The New Europe*, Vol.XI, No.133, 1st May 1919.

† S. Hoare, The Government and the Department of Overseas Trade, *The New Europe*, Vol.XII, No. 144. 17th July 1919.

° C. Hardinge, *op. cit.*, p.229.

Admiralty, Board of Trade and Colonial Office ran the members up to 200."* Bertie snapped that the French were complaining about the size of the British delegation. Most of them he considered joy-riders who had got themselves "jobbed" on to some department.† "Just as the war ultimately resolved itself into the triumph of the Professional Strategist over the Amateur, so the Peace Conference registered the defeat of the Professional by the Amateur Diplomat, who has had things all his own way to the point that "experts" who are abhorent to Political Ignoramuses, were snuffed out. ... British Diplomats had no more voice in the Treaty than the present writer."°

Perhaps a more serious complaint however was the way in which the Prime Minister played havoc with the more important diplomatic appointments. Whilst, as in the case of Spring Rice, we can see there were many influences at work the Foreign Service itself can be forgiven for feeling rather sour, particularly since the manner in which outsiders obtained the plums was often less than straightforward. It is not necessary to postulate deliberate malice for this but the suspicion that Lloyd George's motives were not such as to stand scrutiny could not be prevented. In January 1918 Britain had no Ambassador at Paris, Washington or Petrograd. The reasons for each vacancy were complex and not necessarily discreditable, but when unorthodoxy led to such unfortunate results it strengthened the argument that the policy of ignoring the Diplomatic Service was not in the best interests of the country. Lloyd George wanted to do Reading a good turn writes Vansittart about the Washington embassy;+ the attempt to remove Lord Bertie from Paris in order to facilitate changes in the Cabinet was "Another intrigue, which failed only temporarily,"× whilst the suggestion that Henderson should replace Buchanan in Russia was also "mischievous meddling in Foreign

* Hardinge, *op. cit.*, p.230.
† Bertie, *op. cit.*, Vol.2, p.312.
° L. Maxse, *The National Review*, Oct. 1919.
\+ *op. cit.* p.184.
× Hardinge, *op. cit.*, p.214.

Affairs."* In such an atmosphere the suspicion that these actions verged on deliberate spite grew easily and Vansittart put his finger on the real mischief when he wrote that embassies "cannot be misused without taking the heart out of a great service".†

It is clear that an effective Foreign Service requires knowledge; it needs to digest that knowledge and it needs to assess what it knows and to predict and consider the future. For competence in foreign affairs, a modern country requires a vast array of facts and opinions, often on highly technical subjects and a definite branch of government charged with the responsibility to collect, compare, digest, record and consider. The occasions have been many upon which the lack of any effective process of this sort has been remarked, especially by those with experience of how the system actually works.° It will be remembered that Crowe had wanted more systematic information sent home from the embassies and some method of utilising it, but there seems some doubt as to the extent to which the system worked.+ "The responsibility of diplomacy for the collection and digestion of miscellaneous information about foreign countries had been overlooked and forgotten for years."× During the war, the creation of the Political Intelligence Department appeared to hold the promise that this function might come at last to fruition for out of the needs of the moment came recognition of the importance of following the trends of opinion and internal developments in foreign countries; the conscious utilisation of much information for propaganda purposes and the propriety of discussing and formulating the anticipated problems of the peace. The establishment of such a department gave a real impetus to the association of the Foreign Office with creative and purposeful activity despite the drawback that its personnel was largely drawn from outside sources rather than through the transfer of permanent Foreign Office

* *op. cit.*

† Vansittart, *op. cit.*, p.183.

° Thus rather amending the "eminence grise" theory of the rôle of the Foreign Office.

\+ Tilley and Gaselee, *op, cit.*, pp.157–8.

× Percy, *The New Europe*, Vol.XI, No.133.

members and that, being so concerned with immediate problems, it never established the intimacy of contact with the Diplomatic and Consular Services which its real development required. At one time it appeared that perhaps the government recognised the importance of this function for Cecil spoke sympathetically about the work of the Intelligence Department and the need for its growth beyond a hand-to-mouth existence towards more permanent and systematic methods,* but at the very same time, the department was already disintegrating as the outsiders returned to wider spheres of life and no one within the Foreign Office could be spared for such work. It remained a stunted growth for whose development a plea was to be heard from time to time in the ensuing years.† As late as 1960 Sir William Hayter remarked that "The machinery for thinking on long-term lines about the direction of British policy is on an altogether smaller scale, rising and falling in influence and importance in accordance with the varying temperaments of successive Foreign Secretaries and Permanent Under-Secretaries ... Foreign policy is not a suitable theme for planning in the ordinary sense; ... But it is possible to forecast trends and to think what you will do if the logical consequences of them, or of your current policies, occur. The Foreign Office, under various impulses, has in late years begun to try to do more of this kind of thing".° With the closing of the first world war, however, an era was ushered in unconducive to the development of planning. Combined with its lack of control of economic matters, the confused responsibility of government departments and Lloyd George's diplomatic activities, all that opened for the Foreign Service in the peace was a lost opportunity.

---

* House of Commons, 31–7–18, *Hansard,* Vol.109, Col.564 *et seq.* Staff fell from 25 in 1919 to 7 in 1920.

† See e.g. V. Wellesley, Diplomacy in Fetters; *The Spectator*, 29th Dec. 1944; House of Lords, *Hansard* 5th Series, Vol.126, Debate on the Reform of the Foreign Service, 30th March 1943.

° W. Hayter, *The Diplomacy of the Great Powers,* p.46.

IV

A consideration of the course of events against the background of democratic control as described by Dicey suggests that his theory was inadequate for the realities which were overtaking it. Sufficient at a time when the final decision to declare war could still be considered meaningful and when prior defence planning with other states was unnecessary, modern conditions have undermined the simplicity of his approach to the problem of how to combine popular sovereignty with an effective foreign policy. The reconciliation of the needs of the people and the imperatives of diplomacy is a matter of delicate balance requiring constant adjustment as the substance of those needs and the realities of international relations change. The willingness of the executive to be guided by national objectives necessitates their formulation with sufficient precision to be useful yet not with so much that negotiation is impossible. If the aims of foreign policy are a political responsibility yet their execution demands that a country places some trust in its negotiators. The criticisms made of the conduct of foreign affairs during this period, however, too often helped to disguise the fact that a dilemma does exist between the claims of the people to be consulted and the freedom of action necessary to achieve their desires. Perhaps, therefore, they did equally as much harm as good. The widespread acceptance of the need for internal reform of the Foreign Service and the fact that this was never seriously denied, points to the view that a fairly drastic overhaul was necessary, particularly for the Diplomatic Service. The lack of appreciation by the pre-war government and the Foreign Office of the need for "public relations" in a modern sense may well have been a major cause of the lack of confidence which undoubtedly existed in the conduct of the country's foreign relations. To say this, however, is far from suggesting that the Foreign Service was filled with men whose sinister concern was with class rather than with nation and that it was thus the enemy of the people. In so far as this suggestion, containing as it did a theory as to the causation of war, diverted attention from fundamental flaws in the organisation of human society, it did a disservice to the clear thinking about international relations which was so badly needed. In as much as it played its part in destroying morale within a service whose role in modern government had become far more uncertain, it contributed to a loss of effectiveness in British post-war policy from which no one at home can have gained. Mutual confidence between people and executive is, as Dicey saw, a necessity but this demands a higher degree of sophisticated awareness from both parties than we always manage to obtain.

WORKS REFERRED TO IN THE TEXT

B. J. Hendrick, *The Life and Letters of Walter Page,* Heinemann, 1924.
H. W. Steed, *Through Thirty Years,* Heinemann, 1924.
Lord Hardinge, *Old Diplomacy,* Murray, 1947.
The Foreign Office List.
G. P. Gooch and H. Temperley (Eds.), British Documents on the Origins of the War, H.M.S.O., 1926 onwards.
A. Dicey, *Introduction to the Study of the Law of the Constitution,* Macmillan, 1897.
W. S. Churchill, *The World Crisis,* Thornton Butterworth 1927.
Sir Campbell Stuart, *The Secrets of Crewe House,* Hodder & Stoughton, 1920.
Viscount Grey of Fallodon, *Twenty-Five Years,* Hodder & Stoughton, 1925.
J. A. Spender. *The Life of the Right Hon. Sir Henry Campbell-Bannerman,* Hodder & Stoughton, 1923.
Lady Algernon Lennox (Ed.). *The Diary of Lord Bertie of Thame,* Hodder & Stoughton. 1924.
A. Willert, *The Road to Safety,* Derek Verschoyle, 1952.
R. S. Baker, *Woodrow Wilson: Life & Letters,* Heinemann, 1928–35.
Lord Hankey, *The Supreme Command,* Allen & Unwin, 1961.
C. Seymour (arr.), *The Intimate Papers of Colonel House,* E. Benn, 1928.
Hansard.
The History of The Times, Vol. 4, The Times, 1952.
The Times History of the War, The Times, 1915–21.
G. M. Trevelyan, *Grey of Fallodon,* Longmans Green, 1946.
T. Jones, *A Diary with Letters,* G. Cumberlege, O.U.P., 1954.
J. Davies, *The Prime Minister's Secretariat,* R. H. Johns, 1951.
R. H. Bruce Lockhart, *Memoirs of a British Agent,* Putnam & Co., 1946.

J. Tilley and S. Gaselee, *The Foreign Office*, Putnam & Co., 1933.
C. Petrie, *The Powers Behind the Prime Ministers*, MacGibbon & Kee, 1958.
J. Butler, *Lord Lothian*, Macmillan, 1960.
Earl of Oxford and Asquith, *Memories and Reflections*, Cassell & Co., 1928.
Genefal Sir C. E. Callwell, *Field-Marshal Sir Henry Wilson*, Cassell & Co., 1927.
R. Pound and G. Harmsworth, *Northcliffe*, Cassell & Co., 1959.
D. Lloyd George, *War Memoirs*, Nicholson & Watson, 1933.
D. Lloyd George, *The Truth About the Peace Treaties*, Gollancz, 1938.
H. Nicolson, *Sir Arthur Nicolson, Bart. First Lord Carnock*. Constable & Co., 1930.
H. Nicolson, *King George the Fifth*, Constable & Co., 1952.
H. Nicolson, *The Evolution of Diplomatic Method*, Constable & Co., 1954.
S. Gwynn (ed.), *The Letters and Friendships of Sir Cecil Spring Rice*, Constable & Co., 1929.
L. Jones, *Georgian Afternoon*, R. Hart-Davis, 1958.
W. Hayter, *The Diplomacy of the Great Powers*, Hamish Hamilton, 1960.
Lord Percy of Newcastle, *Some Memories*, Eyre & Spottiswoode, 1958
F. Owen, *Tempestuous Journey*, Hutchinson, 1954.
B. Dugdale, *Arthur James Balfour*, Hutchinson, 1936.
Marquess of Reading, *Rufus Isaacs*, Hutchinson, 1945.
Lord Vansittart, *The Mist Procession*, Hutchinson, 1958.
Lord Beaverbrook, *Men and Power*, Hutchinson, 1956.
J. E. Wrench, *Geoffrey Dawson and Our Times*, Hutchinson, 1955.
J. E. Wrench, *Alfred, Lord Milner*, Eyre & Spottiswoode, 1958.
W. Bagehot, *The English Constitution*, King & Co., 1872.
E. D. Morel, *Morocco in Diplomacy*, Smith, Elder & Co., 1912.
E. D. Morel, *The Secret History of a Great Betrayal*, Foreign Affairs, 1922.
E. D. Morel, *Truth and the War*, National Labour Press, 1916.
A. Duff Cooper, *Old Men Forget*, R. Hart-Davis, 1955.
C. Norman, *Britain and the War*, National Labour Press, 1914.
F. Neilson, *How Diplomats Make War*, Huebsch, 1916.
K. Lichnowsky, *Heading for the Abyss*, Constable, 1928.
A. Berriedale-Keith, *The Constitution of England*, Macmillan, 1940.
A. Ponsonby, *Democracy and Diplomacy*, Methuen, 1915.
A. Ponsonby, *Parliament and Foreign Policy*, The UDC, 1914.
G. Young, *Diplomacy Old and New*, Swarthmore Press, 1921.

A. C. BELL, *The Blockade of the Central Empires*, H.M.S.O. 1961.

Cd. 7748. Cd. 7749. C. 4554. Cd. 9005. Cd. 8715. Cd. 8490. Cmd. 325. H.M.S.O.

The Economist, The UDC, The National Review, The New Europe, The Quarterly Review, The Nation.

The Times, The Manchester Guardian, The Morning Post, The Daily News.

In addition to the publishers whose names are to be found in the list above, I have to thank Mr Arthur Page for permission to quote from B. Hendrick, *Life and Letters of Walter Page*; the owners of the copyrights for permission to quote from J. Spender, *The Life of the Right Hon. Sir Henry Campbell-Bannerman,* and from Viscount Grey of Fallodon *Twenty-Five Years*; the Duchess of Portland, D.B.E, in respect of *The Diary of Lord Bertie of Thame*; Sir Winston Churchill for permission to use brief extracts from his letter of August 23rd, 1912; Sir Bruce Lockhart for permission to use two extracts from *Memoirs of a British Agent*; Mrs Wickham Steed and Miss Joan Stevenson for permission to quote from H. W. Steed *Trough Thirty Years* and from Mr Steed's letter of March 12th, 1915, and the Public Trustee for permission to use extracts from the letters of Lord Northcliffe.

INDEX

Made in Great Britain